WOODROW WILSON

AND

THE LOST PEACE

Woodrow Wilson
and the
Lost
Peace

by THOMAS A. BAILEY

Q

QUADRANGLE PAPERBACKS

Quadrangle Books / Chicago

WOODROW WILSON AND THE LOST PEACE.
© 1944 by Thomas A. Bailey. This book was originally
published in 1944 by The Macmillan Company, New
York, and is here reprinted by arrangement.

First QUADRANGLE PAPERBACK edition pub-
lished 1963 by Quadrangle Books, Inc., 180 North
Wacker Drive, Chicago. Manufactured in the United
States of America.

SEVERAL YEARS AGO, after I had delivered what was doubtless too pontifical a lecture on the mistakes of Wilson and others at the Paris Peace Conference, one of the girls in the class came up to the lectern to ask a routine question. When she had gone I noticed that she had inadvertently left behind a copy of the university news sheet, on the margin of which she had scrawled, evidently for the edification of her neighbor, "Too bad Bailey couldn't have been there to tell them how to do it."

Lest others react similarly to the account that follows, I must at the outset deny any claim to superior wisdom. If I had been in a position of authority at Paris in 1919, I am sure that I should have made many of the mistakes I criticize, and a good many more besides. I realize that statesmen who are working under the pressure of an avalanche of events, and often under physical disabilities as well, cannot attain the serenity of mind and detachment of judgment that come to the scholar in his cloistered cubicle. I realize perfectly well that the wisdom of hindsight is not difficult to attain, and that twenty-five years after the event anyone can see a great many things that were not currently evident.

But so costly have been our blunders, and so strong is the likelihood that we shall again run through the same tragic cycle of disillusionment and isolationism, that I regard it as a solemn duty to rise above the inhibitions of false modesty and call spades by their right names. I happen to be among those who believe that history has lessons for those who will read, and that the Paris Conference of 1919 presents many striking illustrations of what to avoid. Every generation of apes begins where the previous generation began, because apes can hand down no record of their experience. Man leaves a record; but how much better is he than the apes if he does not study it and heed its warnings?

This is not a one-volume history of the Peace Conference. It is a critical analysis of the part played by the United States in the making of the world settlement of 1919, with particular attention to Wilson and to American public opinion. For this reason I touch but lightly upon purely European considerations. My account is primarily an interpretation—a critical interpretation. For this reason I do not try to tell the story in great detail, but rather to sketch the general outlines and stress what seem at this distance to have been the most costly blunders made by the negotiators. Finally, the book is an attempt to educate American public opinion to its responsibilities in future peace-making and international cooperation. For this reason I have tried to make the account simple, direct, and meaningful.

I must at the outset confess to a great admiration for many of Wilson's qualities, and to complete sympathy for the broad ends that he sought to attain. I should be profoundly distressed were I to think that what I have to say could be interpreted as giving aid and comfort to isolationism. The fact is that Wilson and his colleagues in 1918 were presented with an unexampled opportunity to make a lasting peace. Something went wrong. I am interested in finding out to what extent and in what way the United States was responsible for what happened, to the end that we may not make the same mistakes again.

Some of the things that I say will no doubt prove offensive to those who hold the memory of Woodrow Wilson in reverence. While I regret that this is so, I cannot permit such considerations to turn me aside from my larger purpose. Surely enough time has elapsed, and enough disaster has befallen us, that we can ask both the Wilson-worshipers and the Wilson-haters to shed the scales of prejudice from their eyes. Surely we are privileged to hope that this great nation will not again plunge the world into despair by the spectacle of a President and a Senate unable to agree on the precise means to attain that which they both profess to desire.

This book is concerned with the making of the peace. I plan to follow it with a sequel on the part played by the United States in the breaking of the peace, and in the subsequent collapse of collective security.

My title is adapted from Harold B. Butler's *The Lost Peace*.

The following publishers graciously extended permission to quote brief passages from the books indicated: Harper and Brothers, from George Creel's *The War, the World and Wilson;* Houghton Mifflin Company, from Charles Seymour's *The Intimate Papers of Colonel House,* vol. IV; and Doubleday, Doran and Company, Inc. (and Mr. Ray Stannard Baker), from Ray Stannard Baker, *Woodrow Wilson and World Settlement,* copyright, 1922.

The following persons, all colleagues at Stanford University, graciously read and constructively criticized all or substantial portions of the manuscript: Thomas S. Barclay (who for several months was Henry White's private secretary at Paris), Harold W. Bradley, Harold H. Fisher, Jere King, George H. Knoles, and Alfred Owen Ulph. Without in any way reflecting on the helpfulness of others, I must single out for special mention Dr. Rudolf Holsti, the distinguished Finnish diplomat who is now on the faculty of Stanford University. His intimate knowledge of persons and places in Paris of 1919, as well as his subsequent relationship with the League of Nations, not only saved me from some embarrassing slips but resulted in a number of constructive improvements.

I am indebted to a score or so of other persons for ideas and suggestions of various sorts. Some of these people are colleagues at Stanford University, or temporary colleagues at Harvard University; some were advisers to Wilson at Paris; others had unusual opportunity for observation, either as officials or as private citizens, in postwar Europe. I do not list their names, because my subject matter is controversial, and I do not want to embarrass them by associating them with views which they would not in some cases fully endorse. I am nevertheless deeply grateful to them.

The staffs of the Stanford University Library; of the Hoover Library on War, Revolution, and Peace; and of the Widener Library at Harvard University cheerfully extended the usual courtesies. Miss Ruth S. Watson, of the Nebraska State Historical Society, provided me with a copy of an important manuscript of Senator Gilbert M. Hitchcock. President Charles Seymour and Mr. Russell G. Pruden graciously made available the materials in the Yale House Collection. I am also indebted to Dr. St. George L. Sioussat, Chief of the Division of Manuscripts, Library of Congress; and especially to Miss Katharine E. Brand, Special Custodian, Woodrow Wilson Collection, the Library of Congress.

My wife, Sylvia Dean Bailey, not only helped prepare the index but painstakingly read and constructively criticized both galley and page proofs.

THOMAS A. BAILEY

STANFORD UNIVERSITY, CALIF.

TABLE OF CONTENTS

xi

LIST OF MAPS

WOODROW WILSON

AND

THE LOST PEACE

CHAPTER ONE

THE ROAD TO WAR

"The military masters of Germany denied us the right to be neutral." WOODROW WILSON, *June 14, 1917.*

I

ON JUNE 28, 1914, a fanatical student, in the Bosnian city of Serajevo, stepped toward the royal limousine, and fired two revolver shots, one at the Archduke Francis Ferdinand, heir to the throne of Austria-Hungary, the other at his blonde consort, the Duchess of Hohenberg. Both died within a few minutes.

The flaming pistol of Princip touched off the European powder magazine, and set in motion a series of earth-shaking events that have not yet run their course, and will not soon do so.

Did the American people even faintly foresee that the death of the Austrian Archduke heralded the death of tens of thousands of their sons in France, and within twenty-five or so years the death of tens of thousands more in a dozen or so different theaters of conflict?

The answer is no. The news of the assassination made the headlines and then gave way to local sensations, including the scandal involving Mme. Caillaux in France. A handful of American observers, it is true, suggested that the resulting quarrel between Austria and Servia might widen into a European conflict. But the rank and file of the American people, busied with their everyday affairs, could hardly take seriously the murder of a seemingly obscure archduke, by an obscure assassin, in an obscure town, in an obscure part of the world. The New York *Sun* was not alone when it boldly predicted that the assassinations would make for peace between Austria and Servia.

Europe suddenly regained the headlines when the Balkan maelstrom sucked all the great powers, with the temporary exception of Italy, into its vortex. The American people still could not recognize the significance of the events that were fast unfolding before their eyes. It is true that for more than a decade the teetering balance of power in Europe had inspired constant speculation in the press about the inevitable world conflict. But the cry of "Wolf, wolf" had been heard so often that we could scarcely believe that the whole pack was at last on the loose.

When the clashing armies and the rolling death wagons finally dispelled all lingering illusions, our first reaction was to rejoice that we were not involved in the bloody mess. We gave thanks to Columbus for having discovered America, and to our ancestors for having had the good sense to come here. Like the Pharisees, we were pleased to know that we were not like other people: contentious, greedy, treacherous, blood-thirsty. We felt strong, smug, secure.

The American people, in line with their traditions, were then fundamentally isolationist. They did not want to plunge into the European blood bath; they did not expect to. President Wilson not only issued the routine proclamations of neutrality, but went further and urged the American people to be neutral both "in action" and "in thought."

Neutrality in action was possible; neutrality in thought was impossible. America, the famed "international boarding house," was "a menagerie of nationalities"; and millions of German-Americans, Irish-Americans, Italian-Americans, British-Americans and others could not be indifferent to the fate of the "old country." Many if not most Americans sympathized with one side or the other, and hoped it would win. But this did not mean that they were willing to back up their sympathies with their life blood.

The leading American isolationist—or perhaps one should say noninterventionist—was the President of the United States, Thomas Woodrow Wilson.

This is a fact of enormous significance in the unfolding of our story, and we shall have to come back to it again. Wilson declared at the very outset that we had had absolutely "no part in making" the war. He repeatedly insisted, in both public and private utterance, that this was not our fight; that its causes and objects were "obscure"; that the announced aims of both sides were "virtually the same."

Not all Americans, especially the red-blooded Theodore Roosevelt, agreed with Wilson. But there can be little doubt that the overwhelming majority believed with their President that this war was not our affair. Wilson was a professional teacher of great persuasiveness and power, and we must record that he taught this lesson well—perhaps too well. When events later forced him to change his mind and become the leading internationalist, he expected that his isolationist following would change their minds too, and march right along behind him.

But the great majority of the American people did not. They remained rooted to their traditions. And this is another fundamental fact of immense importance in explaining what happened to the peace.

2

The task of remaining neutral was not nearly so simple as many Americans had anticipated. The British early established a long-range blockade of Germany, which was clearly illegal under the existing rules of international law. The Germans countered with a submarine blockade of the British Isles, which was clearly illegal under the existing rules of international law. Our Department of State protested against both blockades, but took a much stronger tone against the submarine, because it was feared that American ships and American lives might be accidentally destroyed. The British could pay for confiscated cargoes; the Germans could offer no adequate compensation for the lives destroyed by torpedoes. Murderers are worse than thieves.

The whole issue was sensationally spotlighted when, on May 7, 1915, a giant British liner, the *Lusitania,* was torpedoed without warning off the Irish coast by a German U-boat. The stricken Cunarder plunged to the bottom in eighteen minutes, with a loss of 1,198 persons, 128 of whom were American citizens, and a large percentage of whom were women, children, and babes in arms. The corpse of one woman was retrieved from the sea with a twin baby clutched to each breast.

America, in common with the rest of the civilized world, was horrified by this holocaust. Even sober newspapers burst forth with denunciations of "mass murder" and of "savages drunk with blood," while the well-known acrobatic evangelist, "Billy" Sunday, cried, "Damnable! Damnable! Absolutely hellish!"

Many hot-bloods in the East demanded immediate war; but the entire country was not ready for drastic action, and Wilson was determined not to repeat President Madison's tragic mistake of 1812 and lead a disunited people into armed conflict. Instead he lodged a series of forceful protests demanding assurances against the repetition of such a horror. The bellicose Theodore Roosevelt, who thirsted for war and not words, classed Wilson with the "flubdubs," "mollycoddles," and "flapdoodle pacifists" and branded Wilson's last note as "No. 11,765, Series B." Nevertheless Wilson did extort from Berlin a promise not to torpedo unresisting passenger liners.

In March, 1916, a U-boat commander flagrantly violated this pledge when he torpedoed an unarmed French passenger ship, the *Sussex,* without warning and with serious injury to several Americans. Outraged, Wilson took a step fraught with the most fateful consequences. He presented an ultimatum to Berlin, declaring that unless the Germans ended their barbarous methods of making war on passenger and freight-carrying vessels, the United States would have no choice but to sever relations.

This, of course, was a threat of war—an irrevocable threat. For various reasons, the Germans saw fit to avoid a showdown with the United States, and they thenceforth refrained from torpedoing passenger liners without warning—at least for a time. But the *Sussex* ultimatum still stood.

3

On January 30, 1917, two and one-half years after the German hordes had goose-stepped into Belgium, the United States was still neutral. There seemed good reason to hope that we could continue to be. The German submarine—as far as we were concerned—was muzzled; the military situation in Europe seemed to be in a stalemate; Wilson had just appealed to the belligerents to state their war aims so that the groundwork could be laid for a negotiated peace. He had followed this up with a memorable speech before the Senate in which he ringingly declared for "peace without victory."

On January 31, 1917, with the echoes of Wilson's sensational speech still reverberating around the world, the Imperial German government announced that it would launch an unrestricted submarine campaign against all ships, *belligerent* or *neutral*, entering the European war zones. (The previous campaign had been proclaimed against Allied shipping only.) As a special concession, the Americans might send one vessel a week through a specified part of the war zone, provided it arrived at Falmouth, England, on Sunday, carried no contraband, was painted with wide red and white stripes, and flew a checkered flag resembling a kitchen tablecloth. One American newspaper acidly remarked that "freedom of the seas will now be enjoyed by icebergs and fish."

The staggering announcement of unrestricted U-boat warfare was equivalent to a declaration of war on the United

States. The German High Command knew this; they expected us to enter the conflict; and they had counted the cost—or what they confidently believed would be the cost. They not illogically assumed that they could knock the Allies out of the war before we could raise, train, equip, and transport a formidable army.

To Wilson, who was absorbed in his plans for a negotiated peace, the German announcement came as a body blow. During the nine months following the *Sussex* ultimatum, our relations with Germany had been unusually amicable, more so than with the British, who were blacklisting our merchants and searching our mails. Even Wilson, in a moment of anger, burst out that the "poor boobs" in England had "got on his nerves."

Yet there was nothing that Wilson could honorably do but accept the brutal German challenge, for in the *Sussex* ultimatum he had nailed his colors to the mast. The Germans now threatened to sink all ships, including ours, without warning. They had called Wilson's bluff—if it was a bluff. There was no alternative left to notifying the German ambassador that diplomatic relations were formally severed, and this was promptly done.

A few minutes later on that same day, February 3, 1917, the pale professor-President went before Congress to explain in solemn tones where he stood. He sorrowfully confessed that he still could not bring himself to believe that the German government would actually do what it threatened to do. He would not believe it until American ships and lives were destroyed by actual "overt acts" of hostility. If they were, he would call upon Congress for appropriate measures to protect Americans who were exercising their undeniable rights to sail the high seas.

The British were disappointed by Wilson's speech. Prime Minister Lloyd George exclaimed: "And so he is not going to fight after all!" Theodore Roosevelt burst out: "I do not believe Wilson will go to war unless Germany literally kicks him into it."

The next anxious weeks were spent in waiting for the blow to fall—for the first "overt" act.

4

As one leafs through the yellowing newspapers of early 1917, one is struck with a surprising fact. The full significance of the German declaration seems not to have dawned upon the American people. Like Wilson, they still wanted to stay out of war, and hoped to do so. Like Wilson, they recognized that there was nothing to do but sever relations with Germany. And like Wilson, they refused to believe that the Germans would actually do what they said they were going to do. Clearly public opinion was not yet ripe for war, and until it was, the Administration dared not lead the nation into the bloody abyss.

But within a month the American people were jarred out of their fool's paradise. On March 1, 1917, the Zimmermann note was sensationally splashed over the front page of every morning newspaper in the land.

The German Foreign Minister, Dr. Alfred Zimmermann, had most indiscreetly cabled the German minister in Mexico that *in the event of war* with the United States he was to negotiate for a German-Mexican alliance, holding out to the Mexicans the bait of regaining Texas, New Mexico, and Arizona. He was also to ask the President of Mexico to invite Japan to support the scheme.

This fantastic cablegram was intercepted and decoded by the British, and, when published, caused a tremendous revulsion of feeling in America, more so than the vastly more significant announcement of unrestricted submarine warfare. The East had generally been favorable to war following the announcement of the U-boat campaign; but the South and West had been rather apathetic. The Zimmermann note did more than anything else to fuse the disunited United States.

Ships—even American ships—sunk in the Irish Sea were far away. But this was close to home. Mexicans in Texas! Japanese on the Pacific Coast! Americans deluged with inferior peoples! To one Texas newspaper this was Prussian militarism "writhing in the slime of intrigue."

Few stopped to realize that Japan was already an ally of the Allies, or that revolution-riddled Mexico could put no effective force into the field. Few stopped to realize that when nations are at war they seek allies. And Germany, it must be repeated, virtually declared war on the United States the day she announced her unrestricted submarine warfare.

5

Meanwhile American ships had been clinging to port, afraid to venture into the war zone. Mountains of supplies were piling up on Eastern docks, and the transportation system of the country was becoming badly snarled. This is precisely what the Germans wanted, for our supplies were not reaching the Allies.

The country could not long endure economic paralysis. Wilson therefore went before Congress again and asked for authority to arm our merchantmen. Congress and the country were willing, but a handful of antiwar Senators filibustered the ship-arming measure to death. Stung to the quick, Wilson issued a statement to the country on March 4, 1917, in which he lectured the Senate on its inadequate rules, and intemperately declared that a "little group of willful men, representing no opinion but their own, have rendered the great Government of the United States helpless and contemptible." Wilson, to his regret, was to learn more about the "willful men" in the Senate.

Balked by Congress, Wilson discovered authority elsewhere, and sent American merchantmen to sea with mounted guns, and with orders to shoot at hostile submarines in the war zone. The country waited breathlessly for the overdue "overt" act.

It was not long in coming. In mid-March four unarmed American merchantmen flying the Stars-and-Stripes were sunk

Forced into It!

(From the St. Louis *Republic;* courtesy of the St. Louis *Globe-Democrat*)

by German U-boats on the high seas, with the loss of thirty-six lives. The submarine announcement had been but an announcement; the Zimmermann note had been but a note; but this was an act of war. The German submarines were making war on the United States just as surely as the Japanese bombers were to make war on the United States when they dumped their lethal cargoes on the American fleet at Pearl Harbor.

Again Wilson's hand was forced. He had no honorable alternative to summoning Congress in special session and asking it officially to recognize the hostilities that were being waged on us. It took two weeks for Congress to assemble, but in the meantime the country assumed that we were at war—which we were. The newspapers and the public in general actually united in an unofficial counter declaration of war on Germany before Congress had an opportunity formally to do so.

On April 2, 1917, President Wilson again stood before the packed and hushed audience in the chamber of the House of Representatives. In measured words he stated that the German government was waging war on the United States, and he called upon Congress formally to recognize the state of hostilities that had been "thrust" upon us. He did not then ask Congress to declare war on Austria-Hungary and Bulgaria and Turkey, even though they were allies of Germany, because they were not attacking us. We would fight only those who were fighting us.

Congress responded to Wilson's summons when, on April 4 and 6, 1917, the two houses voted by overwhelming majorities that "the state of war . . . which has thus been *thrust upon the United States* is hereby formally declared."

Why did we go to war with Germany? The answer is that we did not go to war with Germany. She went to war with us. The United States, as a self-respecting, sovereign nation, whose citizens had a perfect legal right to sail the high seas, could not do other than recognize this fact. As Wilson pointedly declared two months later, "The military masters of Germany denied us the right to be neutral."

The submarine was clearly the precipitating cause of our war with Germany, but this does not mean that there were not other and highly important contributory causes. German espionage as betrayed by Dr. Albert's purloined briefcase, German intrigue as nakedly exposed in the Zimmermann note, and German sabotage as high-lighted by such disasters as the Black Tom explosion, mightily aroused the American people against the "Hun."

There was also a widespread and gnawing fear that if the

Kaiser should crush the Allies, he would hardly wait to take a deep breath before coming over here with millions of spiked helmets to make short work of us and our Monroe Doctrine. This view was not too seriously held by those who knew something of Germany's semi-exhaustion, and of the technical difficulties involved in waging a war across the Atlantic. But it made sense to the man in the street, and it was sedulously cultivated by Allied and home-grown propaganda. After all, it was better to fight when one could have strong allies than to wait until one had to fight alone.

These fears and incidents, superimposed upon a strong pro-Ally, anti-German sentiment, caused us to accept Germany's challenge the more willingly when it came. But without the submarine we probably should not have gone to war with Germany, certainly not when we did.

6

In later years, Senator Gerald P. Nye, of North Dakota, achieved great notoriety by alleging, and proving to his satisfaction, that we were dragged into the war by the munitions manufacturers (a German charge of 1917), by the Wall Street bankers, by the war profiteers, and by the Allied propagandists. All such explanations ignore the simple fact that we were not dragged into the war at all. Wilson took an irrevocable stand in his *Sussex* ultimatum; the Germans finally defied him, and then began making war on us. If any "dragging" was done, it was done by the Germans. The decision that we should fight was made in Germany, not in America.

The question naturally arises: Was Wilson wise in issuing his *Sussex* ultimatum? At this distance it now seems that there were only two possible ways of meeting the submarine threat. The first was to forbid our citizens and shipping to enter the war zones, as we later did in the Neutrality Act of 1939. But Wilson, the idealist and moralist, sternly and quite understandably refused to permit such a course. It would, he felt, be dishonorable; and once we began to abdicate certain rights, the whole "fine fabric" of international law would begin to break down.

The second possible course was to build up so powerful an armed force that the Germans would not dare disregard American rights. This Wilson refused to do, for he was a pacifist, or at least an unremitting hater of war. He fought the preparedness movement tooth and nail, and not until November, 1915, fifteen months *after* the outbreak of the war and nine months *after* the opening of the German submarine campaign, did he reluctantly and lukewarmly clamber onto the bandwagon. By this time it was too late.

Actually, Wilson adopted neither of the two courses here outlined. He refused to keep American citizens off munitions-laden belligerent passenger ships. He refused to keep American ships out of the war zone. He refused, until too late, to build up a strong army and merchant marine. His *Sussex* ultimatum in these circumstances was hardly less than a colossal bluff.

When the showdown came, we had a strong navy but a contemptibly small army, ranking in numbers with about that of Spain. Our navy did not worry the Germans, because they controlled the underseas, and Britain already controlled the surface of the seas. Berlin counted on knocking the British out of the war before we could send an effective army to Europe. When the Germans concluded that they had more to gain than to lose by attacking our ships, they attacked them. And America was forced into the war.

7

In still more recent years another plausible explanation has become fashionable. We went to war in 1917, it is alleged, primarily to save the Allies and to redress the balance of power.

The basic difficulty with this explanation is that it is false. The Allies were not visibly collapsing in February and March of 1917. On the contrary, it was generally assumed in the United States that they were winning—or, at the very worst, there was a draw. The capture of Bagdad by the Allies on March 11, 1917, was widely regarded as an offset to the failure of the Dardanelles campaign. The strategic withdrawal of Hindenburg to the famed Hindenburg line, in mid-March, 1917, involved the yielding of 1,300 square miles of French territory on a 100-mile front, and was preceded and succeeded by Allied successes. The Americans not unnaturally regarded this as a great victory, and were pleased to note that the arrogant Germans were developing a "retiring disposition." Submarine sinkings were an old story, and the toll being taken by the new campaign was heavy but not especially alarming.

It is true that the Allies were beginning to scrape the bottoms of their money chests, but this fact was not generally known. The famous telegram of Ambassador Walter Hines Page, describing the alarming financial situation, was not sent from London until March 5, 1917, five weeks *after* the German war lords had announced their intention of forcing the United States into the war.

The naked truth is that the real danger of Allied collapse came *after* we entered the conflict—not before. In the last two weeks of April, 1917, and the first week of May, 1917, the U-boat took a terrifying toll of Allied shipping. Brought face to face with the gaunt specter of starvation, England passed through her darkest hour from Napoleon to Hitler.

Late in 1917, the Italian front crumbled and was reestablished with enormous difficulty. Shortly thereafter Russia withdrew from the war, thus releasing approximately one million German veterans for the Western front, and insuring preponderant man power to Germany for the first time in the war. In March, and again in May, 1918, the gray German flood came within a hairbreadth of breaking through to Paris and knocking France out of the war.

No, America did not enter the conflict primarily to save the Allies, or to reestablish the balance of power. The Allies did not then seem to be in need of saving, and the balance of power was the very last thing in the world that Wilson was willing to fight for. If any one thing stands out clearly in his numerous war addresses it is that he would have none of the old order of armed camps.

America entered the war to vindicate her right to sail the high seas—the historic American principle of freedom of the seas. As Wilson said in his stirring war message, "there are no other means of defending our rights."

If it is true that we were fighting for freedom of the seas, it is no less true that the Allies, notably Britain, were not. Since the imperialistic aims of the Allies were not our aims, why not withdraw from the war the moment Germany agreed to respect our maritime rights?

It is a fact of the highest significance—and one that has been generally overlooked—that during the weeks following the submarine declaration there was widespread expression of this view in the United States. A considerable number of men prominent in public life, as well as a large number of newspapers, gave serious attention to the problem of waging a limited-liability war, and of withdrawing as soon as our rights were acknowledged. There was also serious discussion of the question as to whether we ought openly or officially to join the Allies.

The agitation for a limited-liability war largely died out after the Zimmermann note and the various overt acts, but it was symptomatic of a profoundly important isolationist prejudice. Wilson would have done well to remember this limited-liability sentiment when he outlined his sweeping program for world responsibility.

8

The United States accepted the gage of war in 1917 without overwhelming enthusiasm—certainly not with the enthusiasm that was generated later. The war resolution in Congress actually received the negative vote of fifty-six members. Throughout the country, and especially in the Middle West, influential groups of people were apathetic if not actually hostile to fighting. The conclusion is inescapable that both Wilson and the American public as a whole made their decision to accept the German challenge with the greatest of deliberation and reluctance. It was a dirty job that had been forced upon us, and the only way out was forward.

Wilson realized, just as the American people realized, that the submarine had driven us into this war. But he also realized that the nation, especially the landlocked Middle West, could not be aroused to support a great self-sacrificing crusade with the cry, "Make the world safe against the submarine!" The submarine was the immediate *cause* of the war; but he would have to find some more elevated and inspiring *objective*.

It is highly significant—and also generally overlooked—that in his speeches and letters of the spring of 1917 Wilson was careful to preserve a fine distinction between *causes* and *objectives*. The submarine, of course, was the immediate *cause*, but now that we were in the war we were fighting not only for our rights on the high seas but for our more general rights to go our democratic way in peace. We were fighting to make the world safe for democracy, because our democracy could not be safe—nor could any democracy be safe—in a world in which Prussian militarism was running amuck.

But as the war dragged on, Wilson introduced other objectives which developed logically from his zeal to make the world safe for American democracy. We were fighting also for the "rights of mankind," for the "rights of all peoples," for the "sacred rights of free men everywhere." We were even fighting for "a new international order based . . . on broad principles of right and justice."

When Wilson said that the American people were fighting for the rights of all humanity, he professed to speak for the great mass of his countrymen. But was he faithfully interpreting their views? Had he forgotten the many millions who were reluctant to fight for their own rights, to say nothing of the rights of all peoples everywhere? Had he forgotten the large number who felt that they were fighting for freedom of the seas for the United States, and who were willing to leave the Allies in the lurch once this object was attained? Had he forgotten that the deeply rooted isolationist tradition did not at all square with the ideal that we were our brothers' keeper?

9

It is doubtless true that Wilson was the spokesman for the more liberal elements in the United States. It is doubtless true that his lofty ideals, expressed with glowing conviction in a number of notable war addresses, captivated the imagination of a great many people. But there doubtless is some truth in the charge that Wilson became hypnotized by the eloquence of his own fascinating phrases. Gradually in his thinking the *causes* began to merge with the *objectives*, and before the end of the war he seems to have believed—and he certainly carried a great many with him—that we had actually entered the conflict to save the world from Prussian autocracy, to make the world safe for democracy, and to end all wars.

In view of the blurring that took place in Wilson's mind, is it surprising that present-day students have fallen into the same error? Is it surprising that they have assumed that the *objectives* which we announced *after* we entered the war were the same as the *causes* that brought us into the war?

We must not lose sight of the fact that these exalted objectives did not exist—at least not in clear form—before they were proclaimed by President Wilson. The American people did not accept the war that had been "thrust" upon them with the expectation of embarking upon a great world crusade. They did not even have clearly in mind sending over a large expeditionary force. It was generally assumed at first that, since the Allies were winning, our chief contributions would be financial and naval, while we took steps to raise an army for defense. But the flaming sword of Wilsonian idealism aroused the American people from their apathy and confusion, and united them behind a cause for which men willingly sacrificed their lives.

At this distance it seems as though one of Wilson's gravest mistakes was to lose sight of the distinction between the fundamental *causes* of the war and the possible *objectives* of the peace. He pitched his objectives on too high a plane—objectives which did not command the support of the American people, at least not in their quieter moments. It is true, of course, that his exalted words exercised unprecedented power in arousing men to fight. But unfortunately wars do not end with the shooting, and people often see things differently in the cold, gray dawn of the morning after.

Wilson declared that we were fighting to make the world safe for democracy. Theodore Roosevelt, who was nearer the grass roots, went around the country shouting through clenched teeth that we were not fighting to make the world safe for anything. We were fighting because we had been attacked. We were fighting to beat Germany—not to attain a new international order.

Few forward-looking persons will argue that Wilson should have formulated his war aims in line with the narrowest isolationist sentiment in the country. But a formidable body of such sentiment did exist at that time, and Wilson, as the event was to prove, should either have reckoned with it or have educated it. Nothing was to be gained in the long run by ignoring it. When a President is determined to commit the American people to a self-denying program of world responsibility, he should make sure that he is not out too far ahead of the parade.

CHAPTER TWO

THE PEN IS MIGHTIER

*"The phrase [self-determination] is simply loaded with dyna-
mite. It will raise hopes which can never be realized. . . . What
a calamity that the phrase was ever uttered! What misery it will
cause!"* ROBERT LANSING, *December 30, 1918.*

————————

1

AN INCREASING number of writers, especially in recent
years, are disposed to censure Wilson for what they consider a
lamentable oversight. Why, they ask, did he not drive a bargain
with the Allies as to the specific terms of the peace at the time
we entered the conflict?

The argument is that the Allies were in such critical need
of our financial and naval assistance early in 1917 that they
could have been forced to make definite pledges in line with
our desires for a non-imperialistic peace. If such promises had
been extorted—and kept—the tragedy of the peace table might
have been avoided.

On the surface, this argument appears plausible. Certainly
the time to drive a hard bargain with one's future associates
in a war is when they are in desperate need of your help. When
the common enemy is crushed, they are much less likely to
respect your ideas about the writing of the peace.

Yet there are sound reasons why we should not censure
Wilson for having failed to exact his pound of flesh before
clasping hands with the Allies. First and foremost, we did not
enter the conflict primarily because we desired to, or because
we wanted to help the Allies, but because Germany had picked
a fight with us. Our quarrel was with the Imperial German
government, not with the Allies over the prospective spoils.

We should also note that Wilson did not have his long-range
war aims clearly thought out at the time we were pushed into

the struggle, and he could hardly have taken the time to work them out and integrate them with those of the Allies before consenting to give immediate assistance. By late April, 1917, the submarine peril had become desperate, and there was no time to be lost in getting our destroyers into action.

Finally, once we had entered the war on the side of the Allies, we were all in the same boat together, and from the military point of view it would have been foolhardy to withhold essential aid from our Associates while haggling over the terms of a peace that lay in the uncertain future. To have done so might well have meant the loss of the war, with Germany on the giving end of the terms.

It is true, of course, that the decision to send a large expeditionary force to France was not taken until some months after our declaration of war, and by that time Wilson could conceivably have discussed peace terms at length with the Allied leaders. Even so, we must not forget that the race to get the A.E.F. to France was a race to meet the impending German spring drive made possible by the collapse of Russia. "A terrible blow is imminent," Georges Clemenceau, the French premier, warned an American newsman early in 1918. "Tell your Americans to come quickly."

We should also remember that by early 1918 the American people had worked up tremendous enthusiasm for "licking the Kaiser," and they would have tolerated no hairsplitting over peace terms at this critical hour. They had also developed a sentimental attachment for their associates, especially France, and they doubtless would have regarded it as dishonorable to take undue advantage of the necessities of their friends. Promises extorted under these conditions certainly could have been repudiated with good conscience in the hour of victory.

Let us suppose, for the sake of the argument, that Wilson had publicly demanded of the Allies a specific renunciation of their territorial and other imperialistic aims before advancing a single dollar or sending a single destroyer to the submarine-infested waters. Let us also suppose that the Allied governments—and very probably this would have happened—had said that they did not dare fly in the face of home opinion by renouncing all such aims. Then where would Wilson have been? He could not withdraw the United States from the war. He could not fight a separate war. In short, it would have been the supremest folly to do other than cooperate wholeheartedly and unreservedly with the Allies—and they knew it.

2

In connection with America's attitude toward the Allies, it appears that Wilson made one avoidable mistake which on the surface seems to have been of a trivial nature. This was his insistence that we be not "allied" with the Allies as "allies," but "associated" with them as "Associates." From this distinction was born that awkward official phrase, "the Allied and Associated Powers."

Wilson was much more than a superficial student of American history and government, as his five-volume *History of the American People* attests. He was keenly aware of the power and persistence of the isolationist tradition, and particularly the antipathy against entangling alliances which had grown out of our military alliance of 1778 with France. He was fully aware that there were few subjects on which the American rabble-rouser could shout with more damaging effect than by misquoting Washington's Farewell Address on the dangers of foreign entanglements.

Wilson therefore insisted that a verbal and psychological barrier be erected between us and our allies in the wordy phrase, "Allied and Associated Powers." In common conversation this circumlocutory mouthful was conveniently discarded, and people referred simply to the Allies as "our Allies"—which was the truth, though the bond was not sealed by a formal alliance. Self-interest and a common enemy were bond enough. Yet Wilson was constantly on the alert to scotch such evidences of loose thinking as were betrayed by the term "our Allies." When careless subordinates lapsed into the colloquial and used this forbidden expression, Wilson rapped their knuckles with a stern and magisterial rebuke. The frustrated Theodore Roosevelt, who hated Wilson and all his works, frothed at this latest exhibition of pedantry. He publicly demanded to know "what the President means by continually referring to this country merely as the associate instead of the ally of the nations, with whose troops our own troops are actually brigaded in battle . . ."

Wilson's insistence on this wordy distinction is further proof that he was well aware of the hereditary American prejudice against making alliances with "wicked furriners." Yet his later effort to lead the United States into the League of Nations and the Security Treaty with France suggests that he forgot the lesson he had once known so well. The Scripture speaks of men who strain gnats out of their drink while swallowing camels. Wilson carefully strained the Allied and Associated Powers 'through his thinking, while gulping down the League of Nations and a military alliance with France.

We know that Wilson strongly urged the adoption of a League of Nations even before the United States entered the war, notably in his masterly "peace without victory" address of January 22, 1917. Immediately an outburst of criticism and denunciation arose from the bitter isolationists in the Senate. If Wilson was interested in leading us into the League, he would have done well to insist that we were allied with the Allies in a common cause, after April, 1917, both in war and in peace. An entanglement forged in the heat of war, and sanctified by victory, would win acceptance more easily in time of peace than one newly forged after the fighting had stopped.

The ancient American prejudice against alliances may be unreasoning, and it may even be childish, but there it was. One could not overcome it by ignoring it or by paying obeisance to it. Wilson certainly adopted a curious approach for one who had already decided to forsake old traditions and embark on the uncharted sea of international cooperation. His emphatic insistence upon our not becoming allied with the Allies did nothing to break down the hoary isolationist ideal. It did nothing to remove the ingrained suspicion that faithless foreigners on the other side of the Atlantic were people unclean, not fit to be "allied" with, fit only to be "associated" with. By merely "associating" ourselves with the Allies, we could the more easily disassociate ourselves when the fighting ended— and we did.

3

It is one of the prettiest ironies of history that the peace-loving President Wilson, with his pacifist Secretary of War, attained far greater success in making war than in making peace.

As a war leader, Wilson achieved what was probably his greatest triumph in public life. The man and the hour providentially met. Endowed with a fine voice and a splendid platform presence, blessed with a gift for telling phrase, and radiating the sincere spiritual fervor of his Presbyterian forbears, he aroused the American people from their apathy and launched them on a crusade of unprecedented power.

Before we were plunged into the war, Wilson had developed certain ideas about a lasting peace, and from time to time he outlined these in eloquent public addresses. After we entered the war, he clarified and elaborated these same ideas, and added others. Few of these statements attracted much attention: the world was full of announced peace aims, and Wilson's were too vague and too lengthily worded.

By early January, 1918, the situation called for the publication of a peace program with a "punch." The Russian revolutionists were insidiously calling for "peace without annexations or indemnities." They had ripped open the musty archives of the Tsar, and had nakedly exposed Russia's secret and imperialistic treaties with the Allies to the gaze of a shocked world. The Allies, who professedly were fighting for nobler things, suffered a severe moral defeat. Wilson's advisers urged him to frame a specific platform in "snappy" placard paragraphs which could be used for propaganda purposes, and which would serve to offset the propaganda and the damaging revelations of the Bolsheviks.

The Peace Terms

(From the New York *American;* courtesy of the New York *Journal-American*)

Wilson responded magnificently when, on January 8, 1918, he appeared before Congress with his memorable Fourteen Points. The first five were general in scope: open diplomacy; freedom of the seas; the beating down of economic barriers; the reduction of armament; and the adjustment of colonial claims on a fair basis. Then followed a series of formulas for applying justice to specific countries or areas. The fourteenth and capstone point was a declaration in favor of an Association of Nations to guarantee world peace. (For texts of Wilson's points, see note accompanying this chapter, pp. 333-336.)

In three subsequent addresses, Wilson set forth at least thirteen other points, bringing the total to twenty-seven. Some of the later points were merely a repetition, elaboration, clarification, or contradiction of the earlier ones. When we eliminate the overlapping, the total is about twenty-three.

Among the latter-day points were persuasive declarations in favor of a just and lasting peace; of no bartering of peoples; of the satisfaction of legitimate national aspirations; of honorable international dealing; of the destruction of arbitrary power; and of territorial adjustments in the interests of the peoples concerned. This last point, self-determination, was destined to arouse a vast amount of unrealizable nationalistic sentiment.

Yet did the American people, despite wide editorial acclaim, really understand and approve the Fourteen Points? Was Wilson expressing the aspirations of his countrymen, as he repeatedly claimed, or was he merely setting up a high-sounding goal to which they might aspire, and in which they could acquiesce as long as their enthusiasm was at a high pitch? Colonel House was present at the last of Wilson's great war-aims addresses, that of September 27, 1918, in the Metropolitan Opera House at New York, and he recorded that most of it seemed to be "over the heads of the audience," and that the parts which were least important brought forth the "most vigorous applause." Ominously, the passage which the press reported as most enthusiastically received was that promising stern treatment for Germany. The American people were evidently more interested in dethroning the Kaiser than in enthroning Wilsonian idealism, and it is unfortunate that Wilson did not grasp this crucial fact.

Below the surface, and even above the surface, there were some rumbling criticisms of the Fourteen Points, especially from Republicans who did not like the idea of a Democratic President reordering the world. There were some sneering comments about the "fourteen commandments" of "God Almighty Wilson," and there was considerable disquietude in the ranks of the high-tariff Republicans over Point III, which aimed at the lowering of economic barriers. But it is significant that this muttered opposition did not break out into the open until the fighting had ended, or had nearly ended.

4

Wilson has been frequently criticized for not having worked out a joint statement of war aims with the Allies, rather than stealing the spotlight with a prima-donna performance.

The truth is that Wilson attempted to secure such a joint declaration, and the Allies were unable to agree upon one. It was only after all efforts in this direction had failed that he decided to go it alone.

One must also correct the rather general misconception that the Fourteen Points were original with Wilson. Three days before the President's memorable address, Prime Minister Lloyd George had partially stolen Wilson's thunder by delivering a hardly less spectacular speech in London before the representatives of the trade unions. He mentioned essentially all of Wilson's Fourteen Points, except three: open covenants openly arrived at; a lowering of trade barriers; and freedom of the seas. On the other hand, he strongly stressed reparations for damages caused by the Germans.

It is most interesting to note that the three points not mentioned by Lloyd George appeared in the Bolshevist statement of war aims, published a week earlier. Both the Russian and the British spokesmen had already stressed self-determination for submerged minorities, and Lloyd George out-Wilsoned Wilson when he advocated the extension of this principle to the half-naked natives of Africa. Later, at the Paris peace conference, Lloyd George heatedly told Wilson that self-determination was one of his own points. He might just as well have claimed authorship of the Bible; self-determination is as old as nationalism.

While it is clear that we cannot blame Wilson for inventing the principle of self-determination, he did give it a new emphasis and a new impetus. This, in fact, may be said of most of his Fourteen Points. What he actually did was to codify the best of existing war aims, even including some announced by the Germans and the Bolsheviks, and to add a few of his own.

Some of the Fourteen Points were precise, shockingly precise for old-school diplomacy; others were vague or contradictory. This was especially true of the latter-day points. Poland, for example, was promised free access 'to the sea in Point XIII. But the only possible corridor to the sea ran through territory inhabited by a considerable body of Germans. If Poland did not get the corridor, one of the points would be violated; if she did get it (with Danzig) the point relating to self-determination would be at least partially violated.

In short, the Points were idealistic enough and vague enough to make a splendid platform for waging the war; but they were too illusory and contradictory to make an adequate platform upon which to construct the peace. "He [Wilson] could have preached a sermon on any one of them," writes John Maynard Keynes, "or have addressed a stately prayer to the Almighty for their fulfilment; but he could not frame their concrete application to the actual state of Europe." One of the most unfortunate aspects of this whole story is that the Fourteen Points were finally used for a purpose that was not originally intended.

Admirable though the Wilsonian points were for arousing the American people to a supreme effort, it now seems that from the long-range point of view Wilson made a mistake in pitching them on so high a note. God is on the side of the big battalions; and the American divisions would probably have got to France and the Allies probably would have overborne the enemy about as rapidly if Wilson had held his idealism somewhat in leash—if he had been more temperate, more precise, more realistic.

One danger inherent in the Fourteen Points was that reaction was inevitable. The ideals that Wilson set forth were, under the best of circumstances, not wholly realizable. Disillusionment—"the slump in idealism"—was bound to come with the cold gray dawn of victory; and unhappily it did come under circumstances that will be described later. The higher the idealism the greater the slump, and if Wilson had fixed his aim on the peace table rather than on the battlefield the reaction might not have been so violent.

5

Wilson not only preached ideals which were clearly unrealizable in this our world, but those who re-preached them grossly "oversold" them.

The dynamic George Creel, who as head of the Committee on Public Information mobilized emotion, took over Wilson and his Points, and advertised him and them all over the world as no one person or program has been advertised before or since. These great "verbiage drives" or "moral offensives" had all the earmarks of a glorified campaign to sell some patent medicine—a development that could hardly have pleased the dignified and sensitive academician in the White House.

More than sixty million leaflets, pamphlets, and booklets—largely featuring "Wilsonisms"—were showered upon Latin America, the Far East, and Europe. They were translated into a veritable babel of tongues. A volume of Wilson's speeches became a "best seller in China"; a leaflet containing one of his addresses was adopted as a textbook in a Madrid school. Always it was the thunderbolts of President Wilson.

Ominously, this great crusade began to arouse Messianic hopes—and President Wilson was the Messiah. In far-away Poland, starry-eyed university students met on the streets, clasped hands, and uttered but one word: "Wilson." Creel, while traveling in a mountainous part of Italy, sought refuge from a storm in a peasant's lonely cabin. Above a shrine on one side of the chimney he observed a wax figure of a local patron saint side by side with a poster picture of Woodrow Wilson. A member of the American Embassy ·in Rome saw in some barracks an improvised altar, on which burned four candles, above which hung a poster of Wilson, and before which the soldiers were constantly kneeling.

Nor was the enemy neglected. Wilson's Fourteen Points were rained upon the Central Powers from airplanes, balloons, and cannon shell. Among the highly nationalistic Poles, Czechs, and Slavs of Germany and Austria-Hungary the rainbow of self-determination aroused hope, then resistance, and finally rebellion. The winged words of Woodrow Wilson were worth armies.

The people of Germany at first felt that the Fourteen Points were a masterpiece of effrontery, especially in view of the fact that their legions had won most of the battles to date. But Wilson's high-sounding promises insidiously began to bore like termites at the foundations of German morale. German liberals could applaud a great deal in the Points, for Wilson had stolen much of their thunder. German merchants and manufacturers were pleased with the prospect of economic disarmament, for they lived in daily dread of after-the-war reprisals. German imperialists could not quarrel with the promise of a fair adjustment of colonial claims, for this was seemingly a pledge that they might keep some or all of their colonies. Germans everywhere could not refuse to applaud the principle of freedom of the seas, for that would hamstring the hated British navy.

As the great conflict roared into its final stages, and as German morale began to crack, increasing numbers of hungry Germans began to ask themselves: would not a negotiated peace based upon the principles of the Fourteen Points be far better than the continuance of this fruitless struggle?

6

One of the greatest weaknesses of the Fourteen Points as a peace platform was that they lent themselves to sloganizing. "Freedom of the seas," "open covenants openly arrived at," "self-determination for peoples"—what did all these things mean? The grave danger of slogans is that they shut the door to thinking, while giving people the comfortable feeling that they are thinking. And since people do not ordinarily go to the trouble to find out what slogans mean, and since the Fourteen Points were inadequately explained by their author, it is not surprising that they were made to mean what their readers wanted them to mean. This was splendid—as long as the Points were used to arouse the Allies and seduce the enemy. But a day of reckoning was bound to come.

Obviously, no mortal man this side of the millennium could have hoped to bring about all the things that the world came to expect of Wilson. On the day he sailed from New York for the Paris Conference, a sweatshop worker was heard to remark, "There goes the man who is going to change all this for us." Wilson's own people were bound to feel disillusioned; the peoples of the neutral and the Allied countries were bound to feel deceived; and the peoples of the enemy countries were bound to feel betrayed.

The official authors of war aims should make them clear, reasonable, and as explicit as possible. In the short run, extravagant promises—specific or tacit—may prove effective, but in the long run they cannot but recoil upon the heads of their makers.

7

The Fourteen Points led to another highly unfortunate development. They came to be rather generally regarded as the peace platform of all the Allies, rather than the platform of

Woodrow Wilson, who was merely "associating" with the Allies.

This inference was not wholly Wilson's fault. In his earlier speeches he stated emphatically that he was speaking *only* for the United States. But as time wore on he made this distinction less emphatic, and eventually it was largely lost sight of, certainly in the popular mind. The result probably would have been the same in any event, no matter how many denials he made. The United States was "associated" with the Allies; Wilson was the outstanding figure among the war leaders of the Allied and Associated Powers; therefore Wilson spoke for all the Allied governments. The senior partner is ordinarily presumed to speak for the entire firm.

Perhaps it is unfair to suggest that Wilson should have had the foresight to see that this would happen. But as things turned out it would have been less disastrous if he had been able to work out some common program with the Allies. This would have been difficult, perhaps impossible; it would have taken time; and time was at a premium when the Fourteen Points were issued. But even if no joint Allied statement had been possible, there was no valid reason why Wilson could not have correlated his program with that of the British. We have noted that the original Fourteen Points speech followed that of Lloyd George by only three days; and the program of the British Prime Minister was certainly sweeping enough. The three new points that Wilson added eventually gained little or nothing, and opened a Pandora's box of misunderstanding. From the standpoint of Allied unity it would have been better if Wilson had merely restated Lloyd George's better aims. But this would not have been true from the standpoint of Wilson's prestige or the success of the Allied propaganda campaign.

In truth, the Allied governments did favor the Fourteen Points as a weapon for disarming the enemy, and they viewed with satisfaction how well this weapon was doing its work. But the Allied governments, as distinguished from the more liberal elements in their population, did not favor the Fourteen Points as a platform for the peace they proposed to draw up. They had already made a number of secret treaties among themselves for carving up the enemy's territory; and they had no intention, after long years of bloody sacrifice, of giving up their prospective booty at the behest of the American doctrinaire-President. When the time came for a serious discussion of peace terms Premier Clemenceau of France remarked, perhaps jokingly, that he had never read the Fourteen Points. But, whether joking or in earnest, he betrayed an inauspicious attitude.

So the Allied governments kept quiet, while a large part of the world believed that Wilson was speaking for the entire coalition. What else could the Allied leaders do? Could they rise up and loudly aver that they did not believe in what Wilson was saying, and thus arouse the Central Powers for a last-ditch struggle? Could they rise up and proclaim that they had secret aspirations for which they—and indirectly the American people—were fighting?

Wilson himself kept quiet at one critically important time. In October, 1918, when the Imperial German government sued for peace, three supremely important interchanges of notes took place between Washington and Berlin. In the second, that of October 12, the Wilhelmstrasse said: "The German Government believes that the Governments of the powers associated with the United States also accept the position taken by President Wilson in his addresses."

Then was the time for Wilson—for he helped prepare these crucial notes—to make it emphatically clear that he spoke only for the United States. But the American reply completely ignored this whole point. Silence is usually assumed to give consent. In any event, the Germans were not without some grounds for complaint when they discovered to their lasting regret that this presumption was wrong.

8

A final word about war aims in general, and the Fourteen Points in particular.

A vast number of people, especially in America, regarded Wilson's declarations as a hard and fast contract with the public that he would carry out to the strict letter every one of his announced war aims. When he failed to do so—no mortal man could have done so—he was widely and bitterly accused of having broken faith.

The longer and more specific a list of war aims becomes, the more difficult it is to realize it in its entirety. Conditions may so change as the war goes on—and this happened in 1917 and 1918—that what once seemed feasible is no longer feasible, what once seemed desirable is no longer desirable.

A statement of war aims is a statement of what one hopes to attain. In this workaday world one would be both foolish and naïve to assume that there must be no leeway for adjustment in the light of changing circumstances. War aims are to warfare what political platforms are to politics; no one ever expects the latter to be carried out completely. In some cases it would be actually harmful to do so. Why we should expect a different standard in the even more complex field of international relations, it is difficult to say, except perhaps that we have had far more experience with politics than with war.

Wilson, it seems, never promised to carry out to the letter every one of his war aims. He was far more concerned with their spirit than with their letter. "They were articles of faith," writes George Creel, "rather than the hard and fast clauses of a commercial agreement, and if they were to be dealt with in a mean, legalistic spirit, every one of them could be denied without loss of face."

It is difficult enough to carry out literally a long and specific list of war aims when a nation is fighting without allies. It is literally impossible when a nation is fighting with a coalition of nearly thirty other belligerents. The Allied leaders, notably Lloyd George (who wore his promises lightly), had now and again made a passing bow to the Fourteen Points. But Wilson knew perfectly well that our Associates had not formally or even informally subscribed to them in their entirety. To force them to do so, even with reservations, was one of the great diplomatic battles that lay ahead, and he knew it. That struggle won, the next step would be to try to make the Allies live up to as many of their promises as practicable.

If Wilson had made it clear, time and again, that the Fourteen Points were not to be taken too literally, he might have dampened America's war enthusiasm, but he would have cushioned the disillusionment which finally ruined the Treaty of Versailles in America.

CHAPTER THREE

AN ARMISTICE THAT WAS NOT AN ARMISTICE

"We have no quarrel with the German people. We have no feeling towards them but one of sympathy and friendship. It was not upon their impulse that their government acted in entering upon this war." WOODROW WILSON, *April 2, 1917.*

1

THERE ARE many who now feel that it was a mistake for Wilson to insist in his public addresses that we were not really fighting the German people but their "military masters." This pleasant fiction led ultimately to tragic consequences.

Governments are the responsible spokesmen—in fact the only spokesmen—for the peoples they presume to govern. Not infrequently, to be sure, those governments do not faithfully represent the wishes of their people. When this happens, it is assumed that the people will cause the government to change its policy, or failing that, change the government, either by ballots or by bullets.

It often happens that peoples, through inertia or ignorance or fear, tolerate governmental policies of which they do not approve. It also happens that governments, through control of the press and other agencies of propaganda, deliberately deceive their own people. But in international relations the only practicable course is to assume that a government speaks for the entire nation. To go behind the returns will almost invariably create more problems than will be solved.

The German people bitterly resented and heatedly denied Wilson's assertions that they were not supporting the Imperial German government. One has only to turn to the contemporary German press, from the most liberal journals to the most conservative, to find abundant evidence that Germans of all classes, except for a few pacifists and left-wing Socialists, were loyally backing their leaders. And we must remember that there was an extraordinary amount of free speech in the Germany of 1917–1918. Almost to a man it was felt that the Fatherland was fighting a legitimate war of self-defense, against an encirclement of powerful, unscrupulous, and vengeful enemies. This, naturally, was the theme of official German propaganda.

Wilson's attempt to drive a wedge between the people and their leaders, if anything, strengthened the will of the Germans to resist—as long as they were in a mood to continue fighting. But there can be little doubt that the distinction which Wilson made between the German people and their "military masters" added to the enthusiasm of the American war effort. It also undoubtedly reconciled the millions of German-Americans to the thought of killing their own kinsmen.

While the American people undoubtedly generated a great amount of bitterness against Germans as such, it would have been difficult if not impossible to arouse a blind and overwhelming hatred against the German people as a whole. We in America had welcomed millions of them as neighbors, and we knew them as clean, industrious, and law-abiding citizens. But the "military masters" of Germany—the arrogant, goosestepping, Junkerized, Prussianized aristocracy—could be epitomized in the person of the Kaiser, with his sneering, snarling, upturned mustaches. The cartoonists and orators had a field day. Against this unfortunate representative of royalty the American people worked up a paroxysm of hate without parallel in our history.

Nothing could better illustrate the dangers of overpersonalizing a great war. When the villain is removed or destroyed, the victors are at a loss how to deal with the underlying forces that brought him into being or gave him strength.

2

Then came October, 1918. Bulgaria had collapsed; Austria-Hungary was near collapse; the German defenses in France were crumbling. The Berlin government approached Wilson seeking an armistice and peace negotiations. With stern, uncompromising words the President replied that if the United States had to deal with "the military masters of the monarchical autocrats of Germany," it "must demand, not peace negotiations, but surrender."

This biting reply was undoubtedly Wilson's own idea, for the Allied leaders were completely in the dark as to what his answer would be. Its uncompromising tone was doubtless due in part to the continuance of submarine warfare while the negotiations were in progress, and particularly to the brutal torpedoing of a British passenger ship, the *Leinster,* with a loss of over four hundred men, women, and children.

It is important to note that Wilson did not specifically warn the German people that they must throw the Kaiser overboard, and it is quite possible that he did not intend that they should do so. If this is true, he made a serious error in not specifying more exactly what he wanted. But the inference to be drawn from Wilson's ambiguous injunction was unmistakable, at least to the Germans. If they continued under the yoke of their Kaiser and "military masters," they could expect nothing but unconditional surrender; if they got rid of them and established a republic, there might be negotiation—and lenient terms. There can be no doubt that this general feeling hastened not only the German revolution but also the establishment of a more liberal government and the expulsion of the discredited Kaiser.

Once the German people had lived up to what they thought was their end of the bargain—but which was no bargain at all—they counted on generous peace terms. When the hour of disillusionment came, they vehemently denounced Wilson and the Allies for treachery and betrayal.

The official Allied reply at Versailles in 1919 was a classic of envenomed realism. It pointed out that the German people had supported the war from beginning to end, which was true, and that they could have overthrown their government and its policy at any time they had willed it, which was also true. The German people had kept up the fight as long as there was promise of victory and conquest, and they could not expect to escape responsibility for their misdeeds merely by changing rulers, as one would change clothes, in the hour of defeat.

In the dark days of 1917 and 1918 Wilson had repeatedly proclaimed that we were not fighting the German people but their "military masters." In the glorious days of victory the Allied spokesmen bluntly denied that this was true. They sincerely believed that the German people were guilty as well as their rulers. And even if they had not believed this, they would have found it convenient to do so, for how could they otherwise justify harsh punishments and heavy reparations burdens?

In this case, as in that of the Fourteen Points, Wilson made the mistake of not squaring his program with that of the Allied statesmen, and keeping closely in touch with them. They could not very well tell him to stop talking; and once he had elevated American morale by making the sharp distinction between the German people and their imperial rulers, the Allies could hardly have issued loud protests that this was not so.

It is highly interesting to note that under the impact of the war and the Conference, Wilson shifted ground. Speaking at Columbus, Ohio, on September 4, 1919, during his fatal tour for the League, he said in reference to the Germans that "a people are responsible for the acts of their Government. If their Government purposes things that are wrong, they ought to take measures to see to it that that purpose is not executed."

The German people would have had less justification for charges of betrayal if Wilson had preached this doctrine during the war rather than after.

3

It would have been much better, as we see it now, if the Kaiser had been allowed to stay and face the music. The long-run results probably would have been less disastrous if his government had been forced to sign the peace; and then, if the tide had turned that way, he could have bowed himself out in the face of a genuine democratic uprising.

The Weimar Republic was more or less imposed upon Germany from above; it did not spring from the soil. This partly explains why it lasted no longer than it did. In addition, this unnatural child of war was made to choke down the Treaty of Versailles—"war guilt clause" and all. That would have been a lethal dose for any government, and it was one from which the German Republic never fully recovered. It would perhaps be going too far to say that this discrediting of German liberalism was the primary cause of the rise of Hitler, but no one will deny that he used it as one of his loudest and most effective talking points in his spectacular rise to power.

In the United States, the enforced flight of the Kaiser had far-reaching psychological results. The American people were all keyed up to march on Berlin, assault the proud capital, and put the hemp around the imperial neck. "Hang the Kaiser" was the reiterated promise of song and slogan. Not only did we not get to Berlin, but we did not get the Kaiser. He fled to Holland, and the Dutch government stubbornly refused to deliver him up. Several months later the Brooklyn *Eagle* lamented: "The ex-Kaiser is still at large; unwept, unhonored, and unhung." Not only was he left unhung, but he was never punished, except to remain an exile and saw wood at Doorn and brood for twenty-three years over the glories that were gone—which was perhaps a cruel and inhuman form of punishment.

It would be a mistake to overstress the feeling of frustration that came to America, but it is probably not far from the mark to say that the premature deposition of the "Beast of Berlin" had something to do with the feeling of disillusionment which found vent in the reaction against the League of Nations. We did not hang the Kaiser, but in a very real sense we did hang the League of Nations.

4

We come now to a phase of Wilson's career which involved a decision of momentous consequences, one which could just as well have been made either way. This was his part in the Armistice negotiations of October, 1918.

Late in September, 1918, the German High Command became panicky over the military situation and peremptorily demanded that the Foreign Office make overtures to Wilson for a negotiated peace. They insisted that Wilson be approached because they were sure that the Allies would return a blunt refusal, as they already had done in the case of Austria-Hungary. The High Command was not yet prepared to surrender, but it hoped to lure the presumably naïve and idealistic Wilson into an armistice which would at least enable the German armies to regroup and strengthen their lines.

The first German note to Washington, that of October 6, 1918, unqualifiedly accepted the Fourteen Points as a basis for peace and requested the negotiation of an armistice. It is possible that the Berlin government, knowing that the Allies had not yet agreed on war aims, hoped to create dissension in their ranks by appealing to the Fourteen Points, and thus escape severe punishment.

Wilson had two courses open to him. He could have referred this overture to the Allied Supreme War Council, explaining that he was not in a position to speak for the Allied and Associated Powers, which was true. If he had done this, the Allies almost certainly would have rejected the German proposal, and would then have blasted the German armies into submission on German soil.

The other course was to open independent negotiations with

the Germans, and this Wilson did. The Allied leaders were vastly annoyed and angered at being thus short-circuited, and they broke into a cold sweat of apprehension lest this "dangerous visionary" be inveigled into some kind of trap that would throw away the fruits of victory.

Public opinion in the Allied countries seems generally to have favored fighting the war through. This was particularly true of the United States, which had developed an overwhelming war madness. There was a widespread feeling, largely among Republicans, that a negotiated peace meant a lost war. From the bellicose Theodore Roosevelt came the wild cry, "Let us dictate peace by the hammering guns and not chat about peace to the accompaniment of the clicking of typewriters."

"Our answer to the Hun's twaddle," shouted the Cleveland *Plain Dealer,* "shall be more war." Ominously, from the United States Senate arose loud rumblings of protest against a negotiated peace, including muttered threats of impeaching Wilson. One Democratic Senator, evidently fearing that the President would fall into the German "armistice trap," came to Wilson in great perturbation. The President was not flattered. "I said to the Senator," reported Wilson, " 'Do they think I am a damned fool?' "

There seems little doubt, as Colonel House testified, that Wilson underestimated the war hysteria of the American people. There also seems little doubt, as Wilson's private secretary, Joseph P. Tumulty, pointed out, that the President would have strengthened himself politically if he had flatly rejected the German overture. A march to Berlin—an unconditional surrender without parley—was what the country overwhelmingly wanted. If Wilson took the unpopular course, he would put a rallying cry into the mouths of his Republican opponents—and he did.

There can be little question but that Wilson's setback in the Congressional elections of November, 1918, to which we shall come presently, was in large part due to the fact that he had entered upon negotiations with the Germans, and that the war by then was virtually over.

But Wilson sternly closed his ears to the siren song of the politicians. From a moral point of view he could do no other than grasp this opportunity to bring the bloody conflict to a speedy and honorable end. "If I think it is right to accept it," he told Tumulty, "I shall do so regardless of consequences.

The Beast That Talks Like a Man:
"I Demand an Honorable Peace—
No Humiliation, etc."
(Courtesy of the Brooklyn *Eagle*)

As for myself, I can go down in a cyclone cellar and write poetry the rest of my days, if necessary."

5

Wilson pushed ahead with the negotiations, in spite of the vehement outcry at home and abroad, and skillfully evaded the traps that the Prussian war lords had laid for him. Once it

was known that the German government had set peace negotiations in motion, the morale of the people began to crack
wide open. The prospect of a peace of justice based on the
Fourteen Points proved irresistible to this war-weary and starving country. As German morale grew weaker, and as the clamor
in Allied countries for a stern peace grew louder, the tone of
Wilson's demands grew correspondingly stronger. A basis for
understanding was finally reached, late in October, and Wilson
passed this on, *without recommendation*, to the Allied Supreme War Council for their approval or disapproval.

This last point is vitally important. Wilson did not draw up
the terms of the armistice. That was left entirely to the Allied
military leaders, who laid down conditions which the Germans, then torn by revolution, were forced to accept. The final
terms were signed on November 11, 1918, in the same railway
car in the same forest of Compiègne that Chancellor Hitler
used for the same purpose in June, 1940.

At eleven o'clock on the eleventh day of the eleventh month
of 1918, an eerie, numbing silence fell upon the Western
Front, and the Great War was over. Or rather, the formal fighting was over.

Wilson's role as an intermediary in the preliminary armistice negotiations undoubtedly shortened the war by a number
of months, and saved tens of thousands of lives. The ultimate
object of the Allies was to disarm the enemy; and if this could
be done by negotiation rather than by prolonged fighting, so
much the better. The Allied military leaders recognized this
fact, and not unwillingly accepted it. Indeed, it would have
been immoral for them to do otherwise. They could hardly
have said: "No, we cannot stop now. There are two hundred
German towns we want to destroy; there are 500,000 more
German soldiers we want to kill."

Wilson's critics condemned him then and later for having
brought the war to an end before full vengeance could be
wreaked upon Germany. They alleged, as we have seen, that
the disappointment and frustration resulting from the failure

to march on Berlin had much to do with the ultimate defeat of his peace program. They insisted that if the Allies had marched into Germany with fire and sword the German people would have really learned what war was at first hand, and that they would have been less willing in later years to worship the false gods of Adolf Hitler.

A Popular Interpretation of Germany's Peace Overtures

(From the New York *Evening World;* reprinted by permission)

There is unquestionably much force in these criticisms. But Wilson's immediate task was to bring the war to a victorious end as quickly and bloodlessly as possible. If the conflict had been prolonged three to five more months, as Marshal Foch had thought possible, Bolshevism might have engulfed Europe, as it almost did anyhow, and the statesmen of the postwar era would have been confronted with a set of different and more disagreeable problems. In this case Wilson's peace program would have encountered even more stormy weather.

As for the frustration of the American people, and the failure of the German people to experience the devastation of war at first hand, these, it seems, were problems that could conceivably have been solved by sane and constructive leadership. Mankind will never get anywhere if it insists on needlessly protracting current evils in order to avoid possible future evils which may be removed by statesmanlike vision.

6

We must return once more to the Fourteen Points before leaving the subject of the Armistice.

The Berlin government, in its first peace feeler of October 6, 1918, announced its unqualified acceptance of the Fourteen Points as a basis for the peace. Wilson, of course, was quite agreeable to this suggestion, but the Allied leaders, who had been preaching the gospel according to Wilson for the purpose of disarming the enemy, were visibly embarrassed, just as the German strategists may have hoped.

The first question of the Allied statesmen was: What do the Fourteen Points mean? There had been little necessity for clear definition earlier in the war: indeed, the more nebulous they were, the easier it was to deceive and disarm the enemy. Colonel House, as Wilson's personal representative in Paris, had Walter Lippmann, the well known journalist, and Frank Cobb, editor of the New York *World*, draw up an elaborate commentary on the Fourteen Points which was cabled to Washington and approved by Wilson on October 30. It was on the table before the Allied leaders during these pre-Armistice negotiations, and was constantly referred to by them as the official interpretation.

The British flatly refused to accept Point II, on the freedom of the seas, because they felt that it would shackle their navy in a future war; and they were determined to continue fighting rather than throw away their most powerful offensive weapon.

Clemenceau had little faith in the Fourteen Points, and he is reported to have sneered: "God gave us the Ten Commandments, and we broke them. Wilson gives us the Fourteen Points. We shall see." He actually issued instructions to draw up a detailed statement of France's objections to the Wilsonian program, but this document was never presented. Italy suspected that the Fourteen Points might stand in the way of realizing her territorial aspirations. Belgium feared that Point III might adversely affect her trade, and Point V her colonies.

But Colonel House, representing the aroused Western giant, held strong cards in his attempts to secure acceptance of the Fourteen Points. The bankrupt Allies, in the hour of victory, were scarcely less in need of American moral and economic support than they had been in the shadow of defeat. House finally threw his ace of trumps on the table when he suggested that the United States might have to withdraw from the war, make a separate peace, and leave the Allies in the lurch. Such a desertion would be disastrous, for the Germans would be enheartened, the Allies would be weakened and demoralized, and the war might result in a stalemate, with the victors unable to gather the fruits of victory. This is so obvious to us now that Colonel House has been bitterly criticized for not having pressed his advantage more relentlessly.

After prolonged debate, the Allied leaders finally accepted the Fourteen Points, with one reservation and one elucidation. The British reserved the right to discuss the issue of freedom of the seas at the Peace Conference. Wilson was most reluctant to make this concession, because next to the League of Nations he seems to have regarded it as his most important point. It was in fact the issue that had plunged the United States into the war. After much hesitation, and after toying with the idea of an appeal to public opinion, Wilson grudgingly acceded to the British reservation.

The one elucidation was presented by the French. Point VIII stipulated, "All French territory should be freed and the invaded portions restored . . ." But this did not specifically say that the Germans would have to make reparation for the devastation they had inflicted. The French insisted upon an elucidation to the effect that the Germans would have to pay "compensation" (reparations) for "all damage done to the civilian population of the Allies and their property . . ." This seemed like a reasonable interpretation to Wilson and the American representatives, and they accepted it without undue difficulty.

The Italians had a reservation regarding their Adriatic territorial aspirations, but they presented it so bunglingly and pressed it so hesitatingly that it was never officially entered on the record. Out of this grew a vast amount of misunderstanding and ill will.

Colonel House was not altogether happy over the result, for he had hoped to secure an unqualified endorsement of the Fourteen Points. Yet it was undoubtedly a triumph for Wilsonian idealism to force an acceptance of all but one. House consoled himself by saying that perhaps it was best to have these reservations after all; they underscored the fact that the Allies had unreservedly accepted all the other points.

The Allied and Associated Powers then presented their reservations on the Fourteen Points to Germany, and this statement forms the basis of what present-day scholars refer to as the pre-Armistice contract. In other words, the victors bound themselves by a solemn legal and moral contract to make peace with Germany on the basis of the Fourteen Points, with one reservation on freedom of the seas, and one elucidation on reparations.

This, it must be emphasized, was not unconditional surrender. There were numerous if vaguely defined conditions in the Fourteen Points which the victors were honor bound to observe. It is incontestable that there was a contract; but what it meant is by no means incontestable.

7

The lawyer will tell us that the basis of any contract is a meeting of minds. There was no meeting of minds in connection with the Fourteen Points. The Germans formally accepted the Fourteen Points of Wilson, points which they read in the light of their own hopes and fears. The Allies formally accepted the Fourteen Points as explained by the Lippmann-Cobb memorandum, but this memorandum was apparently not shown to the Germans. How can there be a contract in good faith when the meaning of its most important clauses is withheld from one set of signatories?

Then there were the mental reservations. As one reads the record of Colonel House's parley with the Allied leaders it becomes perfectly clear that they did not really accept the Fourteen Points. It is perfectly clear, as the Peace Conference was to reveal further, that they and their people all had aspirations regarding security, reparations, colonies, and territory that went far beyond the letter and spirit of the Wilsonian program. To put it baldly, ardent nationalists like Clemenceau, whose people had been bled white by the "Hun," had no intention of carrying through the contract in good faith, at least not in the sense that both Wilson and the Germans interpreted it. Having accepted the points against their will, they were of the same opinion still. Yet they could not stultify themselves before the bar of world opinion, after all the publicity given to the Fourteen Points, by openly announcing that they did not believe in them.

We have already noted that House was later condemned for not using the financial and military resources of the United States to extort a more complete acceptance of the Fourteen Points at the time of the pre-Armistice negotiations. Even if the ethics of using such a club on one's colleagues be granted, it is difficult to see how the final result could have been different. No matter how many or how powerful the clubs, the mental reservations still remained; and they were bound to come out around the peace table. The immediate task was to disarm the enemy; and if the brutal and unscrupulous "Hun" was tricked, that, the American people believed, was what he richly deserved.

The Germans have also been criticized for not having insisted upon a more explicit elaboration of the Fourteen Points before laying down their arms. It appears that they did not want too specific a definition, because it might be phrased to their disadvantage, and because they hoped to interpret the vaguenesses of the Fourteen Points to their advantage at the peace table. As it turned out, they never got to the peace table. But even if there had been a more explicit restatement, the mental reservations of the Allies still existed, and the victors —leaders and people—were in no mood to deal leniently with the Germans. Where the will exists in such cases, "escape clauses" can always be found in the contract, and the Allied statesmen, as we shall later note, were resourceful in finding them.

8

We must touch on one other point before leaving this general subject. Is it true that the Fourteen Points disarmed Germany?

Some writers say that this is completely false. The German armies were being beaten in the field, and the war lords simply sought an armistice so that they could regroup their lines. The Fourteen Points had nothing to do with it.

But this is not the whole story. It is clear that the German High Command sought out Wilson, rather than the Allies, because he, as the idealistic author of the Fourteen Points and moral arbiter of the world, might be easier to handle. And when the news was published that peace negotiations were under way, German morale, already undermined by the Fourteen Points, rapidly deteriorated, and surrender was inevitable.

It seems reasonable to conclude that if the German people had not come to regard Wilson's pronouncements as something more than platitudes, they would not have demanded peace when they did. In this sense, the Fourteen Points disarmed Germany, though forcible disarmament was inevitable within a few months.

As the event proved, it would have been better if Wilson had had fewer points, more clearly defined points, fewer unrealizable points, and more points integrated with the war aims of the Allies and accepted at heart by them. Less delusive and more realistic points might not have lured the Germans into an armistice so soon. But it would have been better to fight the war through to the last barbed-wire entanglement than to make a solemn contract which could not be realized, which the Allies had no intention of fully realizing, and which was not realized.

9

The Armistice of November 11, 1918, with Germany was not a true armistice but a bastard armistice. We must consider this situation briefly because it is fundamental to any understanding of what went on at the Peace Conference. But we need not discuss it at length because Wilson and his advisers had nothing to do with it; in fact, they opposed it.

When the Germans asked for terms, the Allied leaders were anxious to bring about an armistice. Although their armies were moving forward, the current drive was beginning to lose momentum, winter was approaching, and serious problems of man power, morale, and transportation were already at hand. The Allied countries were war-weary, and Bolshevism was sweeping in from the east. Any move in the direction of peace —a victorious peace—could not but be welcomed.

The problem of the Allied leaders was to ask for enough disarmament from Germany to make it impossible for her to renew the war effectively, while not asking for so much that the Germans would be forced to reject the proffered terms. In short, just what the traffic would bear—and no more.

So it was that the German troops were allowed to go home carrying their rifles, and were asked to surrender approximately half of their heavy artillery, machine guns, and other equipment. This meant that, with such military stores as they had captured from their enemies and could manufacture, the Germans were still able to put a veteran army in the field, which would have the advantage of fighting on shortened lines, though without any real prospect of success.

This arrangement was strongly opposed by General Tasker H. Bliss, American member of the Allied Supreme War Council. Bliss favored a formula of complete disarmament and demobilization. General Pershing insisted on unconditional surrender. They both felt that if Germany was beaten she would accept any terms. If she was not beaten, then it was unwise to make terms with her at all.

The American generals were overruled—unwisely many now feel, and certainly to the later regret of at least some of the Allied leaders. After the Armistice was signed, they discovered that revolution-rocked Germany was in much worse shape than they had thought, and that they almost certainly could have imposed far more drastic terms.

This oversight on the part of the Allied generals was partially corrected in the three periodic renewals of the Armistice, in which the French demanded progressively harder conditions. After much protestation and uncertainty, Berlin was forced to yield. The Germans loudly claimed that this was a breach of faith. They had laid down the bulk of their arms on the strength of certain promises, and when they had thus rendered themselves virtually defenseless, they were confronted with new and more onerous terms. President Wilson, Colonel House, and General Bliss were all grieved by what they regarded as "unfair," "unsportsmanlike," and "dishonorable" conduct, not "worthy" of the Allies. The French, on the other hand, advanced plausible reasons for drastic action.

A true armistice ordinarily involves the reciprocal granting of concessions and the imposing of restrictions. In this armistice the concessions were made only by the Germans. A true armistice is generally concerned with military matters. In this armistice a number of political considerations were injected, including an important French reservation on reparations; and in the subsequent renewals the so-called Armistice began to take on the aspect of a preliminary peace.

The net result was that the Germans were increasingly exasperated, while being left with enough to put up some kind of resistance. The soldiers in the Allied armies were clamoring to go home, now that the war was seemingly over, and they were unable to understand the necessity of keeping large armies mobilized against a possible resurgence of defeated Germany. Large bodies of men, notably the Belgians, deserted and went home. Tens of thousands of American boys were eager to return to families and sweethearts, and their plaintive cry was, "Lafayette, we are still here."

In this connection one of the great mistakes of the Allies was in the field of public education. They failed to make it sufficiently clear to their people that the war did not end with the fighting, and that it was imperative to keep huge forces under arms if the bitter fruits of victory were to be properly safeguarded.

But the most distressing feature of the seven months of technical warfare following the Armistice was the continuation of the starvation blockade of Germany, against the remonstrances of Wilson and the vehement protests of Herbert Hoover. The Armistice agreement had actually contained a promise—certainly a tacit promise—that the Allies would "provision" the German people "as shall be found necessary."

The fact is that the blockade, though lightened in March, 1919, was made more severe than it had been during the actual fighting, and it was kept in force until July 12, 1919, three days after Germany actually ratified the treaty, and eight months after the signing of the Armistice. During this period un-counted thousands of German men, women, and children died of starvation, or were physically and mentally blighted. This, of course, could be defended on the technical ground of Ger-man noncompliance with the Armistice, and also on the ground of military necessity, for at no time before the actual signing of the treaty could the Allies be absolutely sure that Germany would not again take the field. Yet if the disarma-ment provisions of the Armistice had been made as drastic as they should have been, and could have been, the hunger-blockade could hardly have been defended on any grounds.

At all events, the whole atmosphere of uncertainty and re-crimination growing out of this situation contributed immeas-surably to the difficulties of the negotiators, and hung like a pall over the Conference. General Jan C. Smuts not unreason-ably concluded that the months of the Armistice were "per-haps" as "upsetting, unsettling, and ruinous to Europe as the previous four years of war."

II

Germany, say the Germans (including the Austrian-born Adolf Hitler), was not beaten but betrayed. The truth is that in a very real sense she was beaten and then betrayed. Her armies were reeling when the High Command sought a truce, though they were reeling on foreign soil. But the circumstances surrounding the Fourteen Points, the pre-Armistice contract, and the renewals of the Armistice gave all too valid a basis to the charges of betrayal, which tended to obscure the fact of the beating. With the wisdom of hindsight we can now see that the beating had advanced so far that betrayal was not necessary.

The German soldiers marched home with their small arms,

and were greeted under evergreen arches as conquering heroes.
Germany had not been seriously invaded; German arms had
won glorious victories against overwhelming foes. After four
years of fighting the Allies had seemingly recognized that the
war was a stalemate, and they were willing to negotiate a treaty
with the German representatives—a treaty based upon peace
and justice, upon Wilson's Fourteen Points. The chivalrous

The New German War-Song
(Knott in the Dallas *News;* courtesy of the Dallas *News*)

Allied foemen, who had learned to respect German steel, could
be counted upon to recognize the Germans as brothers in arms.

So the Germans thought. It was unfortunate that they
thought so, though circumstances gave some reality to their
illusions. It was also unfortunate that the army, which occupied such a prominent place in German pride and national life,
should not have been portrayed as it was—a beaten army. This
misrepresentation of facts gave strength to Hitler's thesis that
the men at the front had been stabbed in the back by the Jews

and Communists, and helped prepare the public mind for another war in which the "invincible army" would bring home more tangible proofs of success.

Germany failed to learn the one lesson that she most needed to learn: war does not pay.

THE MAN WITHOUT
A COUNTRY

*"He [Wilson] is certainly in splendid humor and in good trim—
not worried a bit. And why should he be, for the world is at his
feet, eating out of his hand! No Caesar ever had such a triumph!"*
SECRETARY OF THE INTERIOR LANE, *November 5, 1918.*

1

THE NEWS of the Armistice caused war-taut America to
relapse into a delirium of rejoicing. Streets everywhere were
crowded with laughing, weeping, whooping, whistling, toot-
ing, singing, kissing, drinking, dancing, milling masses. The
canyons of New York City were filled with flags, confetti, torn
paper. The police were powerless to control the crowds bent
on window breaking, bonfire building, streetcar wrecking.

Gloating over the downfall of the Kaiser was everywhere
unrestrained. He was lampooned in effigy, burned in effigy,
tossed from skyscrapers in effigy, trampled underfoot in effigy.
One placard announced triumphantly: "There ain't no
Kaiser." Another proclaimed: "Let him rule in hell." One
imaginative butcher drove about a truck on which he exhibited
a stuck pig labeled: "Kaiser."

The Atlanta *Constitution* passed solemn judgment: "And
somewhere in Holland an old, old man, the greatest criminal
the world has ever known, is shivering before the hosts of ac-
cusing shapes who point their ghostly fingers and brand him
murderer."

But in Washington, Woodrow Wilson was not shivering.
He was responding graciously to one of the greatest spon-
taneous ovations ever given him.

And why not? He was at the dizziest peak of his incredible
career. He had led an unprepared, bewildered, and partially

disunited people through the greatest war in history. He had aroused and united them in a gigantic crusade which had proved that a democracy, in spite of its amateurish awkwardness, could make war, and make war with terrible effectiveness. Two million American boys had hurried ashore in France; they had cracked the German lines; they had driven seasoned veterans out of their trenches, hands in air, whimpering "Kamerad!" The Prussian war lords had sued for peace; Wilson had skillfully evaded their traps. He had forced the Germans to accept his proposals and change their government and evict their Kaiser. All that now remained was to make a just and lasting peace.

He did not know—he could not know—that the rest would be an anticlimax. When one is at the summit, the only possible path is down.

Wilson's triumphant position in November of 1918 was not unlike Lincoln's in April of 1865. Both had led their people through the dark days of gloom and disaster; both had united them with inspiring utterances; both had achieved victory.

But here the parallels break down. Lincoln was shot at the climax of his career, and became enshrined as a martyr, while lesser and weaker hands were left to fumble with the problems of reconstruction. Wilson lived on, toppled from his lofty eminence, and was left to wrestle with the problems of peace singlehanded. If Wilson had been shot on the eve of the Armistice, and if Lincoln had lived to complete his term, it is not improbable that Wilson would now rank higher in popular esteem than the Great Emancipator.

Wilson's wartime leadership had been superb. Despite such blemishes as the lagging aircraft program and the shipbuilding muddle, he had succeeded in inspiriting the people, and getting the job done. He had routed his political opponents when they sought to take the power out of his hands and put it into those of a bipartisan war cabinet. He had done his tremendous task with a minimum of fretting and exertion. He had chosen competent men, like Hoover, Baruch, McCormick, Hurley, and Garfield; had handed the reins of power over to them; and had let them run their respective organizations. During the darkest days of the war he played golf and attended the vaudeville with almost clocklike regularity. By delegating authority, by not overstraining, by concentrating his mind and energies on the over-all organization, he had been able to keep his brain clear, his judgment sound. And success had crowned his efforts.

But from October, 1918, to the end of this great tragedy we see a different Wilson. Something happened to becloud his judgment. Perhaps the strong wine of victory went to his head. Perhaps he was borne down by the responsibility of remaking the world. At all events, he fixed his attention upon the immediate problems with the single-track intensity of mind so characteristic of him, and he undoubtedly worked too hard. During the war he had delegated authority; during the peace negotiations he tried to carry the burden himself. It was too important a job to hand over to subordinates.

Whatever the explanation, he launched out upon an independent and stiff-necked course that brought disaster to his program, and physical prostration to himself. This is not to say that in all of these decisions Wilson was wrong. In some he was right; in some, it seems, he was wrong; in others he took courses which to this day are debatable. But from the vantage point of a quarter of a century after the event we can see some things that we could wish he had done differently.

2

Wilson's first great mistake grew out of his unfortunate appeal habit, which was to backfire again and again during the months that lay ahead.

Like Thomas Jefferson, the founder of his own Democratic party, Wilson had unshakable confidence in the teachableness and reasonableness of the masses, once the situation was clearly laid before them. During the war he had repeatedly appealed to the people, and they had not failed him. He assumed that they would never do so. But the pitcher can go to the well once too often.

By October, 1918, Wilson had definitely decided—though he had made no announcement—to attend the Peace Conference in person. The mid-term Congressional elections were about to be held. If the Democrats should suffer a defeat, the President would be seriously embarrassed at the peace table. He might not be able to command the prestige necessary to force through his program of a just peace capped by the League of Nations. At least, so he feared.

These fears were far from groundless. The Democrats had an excellent chance of suffering a severe reverse, now that the enforced unity of the war had disappeared, and they knew it, especially in view of the fact that they controlled the House of Representatives by an extremely narrow margin. A number of Congressmen whose seats were slipping came to Wilson in something of a panic, and urged him to issue an appeal to the country requesting the election of Democrats to the Sixty-sixth Congress.

Wilson had been toying for some time with the idea of publishing such a statement, and he finally yielded to the avalanche of pressure that was brought to bear upon him. The first draft contained bitter references to outstanding Republican opponents of the Administration, like Henry Cabot Lodge, but Wilson was persuaded by his political advisers to leave these out. After much consultation, some misgivings, and considerable redrafting, the appeal was gradually whipped into final form.

Mrs. Wilson relates that one evening in late October she went into the President's study and found him hammering out the finished draft on his portable typewriter. "I would not send it out," she said. "It is not a dignified thing to do." Wilson replied that he had promised to issue the appeal, and that he could not honorably back out now. So he rang the bell and handed the message to the head usher for delivery to the press.

One wonders why Wilson did not adhere to the plan originally proposed, and address his remarks in the form of a letter to some prominent Democrat, who would then publish it. This strategy would have avoided the impropriety and offensiveness of a direct appeal, while serving essentially the same purpose. Wilson evidently preferred less devious methods.

The momentous October appeal asked bluntly for the election of a Democratic majority to both houses of Congress. But Wilson was careful to explain—a point later overlooked—that he did not impugn the patriotism of the Republican party; they had supported the war loyally, although they had tried to embarrass the administration. They were, he said, "pro-war" but "anti-administration." "In ordinary times," Wilson apologized, such an appeal would be out of place. But this was "the most critical period" in the history of the country, and "no scruple of taste" should stand in the way of plain speaking.

Most significantly, the appeal stressed foreign reactions to the outcome of the election. In four different passages, Wilson referred to what people on "the other side of the water" would think. If the Republicans won, he declared, the result would be interpreted abroad "as a repudiation of my leadership." So he asked the American people to vote for Democrats, if "you have approved of my leadership and wish me to continue to be your unembarrassed spokesman in affairs at home and abroad . . ." In short, Wilson was asking for a vote of confidence.

Wilson may be pardoned for perhaps exaggerating the nature of the crisis, but there can be little doubt that this was one of the most important Congressional elections in our history. From the standpoint of foreign affairs, it was up to that time undoubtedly the most important.

3

During the war the catchword had been—in Wilson's own pedantic phrase—"Politics is adjourned." It was unpatriotic to criticize the president.

Upon publication of the October appeal, a Republican roar of anger reverberated from coast to coast. Wilson had wantonly and flagrantly violated the political truce; he had reconvened politics with a vengeance.

Chairman Will Hays of the Republican National Committee (later guardian of movie morality) cried, "Mr. Wilson wants only rubber stamps." Ex-President Taft remarked privately that Wilson had revealed the spirit of the "German autocracy which he claims to be fighting." The envenomed Theodore Roosevelt wrote exultantly to his bosom friend, Henry Cabot Lodge: "I am glad Wilson has come out in the open; I fear Judas most when he can cloak his activities behind a treacherous make-believe of non-partisanship." More urbanely, the Wheeling *Intelligencer* observed: "There is a growing impression that one Woodrow Wilson spilt a large bucket of beans about 3:00 P.M., Friday, October 25, 1918."

As a matter of fact, politics had never been adjourned during the war; politics never are in a democracy, war or no war. They are always present, though at times not trembling so unpleasantly near the surface as others. As early as the spring of 1918 the Republicans had begun a determined and bitter campaign to capture the next Congress. Even the amiable ex-President Taft was writing privately of Wilson's "peanut soul." The less amiable ex-President Theodore Roosevelt had been rampaging around the country against Wilson and his Fourteen Points, and by October was making such unrestrained statements as to suggest that he hoped to goad Wilson into some such blunder as the October appeal proved to be.

Yet until October the partisan activity of the Republicans was not generally known, and they could make a strong point of their nonpartisan record. During the conflict they had backed Wilson's war program, and in certain cases, notably in connection with the Selective Service Act, their aid had saved critically important legislation. The Republicans could now say that they had loyally supported the war, which they had; that they had sent their boys to France, which they had;

that it had been an American war, which it had. But now it was going to be a Democratic peace.

In brief, the Republicans were good enough to help fight the war, but they were not good enough to help make the peace. It was going to be Woodrow Wilson's private peace. At least, this was the charge.

Election day came, and the Republicans won a moderate victory in the House, gaining twenty-five seats and outnumbering the Democrats 237 to 190. The margin in the Senatorial contests was much closer. The Republicans picked up five seats, thus insuring control of the Senate by two votes. Several of the Senatorial elections were very close, and if any one of them had gone for the Democrats, there would have been a tied vote in the Senate, the Democratic vice president would have broken the tie in favor of the Democrats, and the Senate would have been organized along Democratic lines.

The most spectacular Senatorial contest was in Michigan, where the Democratic Henry Ford, the "flivver" magnate and pacifist, was narrowly defeated by the Republican candidate, Truman H. Newberry. The victor enjoyed a majority of fewer than 8,000 votes out of over 430,000 cast. Newberry was later convicted of having spent too much money (or having it spent for him), but was freed on a technicality. In 1922 he was finally forced from the Senate by the pressure of public opinion.

But by that time the Republicans had organized the Senate committees; and, thanks to Newberry's questionable vote, Henry Cabot Lodge, Republican, became chairman of the Senate Committee on Foreign Relations, from which vantage point he could help engineer the defeat of the League of Nations. In many ways, this was the most important single result of the election.

When the returns were all in, the Republicans exultantly announced that Wilson had been repudiated by the country. He had asked in effect that the election be made a vote of confidence. The country had voted for the opposition party; hence

Wilson could no longer be regarded as the spokesman for his country. He had forfeited his leadership—at least so the result was widely interpreted both at home and abroad.

4

The assumption is general that if Wilson had not issued the appeal the Democrats would not have lost Congress in 1918.

This hypothesis is impossible to prove. In fact, it would be just as reasonable to state, and just as impossible to prove, that if Wilson had not issued the appeal the Democrats would have lost the Senate and the House by an even wider margin, perhaps by a landslide. It is highly significant that a considerable number of Democrats whose seats were in doubt warmly thanked Wilson for the assistance that the appeal would presumably give them. When it was all over, a leading Democratic newspaper, the New York *Times,* was of the opinion that the appeal had saved seats.

There were many reasons, entirely apart from Wilson's appeal, why the Democrats should have suffered a serious setback. Even the most superficial student of our political history knows that there is normally a marked reaction against the party in power during the mid-term Congressional elections. He also knows that the party in power has always suffered a sharp reverse when the mid-term Congressional elections have come during a war.

We must also observe that there were extraordinary reasons why the Republicans should have made desperate efforts to recapture control of Congress in 1918. Since 1897, the country had been normally Republican; and Wilson was able to win in 1912 only because the unseemly row between Taft and Roosevelt had split the Republican vote. Four years later foreign affairs were still in a critical state, and even with the cry, "Don't swap horses in the middle of the stream," Wilson had been able to defeat the Republican candidate, Charles E. Hughes, only by the narrowest of margins.

In 1918, Taft and Roosevelt met publicly, shook hands, and buried the hatchet. The discordant factions of the Republican party were drifting back into the fold, and looking forward to the fatted calf when the Democrats should be thrown out. And how the Republican leaders hated Wilson! As the only

German "Repentance"
(Knott in the Dallas *News;* courtesy of the Dallas *News*)

Southerner elected President since Zachary Taylor, and the only Democratic President since the Civil War except Grover Cleveland, he had driven through a sweeping program of social and economic reform which trod heavily upon the toes of Republican big business. Wilson and his works must be defeated at all costs, and the hands of the clock set back to where they had been in the golden days of Republican standpattism.

The collapse of Germany came at a most inopportune hour for Wilson's political fortunes. By the time he had issued his appeal, it was clear that the enemy was beaten, and that the turbulent stream had been crossed. The old slogan about swapping horses now carried little weight.

We should also note that Wilson's dickering with the "Hun" in October for a negotiated peace added immeasurably to his vulnerability. Republican leaders like Roosevelt and Lodge were identifying the party with a drastic peace dictated in Berlin at the point of American bayonets. They much preferred an American victory in the field to a diplomatic victory by a Democratic President. They scoffed at the dreamy idealism of the "Fourteen Commandments"; they deprecated a "soft peace." "Unconditional Surrender Clubs" were formed throughout the country by Republicans: Germany must be made to pay for her misdeeds. There can be no doubt that this was the popular mood.

The Republicans insisted that a vote for Republican Congressmen was a vote in support of the President at the peace table. They were not only behind him; they were way ahead of him—in their insistence on Carthaginian terms. When it was all over, they claimed that they had won because they were the "unconditional surrender" party.

5

One important reason why Congressmen lost seats—this point is generally overlooked—is that the country as a whole regarded the incumbent Congress as an unusually poor one. It had been dilatory and inept in dealing with critically important war legislation. Its important committees had been headed by long-lived "Dixie" Democrats, "parochial politicians," and "political nondescripts." The chairman of the all-important House Committee on Ways and Means, Claude Kitchin of North Carolina, had been accused of "a fierce joy" in devising schemes for "soaking the rich"—the Northern Republican rich. The Southern Democrats had embittered the

Northern wheat-growing sections by voting to put a ceiling on the price of wheat, while refusing to put a similar ceiling on cotton. Northern resentment against Southern sectionalism unquestionably contributed to the November debacle.

Finally, the country was in an angry mood, tired of the necessary wartime dictatorship and "the patriotism of the lean garbage can." It was wearied of heatless, wheatless, meatless days, and determined to "take it out on someone." The party in power happened to be a convenient if illogical target.

Yet when all these things are said the fact remains that the contest was basically fought out over local issues. While there was some talk about letting the Germans off too easy, about the possibility of free trade under the Fourteen Points, and about the ineptitudes of the Administration, the average voter was not concerned with remaking the world but with electing a man that would look after the local interests of, say, the Nineteenth Illinois district. There is no evidence that the electorate believed that a vote of confidence for Wilson was the real issue, or even a primary issue, though the Democratic leaders tried to make it so.

Whatever interpretation one may wish to place upon this election, it seems reasonably clear that Wilson was stronger than his party. The vote was more pro-Republican and anti-Democratic than it was anti-Wilson. It is entirely probable that if a parliamentary form of government had existed in America, and the issue had been a vote of confidence, the President would have polled a comfortable majority.

Wilson asked in effect for a vote of confidence, and he got neither a vote of confidence nor a vote of lack of confidence. Under our presidential form there can be no true vote of confidence. In Congressional elections the issue is normally the vindication of incumbent Congressmen, not the vindication of a President. The rank and file of the electorate did not have the remotest idea that their vote would have any bearing upon the subsequent defeat of the Treaty of Versailles.

6

Some critics have charged that Wilson made a mistake in putting his appeal on so narrow a basis. Why did he not adopt the strategy later used by President Franklin D. Roosevelt and ask for the election of men, whether Democrats or Republicans, who would loyally uphold his hands in the making of the peace? This is what Colonel House and some of his other advisers urged, because it would have avoided making an issue of Republican patriotism.

We may well doubt whether a nonpartisan appeal of this sort would have worked out successfully. Wilson was a deep-dyed partisan, and he had a profound distrust of Republicans. His Democratic followers needed his support; and what would their feelings have been if Wilson had proclaimed that it was quite all right to elect Republicans, as long as they favored his peace aims as announced in the Fourteen Points? It is altogether probable that Wilson would have lost more through Democratic anger than he would have gained through Republican support.

Nor do those who point to the superior political finesse of President Franklin D. Roosevelt choose too happy a comparison. Roosevelt was conspicuously unsuccessful when he intervened in the state elections of 1938 for the purpose of securing Congressmen and Senators to his liking. In general, our people regard the election of members of Congress as their own local business, and they resent interference by the President or any other outsider.

The blunt truth is that the Republican leaders hated Wilson, and they were out to "get" him at all costs. They probably would have been just as determined if he had issued the appeal on a broad, nonpartisan basis. Indeed, they probably would have voted Republican just the same and just as hard, even if there had been no appeal of any kind. From their point of view the ides of November witnessed the fall of two great autocracies: that of the Kaiser and that of Wilson.

It now seems evident that Wilson committed a serious error when he issued the October appeal in the form that it took. All fair-minded persons will recognize, of course, that the decision was a difficult one to make. If he had kept quiet, his followers would not have had the benefit of his support; and, whether they won or lost, he would have earned their lasting resentment. There was in fact considerable grumbling already among the leaders of his own party.

At best, the appeal was a gamble. But from the point of view of foreign affairs Wilson could not have lost at all, or could not have lost much, if he had kept quiet. If he had issued no appeal, and the result had been the same, he could have waved aside the result as the normal, mid-term reaction against the party in power, in this case accentuated by wartime restrictions and local issues. As it was, he burned all his bridges behind him.

If he had kept quiet and won, as is conceivable, then he would have been in an extraordinarily strong position. He could have triumphantly announced that the result was a vote of confidence in his administration, and a mandate from the people to go ahead and make the kind of peace he had been preaching—a peace based on the Fourteen Points. This, of course, would not have been true, for, as previously noted, a Congressional election is primarily an election of Congressmen. But it is the privilege of the victor in politics to place his own interpretation on the result, whether sound or not. And when this interpretation is proclaimed loudly enough in the moment of victory, and repeated frequently enough under the sanction of victory, it is more often than not accepted as the gospel truth.

7

Next to making the appeal itself, Wilson's most costly error was in declaring so pointedly that a loss for the Democrats would be regarded as a repudiation of his leadership. Wilson

was one of the greatest living authorities on American government. He knew that we did not have a parliamentary system;
he knew that a Congressional election could not be a vote of
confidence. Then why did he lend the weight of his own
authority, even by indirection, to this false interpretation?

We know that he admired the parliamentary system of England, and felt that a government could not function smoothly
unless the executive and legislative branches were of the same
party. He planned to attend the Peace Conference in person;
and if he sat down with the prime ministers and premiers of
Britain, France, and Italy after a defeat in the November elections, he would be embarrassed by knowing that he was the
only one there not entitled to his place under a parliamentary
arrangement.

Immediately after the election, and several weeks before
Wilson reached Paris, his critics on both sides of the water
were clamorously claiming that he had no business to go
abroad as a delegate, because he had been repudiated by the
electorate. He himself had implied that he would be if the
Democrats were defeated; and these critics, both domestic and
foreign, could hardly be blamed for taking his own words at
their face value. It is an ironical fact that this great authority
on American government, by giving a misleading interpretation to our electoral system, thrust a lethal weapon into the
hands of those who wished to attack him. They undoubtedly
would have seized upon it even if he had issued no appeal, but
his unfortunate emphasis undoubtedly gave it greater potency.

In mid-December, 1918, following an appeal to the country
by Prime Minister Lloyd George, the British held a rousing
general election, and vindicated the administration by a landslide. Late in December, Premier Clemenceau asked for a vote
of confidence in the Chamber of Deputies, and was supported
by a thumping majority of 380 to 134.

The essential difference between the appeals of Lloyd
George and Clemenceau on the one hand and Wilson on the
other was that the British and French leaders were trium-

phantly successful, whereas Wilson was apparently repudiated. There can be no doubt whatsoever that the outcome of
the November election, and particularly Wilson's implied insistence on a vote of confidence, was extremely damaging to
his prestige. Premier Hughes of Australia said that Wilson
"had no claim to speak even for his own country," and certainly not for the whole world.

He Got There!
(Courtesy of the St. Louis *Post-Dispatch*)

Wilson's own seat was secure until March, 1921, but for
whom did he speak? The taunt was thrown in his face that in
no other great nation in the world would he even be in office,
much less at the peace table. His threats at the Paris Conference to appeal to American and world opinion over the
heads of the Allied leaders were greeted with cynical and
incredulous smiles.

Foreign criticisms to the effect that Wilson was a repudiated leader were largely ill informed or for political effect, designed to humiliate and embarrass the President. Discerning Europeans knew perfectly well that Wilson was still a power to be reckoned with; they knew perfectly well that we did not have the parliamentary form of government; they knew perfectly well that Wilson had not been legally repudiated.

Those who think otherwise will have to explain how it was that the French and the British accepted commitments from Wilson of the most vital importance to themselves merely on his verbal assurance that he could persuade the American people to endorse them. A repudiated leader cannot be relied on to make such deliveries.

Ominously, the apparent rebuke at the polls merely made Wilson more obstinate. He wrote with the utmost cheerfulness that he was not at all "dismayed or disheartened" by the results, and he boasted that "you may be sure that the stubborn Scotch-Irish in me will be rendered no less stubborn and aggressive . . ." This, unfortunately, was all too true.

CHAPTER FIVE

JOVE STEPS DOWN FROM OLYMPUS

"When he [Wilson] stepped from his lofty pedestal and wrangled with the representatives of other states upon equal terms, he became as common clay." COLONEL HOUSE, *June 29, 1919.*

1

THE OCTOBER appeal was sensational; the November election no less so. But the sensations did not end here. On November 18, 1918, less than two weeks after Wilson's presumed repudiation at the polls, the White House made the startling announcement that the President was going to attend the Peace Conference in person.

A heated debate immediately started as to the wisdom of this move, and it continues in an academic way down to the present time. But one thing is certain. The critics of Wilson are virtually unanimous in agreeing that the trip abroad was one of his most serious blunders—perhaps the most serious in a long sequence of blunders. If he had not gone, they say, the peace would have been a more lasting one, and it undoubtedly would have been accepted by the United States Senate.

At precisely what time Wilson made this momentous decision it is difficult to say. But we do know that from an early date he thought of himself as an important influence at the peace table. His futile attempts to mediate between the Allies and the Central Powers late in 1916 showed him how difficult it was to exert effective pressure while the United States was a mere spectator of the great events which were then unfolding. Reluctant as he was to accept the arbitrament of war, he found some consolation in the thought that as an active belligerent, and as a leader of the strongest of the victor nations, he would have a far better opportunity to remake the world along the lines of a just and permanent peace. As he told Jane

Addams, the voice of the United States would be more compelling at the peace table than calling through the crack of the door.

When Germany began to sue for peace terms in October, 1918, this question of attendance was thrust prominently to the fore of Wilson's mind. He discussed it with a number of advisers, and even sought the counsel of several Democrats in the Senate, though there apparently is no record of his having discussed the problem with Republicans. Whatever else may be said about this hotly disputed question, the fact is clear that Wilson was amply forewarned of the probable consequences of his going. A number of his closest advisers begged him to stay at home.

The announcement of Wilson's plans evoked an immediate outburst of condemnation, chiefly from partisan Republicans. There was also a good deal of quieter dissatisfaction among Democrats in the Senate and elsewhere, for they felt that the President should stay at home and rally the shattered and dispirited ranks of the party. One Democratic newspaper let the cat out of the bag when it remarked that it was "frightfully afraid that while we are making Europe safe for democracy the party will lose every post-office in the United States."

The thing that most infuriated leading Republicans was that Wilson should presume to go to Europe and speak for the United States after his recent rebuke at the polls. Ex-President Theodore Roosevelt, who next to Wilson was the most influential American abroad, cried across the Atlantic to the European statesmen in stentorian tones:

Our allies and our enemies and Mr. Wilson himself should all understand that Mr. Wilson has no authority whatever to speak for the American people at this time. His leadership has just been emphatically repudiated by them. . . . Mr. Wilson and his Fourteen Points and his four supplementary points and his five complementary points and all his utterances every whichway have ceased to have any shadow of right to be accepted as expressive of the will of the American people.

Such extreme statements were not only reprinted in the European press; they were played up to the exclusion of news items more flattering to Wilson. All this did nothing to strengthen the President's prestige when he finally sat down at the peace table.

2

Some of the criticisms of Wilson's pilgrimage to Paris were sound, some unsound; some trivial, some weighty; some contemporary, some latter-day. Let us briefly examine some of the principal criticisms, with attention to the domestic scene first:

Wilson's going was unconstitutional.

The argument was that Wilson could not properly discharge the constitutional duties of the President in Paris, and for this reason he should either stay at home or resign in favor of Vice President Thomas R. Marshall. Senator Sherman of Illinois, a violent Republican critic of Wilson, actually introduced a resolution designed to declare the Presidential office vacant. Marshall was urged to assume the Presidency, but he was too good a Democrat to create this kind of schism in the party's ranks.

Wilson's European trip was unprecedented.

Up to this time no other President had ever set foot on European soil during his term of office. Previous Presidents had in fact made extraordinary efforts to avoid leaving the country at all during their administrations. Theodore Roosevelt, with characteristic Rooseveltian love for shattering traditions, had gone down to Panama in 1906 on a battleship to "see the dirt fly." But this was in the Western Hemisphere, the Canal Zone was a leasehold of the United States, and the Republic of Panama (which he also visited) was a creature and virtual protectorate of the United States. Even so, Roosevelt's bold act was criticized, chiefly by Democrats, who then happened to be the party of the "outs."

Wilson was needed at home.

The greatest industrial machine thus far in history had just been stopped at full speed, and overpowering problems of domestic reconstruction—finance, railroads, industrial and human demobilization—were clamoring for immediate solution. The country was eager to get back to a normal footing after the orgy of war. Wilson should stay in Washington, provide Congress with the necessary leadership, and devote the major portion of his energies to the pressingly important domestic difficulties. Of course, the Republicans did not care for the kind of attention that Wilson would give these problems, either at home or abroad, but they felt that they could keep a closer watch on him if he stayed in the United States.

Wilson was needed to guide public opinion in the problems of peacemaking.

No treaty could be ratified that was not supported by popular sentiment and approved by the Senate. Wilson would do well to keep closely in touch with both these important co-adjutors, provide the necessary information as to the progress of the negotiations, and carefully educate both the Senate and the public to the new responsibilities which he was asking the country to assume. As we shall see, both public opinion and the Senate were kept largely in the dark, and herein lies one of Wilson's greatest failures.

Wilson's venture abroad was merely an unseemly display of swell-headedness.

The President's moral leadership of the world, it was alleged, had inflated his vanity and had given birth to a Messiah complex. The wine of world domination had affected his head. His junket abroad was additional evidence of a desire "to hog the whole show"—to use the earthy phrase of William Howard Taft.

3

We come now to certain objections which bear more directly upon the actual negotiation of the peace.

The Old Girl Who Wasn't Invited to the Show
Turns Up Her Nose at the Program
(Courtesy of the St. Louis *Post-Dispatch*)

Wilson was a poor negotiator.

Although he had visited England and Scotland a half-dozen times, he knew little of Europe at first hand, having made only one hurried summer trip to the Continent sixteen years ago. No American, it was currently said, could ever understand Europe, yet this egoist-idealist was going to reorder not only

the mother continent but the whole world. He could understand or speak no European language, and his Ph.D. "reading
knowledge" of French and German had grown rusty since his
graduate years at the Johns Hopkins University. He was a rank
amateur as a diplomatist. He was an idealist and a chaser after
moonbeams. He was a poor horse trader, inept in the give
and take of the conference table. The "slick" European diplomats would wrap this honest greenhorn at the poker table
around their little fingers, and "trade him out to his eyeteeth."

Wilson would make a "soft peace."

A great many Americans, preponderantly Republicans, felt
that Wilson had robbed them of a satisfying victory, and they
were afraid that this "mushy" sentimentalist would now rob
them of a victor's peace. He would be too lenient with the
Germans, who admittedly were rejoicing at the coming of their
American savior. The Allied diplomats would, of course, favor
stern terms, but the strong-willed and imperious Wilson
would use the enormous influence of the United States to "put
over" a "soft peace." (This, it will be noted, rather contradicts
the charge that he would be putty in the hands of the wily
European diplomats.)

Wilson would jeopardize his overshadowing moral ascendancy.

Sitting quietly in the White House, at one end of the wire
and aloof from the hurly-burly of the conference, he would
still be the arbiter of the world. His voice would resound across
the Atlantic with the authority of Jove. He could appeal to
the peoples of Europe, to his own people, to the people of the
world—and they would listen. But to go down from Mount
Olympus to Paris, to sit at the same table with tricky and unscrupulous diplomats, to haggle over the sordid details of the
loot, to rub elbows with treacherous and dishonest wirepullers
—all this would sully his raiment and undermine his authority.
What would the European masses think of their new Messiah

if he had intimate converse with this discredited breed of publicans and sinners?

If things did not go well, and Wilson bolted the Conference and appealed to the people, he would be jeered at as an egoist who was piqued because he could not have his own way all the time. If he stayed at the Conference, he would be outvoted; at best he could expect only a shabby compromise. If he stayed at home and played the game his own way, he could not lose; if he went abroad and played the game their way, he could not win. And all the disappointed peoples in the world would condemn him for not winning.

Wilson could work more efficiently at home.

Securely ensconced in his ivory tower at the White House, receiving cabled reports daily from his representatives, issuing instructions over the same wire, and keeping closely in touch with public opinion, he could preserve detachment and sound judgment. This is what McKinley had done in 1898 during the negotiations with Spain in Paris, and the results had been satisfactory.

At Paris, Wilson would come to know the other negotiators personally. He would have to say "No" to them so often that he would become seriously embarrassed; the pressure to say "Yes" would finally become so great that he would have to yield occasionally against his better judgment. It is much easier in such circumstances to say "No" by cable.

The Paris Conference was bound to be a madhouse of confusion, with hundreds of people desperately seeking something, and with little or no opportunity for Wilson to get off and view the whole scene with sanity before making an earth-shaking decision. He could not ask his colleagues to wait while he appealed to Washington for instructions. He was the source of instructions; there was "no appeal from himself."

In Washington, at the other end of the wire, he could make his decisions impersonally, without the "pneumatic hammer of daily personal contacts." His representatives could bring about a wholesome delay by cabling to him for instructions. And he could drive off into the arboreal quietness of Rock Creek Park and have a chance to think.

4

A final argument against Wilson's going—though not generally known at the time—was that the leading European statesmen, as distinguished from their people, did not want him to come. This feeling is quite understandable. Wilson overshadowed Clemenceau of France, Lloyd George of England, and Orlando of Italy like a veritable colossus. This stiff-necked schoolmaster would doubtless lecture heathen Europe on its congenital wickedness and hold out for a "soft peace"; he might even arouse the people against their leaders by stirring appeals; he would almost certainly throw all kinds of monkey wrenches into the plans of the Allies for partitioning the spoils of war. And who was this eleventh-hour laborer in the vineyard to come to them, after they had sacrificed millions of their sons on the altar of Mars, and tell them what they might or might not keep?

The idealist-professor was all well enough in framing and preaching the Fourteen Points, which had proved terribly effective in disrupting and disarming the enemy. But when it came to the cold, hard, realistic business of peacemaking he had better stay at home and let Europeans settle the affairs of Europe. They were old hands at the game; they knew best.

When Wilson announced that he expected to attend the Conference, Clemenceau and Lloyd George could not very well make their real objections known. So they resorted to a quibble. Wilson, they said, would be the only "head of a state" present, and the head of a state could properly negotiate only through accredited agents. If he insisted on coming, then it might be necessary to invite the King of England, the President of France, the King of Italy, and others. Premier Clemenceau was insistent that his implacable political foe, President Poincaré, be given no opportunity to attend the Conference in an official capacity.

Wilson was clearly much annoyed by this transparent attempt to sidetrack him. He was determined to go; he expected to preside; he planned to take an active part in the deliberation; and he had no intention, so he said, of hanging around the Conference as "the centre of a sort of sublimated lobby." The sharp cablegram he sent to Colonel House in Paris on this point suggests that the enormous power which he was then wielding had to some extent affected his ego.

The quibble about being the head of a state was especially annoying to Wilson. The United States had the presidential system of government, and the head of the government, unlike the prime ministers of Europe, happened also to be the head of the state. Wilson, as we have seen, admired the parliamentary system, and liked to think of himself as a prime minister. If the other prime ministers and premiers were entitled to go, he felt that he should enjoy the same privilege, not as the head of the state, but as the head of the government—and also as the herald of a new age. He had no intention of being kept at home by this hollow subterfuge, which his opponents knew very well was a subterfuge. If anything, this attempt to "pocket" him— to use his own word—aroused his Scotch-Irish stubbornness, and made him all the more determined to go.

Clemenceau's opposition to the coming of the inconvenient idealist waned with the passage of time. Wilson tactfully yielded the presidency of the Conference to the doughty French premier, an honor which could not be denied France once Paris was made the seat of the Conference. Clemenceau also perceived that "the theocrat of the White House" would prove more manageable than he had been led to suppose. What more could he ask than that Wilson should forsake the lofty advantages of Mount Olympus and go to the mat with him—a mat which Clemenceau would dominate as both wrestler and referee? If Wilson opposed French demands, he could be (and was) branded a pro-German. And, as President Poincaré shrewdly observed, if he did not come, all the failures of the Conference "would be attributed to his absence."

5

Many, if not most, of the arguments advanced by Wilson's critics could be strongly challenged.

It is a debatable point whether his going was unconstitutional; and Wilson secured competent legal advice on this question before departing. The Constitution does not forbid the President to leave the country; and Wilson's being physically absent probably did not amount to disability within the meaning of the Constitution, because he could arrange to keep in contact with Washington by wire and sign bills on his return trips. Besides, the Constitution does not vest in any person or body the authority to declare the office of President vacant.

It is true that Wilson's trip to Paris was unprecedented, but what of it? Times had changed. America, as Wilson now recognized with increasing clearness, was no longer isolated but was part and parcel of the rest of the world. The making of the peace concerned our future welfare as well as that of Europe and the other continents. It has often been said that the United States wanted nothing and asked for nothing at Paris, and had no direct stake in the terms of the settlement. Nothing could be farther from the truth. We had invested billions of dollars and tens of thousands of lives in a war to end wars, and we had a direct and vital interest in the task of making sure that it would not all happen again.

Nothing could be more silly, Wilson's defenders say, than to argue that America should not play the role that was rightfully hers simply because of a horse-and-buggy precedent. President Coolidge went to Cuba in 1928, while Franklin D. Roosevelt ranged by boat and by plane from Buenos Aires in

South America to Casablanca and Cairo in North Africa, and to Teheran in Asia. If there should be a great peace conference today in Paris, no one would think it strange that a President of Franklin D. Roosevelt's stature should go. On the contrary, he would be expected to go. Every trail-blazer, every precedent-breaker, is criticized for what his successors are frequently praised, and Wilson was no exception.

No one could deny that the problems of reconstruction were pressing, but they could be worked on by Wilson's able administrative assistants, who would keep closely in touch with their chief in Paris. Domestic reconstruction could wait; world reconstruction could not. As Wilson told Congress on the eve of his departure, he could think of no other "business or interest" that should take precedence. Foreign affairs, for one of the few times in our history, seemed to be of more pressing importance than domestic affairs. It was eloquent testimony of the changed position of the United States in the world theater that this should be so. Those who thought that wars end when the fighting ends were living in a fool's paradise. From the long-range point of view, it was of paramount importance that a just and enduring peace be made. Otherwise, as Wilson himself told Congress, we should break faith with those boys who had joyfully sacrificed their lives for such a noble end.

It is self-evident that Wilson could theoretically have remained in closer contact with public opinion, and could have guided it more surely, if he had stayed in the United States. Whether he would have done so had he remained behind, one cannot say. As we shall repeatedly observe, one of his gravest mistakes was to fasten his eyes so steadfastly on the distant vistas of a new world order as to ignore the mundane problem of keeping up his fences at home. Star-gazing is just as easy on either side of the Atlantic. Even while in Paris, Wilson was kept constantly informed as to the state of public opinion by Joseph P. Tumulty and others, though he evidently did not pay much attention to what they reported. At all events, he could not be in two places at once; and for reasons that were undeniably weighty he thought it best to be on the other side. It seems reasonable to suppose that Wilson's new earth-shaking role had to some extent gone to his head. But what mortal man, for that matter, would have been completely immune? Lloyd George chucklingly and perhaps inaccurately recalls that at Paris the President once startled Clemenceau by telling how he was going to avoid the mistakes that Jesus had made.

Wilson was undoubtedly aware of the charges that he was going to the Conference merely to gratify his Messiah complex. But why should he turn aside from the noble deeds that only he could do because of the cavilings of mean spirits? He was moral arbiter of the world, and why should he not go and don his mantle? The common people of all lands were counting on him to do so, and he could betray neither the living nor the dead. A stern sense of duty, rather than selfish motives, probably more than anything else sent Wilson to Paris.

6

No one will dispute the fact that Wilson knew little at first hand of the machinations of European chancelleries. But he was no babe in the woods when it came to either politics or foreign affairs. His public career had been relatively brief but spectacular and concentrated. Two years as governor of New Jersey followed by six years of the Presidency of the United States had been an incomparably rigorous training school, and had left him with few illusions about men and their motives. As a politician and political leader Wilson had up to this time established a record which still ranks among the most sensationally successful in American history.

It is true that Wilson was not a professionally trained diplomat, and that he was not at his best in the give and take of a free-for-all discussion. It is also true that he did not speak foreign languages; but interpreters could be used and were used. Although he did not know a great deal about Europe at first hand, he had an unusually wide theoretical knowledge, and when he reached Paris he gave the more important problems intense study. It was not unusual to find him on all fours over a geographical or ethnological map. He had a keen, perceptive mind, which kept on the main track; he was a comprehending listener; and he spoke with precision, intelligence, and force. This is the well-nigh unanimous testimony of the American experts who were intimately associated with him at Paris.

In all fairness to Wilson, one must point out that the problems harassing the world were so complex and far-ranging that no mortal mind could master them. Lloyd George made the incredible confession at the Peace Conference that he had never heard of the notorious Twenty-one demands presented by Japan to China in 1915. On the floor of Parliament he also made the no less incredible admission that before going to Paris he had never heard of the industrially important area of Teschen, the bone of contention between Poland and Czechoslovakia. Lloyd George may not have known some things, but he knew enough to keep up his fences at home, which Wilson did not.

English writers like John Maynard Keynes and Harold Nicolson have done the cause of truth no service by stereotyping Wilson as an ignorant fumbler who was "bamboozled" by the European frock coats. He made his errors, as they all did, but his average of constructive achievement was high. And he was far from being dull-witted. His mind did not scintillate as sparklingly as that of Lloyd George, who darted from point to point with kingfisher rapidity, and who reversed himself with the greatest of ease when he found his information incorrect. Wilson preferred to get the facts first, and then move more slowly in one direction.

It is clear that Wilson was an idealist, but idealism may be—and much of Wilson's was—long-range realism. The pothouse politician, who sees only one move at a time, brands anyone an idealist who spurns the short-run advantage in favor of the larger, less immediate gain. Wilson was dealing in long-range realities, and he failed largely because the great mass of humanity is unable to see more than one jump ahead. From a practical point of view he should have recognized this fact, and trimmed his sails accordingly.

Wilson, his critics to the contrary, did not favor a "soft peace." He favored a just peace—just retribution for Germany's misdeeds—and this meant a stern peace. We shall have occasion to refer to this later.

It is perfectly true that Wilson risked his political standing at home and his moral ascendancy abroad when he went to Europe. He knew that the popular thing to do would be to stay in America. He knew that he would be throwing his enormous prestige on the gaming table if he went to Paris. But the problems to be solved were so tremendous, and the chances of establishing a new world order were so unprecedented, that he decided to take the risk. This was no time to be selfishly thinking of one's popularity. This was no time to stay at home mending political fences when the entire world needed mending. There was no one else whom he could entrust with such a colossal responsibility. To shirk this tremendous task would, to him, have been nothing short of immoral.

7

On the positive side, there were weighty reasons why Wilson should go.

He had been the leading spokesman of the Allied and Associated Powers, and his peace aims had commanded general popular acceptance. The Germans had laid down their arms on the basis of the Fourteen Points, and it was perfectly natural that Wilson should go to Paris as the author of the Points, explain them more fully, and see that they were written into the peace. This was all the more true since he knew that they had been accepted with mental reservations by the Allied leaders.

Wilson was the moral arbiter of the world, and the masses everywhere, not just in the United States, expected him to go to Paris and give them a lasting peace. They did not trust the Old Diplomacy, but they had a childlike faith in his ability to usher in the new era. How could he disappoint this tremendous and expectant following? Like Jesus, Wilson found that a prophet is more honored abroad; and it is an ironical fact that the Europeans, who knew Wilson least, trusted him more than did his own countrymen.

Could Wilson have worked better through subordinates, as McKinley had done? At the outset we must note that the problem in 1898 was of kindergarten simplicity when compared with the Augean tasks confronting Wilson. In 1919 there were multipartite negotiations, involving not two powers but some thirty; the reshaping of the world, not the crumbs of Spain's once proud empire. With so many hundreds of threads in the tangled skein; with so many different and clashing interests; with so many reasons for moving with the utmost speed, it seemed desirable to Wilson that he be on the ground. There were too many problems that could not be settled, at least not expeditiously, without oral discussion. Terse cablegrams, laboriously coded and decoded, were slow, misleading, and often inaccurate.

The question of working through subordinates may be answered in part by fact and not speculation. In February, 1919, after getting off to a seemingly splendid start, Wilson left Paris for a flying trip to the United States, leaving Colonel House and Secretary Lansing in charge. Though he kept closely in touch with House by wire and wireless, he found upon his return after a scant month that his subordinates, in his judgment, had given ground alarmingly, and he had to struggle desperately to regain what they had lost, or what he thought they had lost. We shall return to this episode later.

Present-day scholars like Dr. Paul Birdsall—and their evidence is convincing—conclude that Wilson, by being present and exercising his great personal prestige, was able to force more of his program into the peace than would have been possible through subordinates. This does not necessarily mean that the peace was better because he did so; perhaps it would have been more workable and more lasting if he had stayed at home and let the Europeans write the kind of treaty they wanted. But for the moment we are concerned with his efforts to incorporate his own ideas in the peace; and, as we shall note in the last chapter, he achieved a very considerable degree of success.

8

When Wilson announced, on November 18, 1918, that he was leaving for Paris, he was at pains to say that he was not going as a delegate, and he was careful to suggest that he might find it possible to take part in only preliminary meetings.

This was hardly candid, for Wilson had every intention of attending as a delegate, and of staying for the main work of the Conference. But knowing that his move was unpopular he took the precaution, at Colonel House's suggestion, of breaking the news gently. It was not until eleven days later that the five American delegates to the Conference were publicly named, and Wilson headed the list.

During this eleven-day period criticism of Wilson was not so severe as it otherwise would have been, and much of that which was expressed quickly waned. There were many who felt that it would be a good thing for him to go to Europe, get the "feel" of the situation, meet the leading statesmen, engage in preliminary discussions with them, and then leave for home to direct the concluding negotiations by wire. If he should do this, his influence would remain unimpaired: in fact, it might be enhanced.

The Cleveland *Press* struck a not uncommon note when it remarked that those who were criticizing Wilson for "going across" should wait to see whether he "puts it across."

CHAPTER SIX

WILSON AND HIS "ERRAND BOYS"

"[The Commission] is a cheap lot of skates. I could swear if it would do any good." WILLIAM HOWARD TAFT, *December 23, 1918.*

1

THE COUNTRY was shocked by the October appeal, and by the announcement that Wilson was going to Paris. It received another rude shock on November 29, 1918, when the personnel of the Peace Commission was announced.

Wilson, of course, headed the list. The other four commissioners were Robert Lansing, Secretary of State; Colonel Edward M. House, confidential adviser to the President; Henry White, an experienced diplomat; and General Tasker H. Bliss, a member of the Supreme War Council in Paris and the expert on military affairs.

The outburst of condemnation that greeted the announcement of these names was loud, prolonged, and insistent.

The first criticism was that the group contained no really big men comparable in stature with Wilson. The Republicans in particular cried that the new Messiah was so determined to remake the world himself in his own way that he did not want the counsel and interference of really competent advisers. He wanted only "rubber stamps"—soft-spoken and self-effacing "yes men" like Colonel House. The Republicans distrusted Wilson's exalted idealism, and they wanted able and hard-headed realists around him to apply the brakes when necessary.

It is true that, politically speaking, there was no really "big" man on the Peace Commission. Robert Lansing had to be chosen *ex officio,* because the other foreign ministers were being sent to Paris, and it would have been an intolerable insult to ignore him. As it turned out, he was taken to Paris and

87

there ignored—at least according to his own embittered book.

Lansing—handsome, prematurely white, fussily precise—was an able international lawyer who had been serving as Counselor for the Department of State when Secretary Bryan resigned in 1915 over the *Lusitania* crisis. Wilson was preoccupied, and rather than comb the entire country for an outstanding successor, he followed the path of least resistance by merely moving Lansing up, though all the time he had grave doubts as to his fitness for the job. In all important matters, Wilson served as his own Secretary of State, and for this reason he probably thought that he needed nothing better than a competent and experienced administrative assistant.

At all events, Lansing was an able rather than an outstanding man. Although he spent much of his time in conference at Paris absent-mindedly penciling sketches and grotesque figures on a pad, he nevertheless gave serious thought to the problems at hand, spoke cogently when the occasion demanded, and grew steadily in the esteem of his colleagues. Being an international lawyer, he was thoroughly out of sympathy with Wilson's flights into the future, and a rift rapidly widened between the two men over the League of Nations and other issues. He probably would have resigned, but was restrained in part by the conviction that this would weaken the hands of the President by advertising dissension within the Commission. Wilson seriously considered asking him to resign, but refrained from doing so, probably for the same reason. In any case, Lansing was a stern realist, with his feet on the ground, and Wilson would have done well to heed some of his advice at Paris.

2

Colonel House was not a big man, though he was far from being a stupid one. The keen but erratic British critic, Harold Nicolson, who was at the Conference in a minor capacity, characterizes him "as the best diplomatic brain that America has

yet produced." While there are many who will quarrel with
this sweeping judgment, it is true that House had behind him
an unusual amount of experience. As Wilson's personal representative and *alter ego*, he had made several extensive trips
abroad, and he not only had come to know many of Europe's
problems at first hand, but had made the acquaintance of many
of the leading European statesmen. They respected him and
had confidence in him. The American people, on the other

Wilson's Peace Delegation
(Malicious satire from *Harvey's Weekly*)

From left to right: Wilson, House, Lansing, White, Bliss,
Baruch, Hoover, Creel

hand, regarded him as something of a sphinx-like man of
mystery.

Small of stature, gentle, soft-spoken, and retiring to the point
of shyness, the quiet Texan Colonel—a geographical not a military colonel—had never run for public office, and had never
been elected or appointed to one, much preferring the role of
the power behind the throne. His portfolio as peace commis-
sioner was the only quasi-official public appointment of any
kind he had ever held. He was the only one of the four commissioners whom Wilson took into his confidence; indeed, on
important matters the other three were virtually ignored.

It may not have been a mistake to take Colonel House to

Paris, but it probably was unwise to appoint him as one of the five official commissioners. If he had not gone in this capacity, Wilson could have made room on the commission for someone else whose political standing would have reassured the country. House had faithfully served Wilson as an invaluable personal and confidential adviser, and there is no good reason why he could not have continued in the same role at Paris. Despite recent criticism, he was generally levelheaded, well informed, and experienced in European statecraft. He has been sneered at as a compromiser; but in complicated human relationships, such as the making of a peace treaty by twenty-seven victorious powers, there can be no agreement without compromise, and no achievement without agreement. But even granting all this, Colonel House's advice would have been just as sound, perhaps more sound, if he had not gone in an official capacity.

3

A word about the remaining two commissioners, General Bliss and Henry White.

General Bliss was a gruff, honest soldier, of medium height, thick-set, and slightly stooping. "Nature," says Ray Stannard Baker, "intended him to be a hairy man, gave him thick eyebrows and bristling moustache and then changed its mind and made him bald—an extreme shiny baldness, except for a bristling fringe of hair at the back and sides of the head." Surprisingly enough, he was a classical scholar, and interlarded his correspondence with erudite Latin expressions. *Harvey's Weekly,* a bitterly critical sheet, remarked that "his presence at an international peace conference is about as fitting as that of an army mule would be in a church choir."

General Bliss was not a big man politically, but he proved to be a lucky "find." He not only had a firm grasp of the military questions involved, but had a broad comprehension of the general economic and political problems that were then vexing

Europe. He was that rare combination: statesman, humanitarian, scholar, and soldier. His advice was sound and farsighted, startlingly so for one who was presumed to be a narrow military man. He was in fact one of the few figures who came out of the Conference with enhanced stature. To this day there are some who believe that he was the ablest man on the American commission.

There is no reason to suppose that it was a mistake to have General Bliss in Paris, but in some ways it was unfortunate that he should have had an official place on the Peace Commission. As a technical military adviser he could have been kept close at hand, like Colonel House, while his place on the Commission could have been taken by a more impressive political figure.

The fact is often overlooked that there were scores of American legal, economic, and other technical advisers at Paris, many of whom overshadowed—at least in the public mind—the four commissioners whom Wilson appointed. The names Herbert Hoover, Bernard M. Baruch, Norman H. Davis, and Vance C. McCormick at once come to mind. There is no valid reason why Wilson could not have added indefinitely to this list, and why he could not have reserved room on the official Peace Commission for men of outstanding stature.

4

Handsome, affable Henry White was not a big figure politically, though he was physically. A man of independent wealth, he had been able to afford the luxury of a lifetime in the diplomatic service, and was unquestionably the outstanding "career" diplomat of his generation. But he had not held a post for about ten years, and there was a tendency to sneer at him as a "has-been."

White was an open-minded and broad-gauged man, with sound judgment, polish, tact, and great conciliatory powers.

He knew Europe, European statesmen, and European problems. Having lived in England and France for many years, and having a daughter married to a German nobleman and suffering from the Allied blockade, he could to an unusual degree sympathize with the conflicting points of view. He had played the leading role for the United States in the critical Algeciras conference of 1906, which is credited with having postponed the World War. In fact, he was the only man in the entire country who had behind him responsible, first-hand experience with the interplay of international forces at a great conference. He was the only American on the commission of five who knew French well enough to carry on an official conversation.

From every possible viewpoint except the political—which we shall come to shortly—Henry White was an excellent choice. His services should have been utilized in some way, either officially or unofficially.

5

The Republicans were not so much disturbed by the small caliber of the men on the Commission as by the fact that there was only one Republican on it, Henry White, and he was not at all prominent in party councils. He was a registered Republican, and when living in the United States, which had been intermittently, he had voted the Republican ticket. Ex-President Taft, an unfriendly critic, thought he was "more of an Englishman than he is an American." He was not a bitter partisan; if he had been, Wilson would have passed him by. The Republicans consequently insisted that they did not have a single representative on the Commission of five. Henry White was a pleasant man, but as a political figure he simply did not count. No one was more surprised at the appointment than White himself.

Harvey's Weekly satirized the whole Commission, and Wilson's domination over it, with diabolical cleverness:

Name	Occupation	Representing
Woodrow Wilson	President	Himself
Robert Lansing	Secretary of State	The Executive
Henry White	None	Nobody
Edward M. House	Scout *	The Executive
Tasker H. Bliss	Soldier	The Commander-in-Chief

Senator Henry Cabot Lodge sneered that Wilson had appointed himself four times—and Henry White.

The charge that the Republicans had been deliberately slighted was, unfortunately, all too true, and it was one of the mistakes which had most to do with the disaster that finally befell Wilson.

The Republicans undeniably had a strong and well founded grievance. They had supported the war enthusiastically and loyally, more so in certain respects than Wilson's party. They now represented, at least on the basis of their recently won Congressional majority, more than 50 per cent of the voters of the country. Yet they were to have only 20 per cent of the numerical representation on the Commission, and not even 5 per cent when one considered the fact that Henry White was not a strong and vengeful Republican. No wonder they cried that the President had been glad enough to have the Republicans fight the war, but he did not want them hanging around when it came to making the peace. The cowboy humorist, Will Rogers, had Wilson say to the Republicans, "I tell you what, we will split 50–50—I will go and you fellows can stay."

The disconcerting truth is that there was only one prominent partisan of either party on the Commission, and that was Woodrow Wilson.

Why, demanded the Republicans, was there not at least one distinguished Republican who could give to the majority party in the country the feeling that their views, as well as those of Wilson, would be written into the peace? Why not take men

* A reference to House's several secretive trips to Europe as representative of Wilson.

like Charles Evans Hughes, Republican presidential standard-
bearer in 1916; or ex-President Taft, an outstanding advocate
of the League of Nations; or Elihu Root, a former Secretary of
State, a friend of international collaboration, and the distinguished elder statesman of the party?

6

It seems reasonably clear that Wilson made a mistake in not
appointing one or more of these three men. But in fairness to
him we must note that from his point of view there were strong
objections to all of them.

They were all distinguished lawyers; and Wilson, who had
begun life unsuccessfully as a lawyer, had a deeply ingrained
dislike for the narrow mental processes of the legal profession.
He wanted to work for a broad, sweeping program, and did not
care to be constantly annoyed by the realistic and legalistic
objections of the precedent-bound "library lawyers." He
bluntly told Robert Lansing, himself a lawyer, that he did not
intend to have lawyers drafting the treaty of peace. Lansing
was hurt.

The three "big-gun" Republicans most commonly mentioned—Taft, Hughes, and Root—were all strong partisans,
though perhaps not narrow and bitter partisans. Theodore
Roosevelt was narrow, bitter, and unbridled, and he had been
ranting around the country making "skin-'em-alive" speeches
against Wilson. But no one seriously proposed taking him
along.

Wilson himself was a strong partisan and a good hater. Born
a Democrat—a Southern Democrat—in the state of Thomas
Jefferson, and dedicated to the principles of Thomas Jefferson,
he believed that Republicans were tolerable people, but not
to be trusted too far in high places. He believed in the two-
party system: one party governing, the other watching—with
the Republicans doing the watching.

During the summer and fall of 1918, Root, Hughes, and Taft had all made speeches attacking the Administration. Hughes and Taft had both assailed the October appeal in public, and Taft had gone so far as to criticize Wilson's Fourteen Points and his thirst for power. As a presidential rival, Taft had thrown some heavy verbal punches at Wilson in 1912, and Hughes had done the same thing in 1916 when courting the German-American vote. And Wilson, despite his policy of hitting such people "with a chunk of silence," took these things to heart.

Root, Taft, and Hughes were all big men, comparable in stature with Wilson. But Wilson did not like to have big men around him giving advice, and therein lay one of his gravest weaknesses. He naturally sought the counsel and enjoyed the company of inferior if not mediocre minds. Colonel House, his most intimate adviser, was not a big man. Most of the time the self-effacing House agreed with Wilson; but when he did disagree he was careful to phrase his objections in the most inoffensive manner. Much of the time he indicated dissent by a period of silence. Wilson, contrary to the popular misconception of the know-it-all professor, was fully able to listen to counsel, and there is abundant evidence that he did so intelligently and appreciatively. But he apparently did not want advice crammed down his throat by men of his own level of ability. He had great confidence in his own undeniably superior mental equipment, and he preferred associates whose minds "went along with his"—to use one of his favorite phrases.

From one point of view Wilson was perfectly right in not asking outstanding Republicans of a strong partisan bent to serve with him. He was responsible to the American people for the kind of peace that was to be made, and he doubtless felt that harmony would be better in the long run than outstanding but contentious ability. He may have remembered that the United States had suffered from such embarrassments in making peace with England at Ghent in 1814. As it was, the Commission of 1919 developed enough disharmony. Taft had been President; and although he was amiable and had an infectious laugh which bubbled up from his abundant abdomen, he distrusted Wilson and had ideas of his own. And men who have been President are not accustomed to taking orders. Root and Hughes also had ideas of their own, and Hughes had come within a hairsbreadth of attaining the Presidency in 1916.

There were additional reasons for not taking along these outstanding Republicans. Taft was a strong and faithful supporter of the idea of the League of Nations, which was coming under increasing attack in the Senate. Would it be wise to weaken the home front, where Taft was doing such effective work, by taking him abroad to serve in a purely advisory capacity?

Several members of Wilson's official family strongly urged that he take Root. But Wilson peremptorily dismissed him as a "hopeless . . . reactionary," whose "appointment would discourage every liberal element in the world."

No one will deny that Root was conservative—perhaps reactionary. But Wilson undoubtedly exaggerated the importance of this objection. Even granting that liberals and labor would have been seriously antagonized, which is debatable, the selection of Root would have done a great deal to mollify the Republicans. The objections to Taft and Hughes were much less applicable to Root; and temperamentally he should have been able to work harmoniously with Wilson. Having recently served a term in the United States Senate, he also would have represented the point of view of that body, and could have used his great influence to get the treaty approved.

In fairness to Wilson it must be repeated that he had reasons —strong reasons in his own mind—for ignoring the outstanding Republicans. It was most unfortunate that he could not bring himself to invite at least one of them, preferably Root. The tragedy is that he was temperamentally incapable either of inviting them or of serving wholeheartedly with them.

7

Two other questions naturally arise. If Wilson could not bring himself to appoint "big" Republicans, why did he not take along several smaller ones? And in particular why did he not invite a Republican or two, perhaps a Democrat also, from the Senate?

One difficulty was that the number of five commissioners was decided upon in consultation with the Principal Allied Powers. The possibilities ranged from three to seven, and the figure finally agreed upon was five. After Wilson had taken care of himself, as well as Lansing and House, there were only two places left, and one of these was earmarked for a Democratic military adviser.

So far as the records show, the idea never occurred to Wilson that he could have appointed House and Bliss as unofficial advisers. He could in fact have taken along any number of Republicans in an unofficial capacity. When he reached Paris he largely ignored both his official and unofficial advisers, and it is just as easy to ignore a large delegation as a small one—perhaps more so. But one danger is that some of them will come back and write bitter books.

If Wilson had put House and Bliss in the unofficial group, this would have left room on the Commission for three Republicans, besides himself and Lansing. The appointment of three Republicans, who could have been ignored if they had proved unmanageable, would have been a master stroke from the standpoint of meeting the charge that the Commission was "packed" with Democrats. On the other hand, the Democrats would have been acutely unhappy over the "packing" of the Commission with Republicans, and Wilson could not afford to antagonize both his own and the opposition party.

Then what about the Senate? Republican President McKinley had appointed three Senators, one of whom was a Democrat; and would not Wilson have flattered that body by the selection of two or three of its members? Would not Senatorial advisers in Paris have been able to tell him at every stage of the negotiations what the Senate would or would not be likely to approve? Would they not have warned him against omitting a reservation regarding the Monroe Doctrine from the first draft of the League of Nations Covenant, and would they not have told him that the Security Treaty with France did not have even a fighting chance in the Senate? Would they not have been able to inform their Senatorial colleagues at home what was going on, and thus forestall the damaging criticism that Wilson was purposely keeping the Senate uninformed?

If Wilson had chosen three Senators, would he not have had three votes assured for the treaty before it was even signed? The influence and votes of McKinley's three Senatorial commissioners had saved the treaty of 1898 with Spain, and certainly Wilson's appointees could not have stultified themselves by throwing out their own handiwork. If Wilson had chosen prominent Senators, would they not have been able to carry their friends with them? And during the debates in the Senate would they not have been able to provide information at every stage as to what certain provisions actually meant and what had really happened at Paris?

8

All things considered, it would have been perfectly feasible to take one Democratic Senator and one or even two Republican Senators. The press rather generally spoke of Senator Walsh, of Montana, a Democrat of high ability, and Senator Knox, of Pennsylvania, a distinguished lawyer who had served under Taft as Secretary of State and who, as a consequence, had a broader grasp of foreign affairs than the great majority of his colleagues. He was passed over, and developed into one of the most unrelenting critics of Wilson's handiwork.

Whether he would have done differently if he had served on the Commission, one cannot say.

Another alternative was to take the Democratic chairman of the all-important Senate Committee on Foreign Relations, Senator Hitchcock of Nebraska, an excellent choice. If this had been done, propriety would have suggested that Wilson also choose the ranking Republican member of the same committee, who would be the chairman when the next Congress assembled. This happened to be Henry Cabot Lodge of Massachusetts.

Aye, here was the rub. Lodge and Wilson were on conspicuously unfriendly terms. The Senator from Massachusetts was a Boston Brahmin of the Charles Sumner tradition, educated at Harvard, and profiting from the social and cultural advantages of inherited wealth. Chauncey M. Depew once remarked that his mind was like the soil of New England, "naturally barren, but highly cultivated."

Lodge had enjoyed the distinction of being "the scholar in politics" until Wilson came along, and then the Senator's scholarly and political attainments were overshadowed by the greater scholarly and political attainments of Wilson. Lodge had openly and enthusiastically supported the idea of the League of Nations before Wilson took it up, and when Wilson came out in favor of it, Lodge somersaulted over into the opposition camp. During the heated presidential campaign of 1916, Lodge had made a not altogether groundless charge as to Wilson's handling of the *Lusitania* affair, and Wilson had politely given Lodge the lie. From then on the two men were at daggers drawn.

There is no evidence that Wilson ever seriously considered the appointment of a Senator. If he had chosen a Democrat, he presumably would also have had to take a Republican. The natural Republican choice was Henry Cabot Lodge—and this may have caused Wilson to shy away from the Senate altogether. If Lodge had been invited, he could have been expected to cause much embarrassment at a time when there was enough embarrassment over larger matters. He might also have been disloyal, for he tried to persuade his delegate-friend, Henry White, surreptitiously to circulate a memorandum at Paris among the Allied statesmen to the effect that Wilson did not really represent the American people. Perhaps, on the other hand, Lodge would have been loyal if he had been invited into the family and stroked the right way; he might have caused less trouble in Wilson's "bosom than on his back."

It probably would have been unwise to appoint Henry Cabot Lodge, but some other leading Republican Senator, such as Knox, could well have been invited. This would have caused some raising of the eyebrows; but the feud between Wilson and Lodge was no secret, and the country would have understood. Of course, Lodge would have been mortally offended, but he was mortally offended anyhow, and out to get his knife into Wilson's back.

The reason that Wilson actually gave to his Attorney General for passing by the Senate was a constitutional one. He remarked that "the Senate was an independent body and that it did not seem fair to him to influence its free judgment of diplomatic negotiations by appointing Senators who would take part in the negotiations and then act upon them as judges."

At the time of the approaching negotiations with Spain in 1898, certain prominent Senators had protested vigorously that it was unconstitutional to have the same men serve as both negotiators and ratifiers. This would break down the fine system of checks and balances in our federal system.

Even granting this point of propriety, there was in 1918 ample precedent for appointing Senators, as there has been since then. And if one may credit the reports of the Washington press correspondents, the Senate would not have been displeased by such a compliment. Some of the Senators expected to have representation on the Commission, and they were deeply disturbed when they were completely ignored.

The stakes at Paris were stupendous. With the future peace

and stability of the world involved, it is strange that Wilson should have been squeamish about an obscure point which was sanctified by precedent. He did not scruple to throw overboard a century of isolationist tradition, yet he was a stickler for a constitutional point which at the most was unconstitutional only in spirit. One is again reminded of men who strain at gnats and swallow camels.

One suspects—though proof is lacking—that Wilson would have found this constitutional argument less satisfying if it had not provided such a convenient excuse for leaving Lodge and other Republican encumbrances at home.

9

It is possible to understand why Wilson should not have appointed Senators, but it is difficult to explain why he snubbed that all-important body in almost every other way. He seems to have made little or no effort to defer to it either on the question of selecting the Commission or on that of shaping the peace.

General Ulysses S. Grant, upon being thrust into the Presidency, thought that Congress and not the Senate approved treaties; but gradually he learned something about the Constitution at the taxpayers' expense. Yet Wilson, the internationally known authority on government, could certainly not plead ignorance.

The simple facts are these. Wilson knew, or should have known, that the Senate is a powerful body, sleeplessly jealous of its prerogatives; that it had defeated treaties before and might do so again; and that only one-third of its membership (plus one) could undo any pact brought before it. He knew, or should have known, that the Senate Republicans were in an ugly mood following his October appeal, and that the Senate was eager to regain the power and prestige it had enjoyed before Wilson had assumed his wartime dictatorship under the Constitution. He knew, or should have known, that the next

Senate would be controlled by the Republicans, with the chairman of the Senate Committee on Foreign Relations none other than the implacable Henry Cabot Lodge. He knew that he was going to try to force a League of Nations into the treaty of peace, and he also knew, or should have remembered, that when he had earlier broached this idea he had stirred up a hornets' nest among isolationist Republicans in the Senate.

As recently as 1908, Wilson had written in one of his better

"Seein' Things"
(Courtesy of the Brooklyn *Eagle*)

known books that there was nothing to prevent the President from making the Senate a useful partner rather than a jealous rival. He received a forceful reminder of his own dictum when, early in November, 1918, ex-President Taft appealed to him publicly to defer to the foreign relations committees of both the House and the Senate.

It is true that previous Presidents had not ordinarily followed the practice of consulting the Senate in advance of negotiating a treaty; but a few had done so, and there was nothing to prevent Wilson's doing so. This, it must be repeated, was to be no ordinary treaty; the destiny of the world hung upon it; money and blood had been poured out like water to achieve it. Then why should the President stand on punctilio?

Wilson, it must be confessed, did not entertain great respect for the Senate, and he viewed it with irritated aloofness. It must also be confessed that he was not discreet in his private references to the "pigmy-minded" gentlemen in that body. He tactlessly insisted in a public speech, after his return from Paris, that he owed nothing to the Senate. Both he and the Senators were elected and paid by the American people to do their respective jobs. His job was to draw up treaties; theirs was to pass upon them. If any accounting was to be made, he would make it to the people who had hired him. The Senate could do likewise.

There can be no doubt, either, that Wilson did not like the two-thirds rule. But the fact remains that the Senate was just as much a part of the treaty-making power as he was, and there was nothing that could be done about it short of amending the Constitution, which, if possible, would have taken too long. As Wilson was condemned to live with the Senate, he would have done well to invite its cooperation rather than excite its antagonism.

10

The members of Congress, and in particular the members of the Senate, were vitally interested in making the peace, as was true of all thoughtful Americans. On December 2, 1918, Senator Cummins introduced a resolution in the Senate designed to send a bipartisan Senatorial committee to Paris for the purposes of watching the negotiations and keeping Congress posted. Administration forces, after sarcastically proposing that all ninety-six Senators go to Paris, were able to sidetrack this unwelcome move.

The members of the Senate would doubtless have been flattered, and made to feel that they were partners in the enterprise, if their advice had been sought in advance of Wilson's going. They would have been able to give some excellent advice as to what to put into the treaty and what to leave out, in order to insure prompt approval. Even assuming that the Senate had not responded graciously to Wilson's gesture, there was nothing to be lost and everything to be gained by making it.

Why, then, did Wilson ignore the Senate?

Perhaps it was because he had not got his fingers badly burned in any previous treaty fight, though he had encountered annoying difficulties over the Colombia indemnity treaty, over the canal-tolls repeal, and over the armed-ship filibuster. Perhaps it was because he felt that the Senate did not matter as long as public opinion was on his side. Perhaps it was because he did not believe that the Senate would dare incur the opprobrium of ruining his plans for world reorganization. This thought cropped out later in one of his public speeches.

Possibly the true explanation is that Wilson, as he himself admitted, had a "one-track" mind, and that he tackled this problem with "single-track" intensity. While he was concentrating on the colossal task of making a new world order, the Senate did not seem important. As has been well said, "he was like the man who knocked the ball into the left-field bleachers, but forgot to touch the home plate."

In any event, either Wilson overlooked what he already knew about the Senate, or he thought it unimportant.

But the Senate was not unimportant—and it was to be heard from again.

11

The uproar over the appointments had not died down when, on December 2, 1918, Wilson appeared before Congress to deliver his annual message. He was to sail for Paris two days later, and it was generally anticipated that he would take the country into his confidence and outline in general terms the kind of peace he expected to bring back.

But the address was largely the conventional and prosaic presidential discourse on the state of the nation. At the very end, Wilson appealed to the people to support him in what he was going to do, but he did not make it at all clear what he was going to do.

The Democrats who were present generally applauded his remarks. The Republicans, and a considerable sprinkling of Senate Democrats, sat in sullen silence. The press voiced keen disappointment at Wilson's secretiveness, and partisan journals remarked that Wilson treated the American people like a class in political economy at Princeton. There can be no doubt that Wilson completely muffed a splendid opportunity to win popular support and acquaint the American people with their new responsibilities.

Two days later he sailed from New York. Ominously, he left behind him an ill-tempered, resentful, and suspicious Republican opposition, and a confused, preoccupied, and drifting Democratic following.

CHAPTER SEVEN

THE COMING
OF THE MESSIAH

"If he [Wilson] has any sense he will get back to America as soon as he can." SIR HENRY WILSON, *December 22, 1918.*

1

O N T H E morning of December 4, 1918, the good ship *George Washington* (a former German luxury liner) nosed slowly out of New York harbor, bearing Woodrow Wilson to Europe on one of the greatest adventures of all time. No argosy—not even that of Columbus—ever ventured out into the unknown more heavily freighted with the hopes of humanity.

Airplanes droned overhead, tugboats shrieked hoarsely, and the black masses of humanity on shore shouted enthusiastically, as President Wilson, standing beside Mrs. Wilson on the topmost deck of the *George Washington,* waved his dark felt hat in response, and flashed his famous smile. Gradually the up-pointing Statue of Liberty hazed into the background, and the great adventure had begun.

On.the way out of the harbor, the *George Washington* met the transport *Minnehaha* bringing home a cargo of khaki-clad American boys from Europe. They waved and cheered as if to remind him that he must not break faith with their buddies who would never come back; as if to remind him that if he succeeded in making the right kind of peace they would not have to go back and do the bloody job again.

But Wilson needed no reminders. He knew full well the ghastly cost of the recent war. He knew full well that it lay within the power of the victorious nations to dictate the terms of settlement and to erect the structure of an enduring peace. This was an opportunity such as had never before come to mortal man—an opportunity that might never come again. If the peacemakers succeeded, their names would be blessed; if they failed, their names would be cursed by generations yet unborn.

No one was more completely convinced than Wilson that there could be no enduring peace without the participation of the United States in his League of Nations. He was therefore determined that the American people should underwrite the military, political, territorial, and financial terms of the yet unnegotiated peace. But would they? He assumed that the American people had changed their minds, much as he had changed his mind, on the subject of close cooperation with the rest of the world. But had they?

We have already referred to Wilson's capacity for changing his mind in recognition of changing realities, and to his assumption that others could change their minds also. We have also considered the "one-track" intensity with which he pursued large objectives, while losing sight of smaller ones. In making up the personnel of the Peace Commission, he lost sight of the Senate. In making plans for the new and enduring peace, he lost sight of the American people.

For some unaccountable reason, Wilson did not properly appreciate the magnitude of the sacrifice he was calling upon his countrymen to make. From the days of George Washington onward, with the single exception of the brief interlude of Theodore Roosevelt, the United States had generally pursued a policy of isolation—a policy of having as little political connection with Europe as possible.

Yet here was Wilson—singlehanded—about to change the main current of American foreign policy, a policy sanctified by time and hallowed by association with the names of the Founding Fathers. To Wilson's penetrating mind the reversal seemed simple, and altogether necessary in the light of changed conditions. To the less penetrating minds of millions of his countrymen, this was a momentous step, not to be taken lightly, certainly not without the greatest of deliberation.

Not the least among the ironies of this great tragedy is the fact that Wilson was sailing to Europe on the *George Washington*—a ship named after the very President whose policy he was seeking to reverse. If this was a gentle warning from the great Disposer of Events, Wilson seems to have paid little or no attention to it.

2

Wilson was by no means without assistance in his plans for remodeling the world. Accompanying him on the *George Washington* were scores of specialists in history, geography, ethnography, economics, finance—a veritable "brain trust," to which Wilson referred as his "brains."

The principal Allied and Associated Powers, including the United States, had been at work for many months on the problems of the peace. Some months after America entered the war, a group of experts, predominantly college professors, was brought together in New York City under the direction of Colonel House. For many months this earnest group, named The Inquiry, had been giving meticulous study to the numerous problems that were bound to vex the makers of the new map of Europe.

There can be no doubt that the American experts amassed a great deal of sound, factual information. The *George Washington* groaned under the cartloads of books, maps, reports, and other data which had been so carefully assembled—"peace conference munitions." But American opinion, suspicious of academicians, was not too favorably impressed. One New York journal irreverently described the whole organization as "Colonel House's troupe of performing professors." William Allen White, another journalist, wrote:

"Down the gangplank walked this Yankee knight errant followed by a desperate crew of college professors in horn-rimmed glasses carrying textbooks, encyclopaedias, maps, charts, graphs, statistics, and all sorts of literary crowbars with which to pry up the boundaries of Europe and move them around in the interests of justice, as seen through the Fourteen Points."

This lurid picture is not only unfriendly but unfair. The nationally known experts who went to Europe were not carrying textbooks; they had advanced far beyond the textbook stage. Harold Nicolson, a minor member of the British delegation, cheerfully concedes that the American delegation was the best informed at Paris. Dr. Charles Seymour, who was one of the specialists in question, relates that at a meeting of a commission in Paris, an American expert proposed that a decision be altered in the light of new facts, and offered to present the evidence. A foreign delegate thereupon suggested "that we accept the amendment without asking for the evidence. Hitherto the facts presented by the Americans have been irrefutable; it would be a waste of time to consider them."

3

Three days before the *George Washington* reached France, Wilson assembled the American experts for a discussion of some of the problems that loomed menacingly on the horizon. He announced at the outset that he was speaking "off the record." Disregarding this injunction, Dr. Isaiah Bowman took careful notes, and immediately thereafter reconstructed the entire speech.

We need not analyze this revealing address at length, but we should carefully weigh two remarks which throw a flood of light upon Wilson's thinking, and which in some measure explain his conduct at Paris.

At the very beginning Wilson declared that the Americans would be the "only disinterested people at the Peace Conference, and that the men whom we were about to deal with *did not represent their own people . . .*"

This is an astonishing statement. What Wilson evidently had in mind was that the greedy and grasping premiers and prime ministers of Great Britain, France, and Italy did not represent the finer aspirations of their people, to whom Wilson had appealed in his Fourteen Points. The actual experience at the Conference revealed that the people not only were behind their representatives but were to some extent ahead of them in clamoring for the spoils of war.

But whether well founded or not, this attitude on the part of Wilson did not augur well for harmonious cooperation with his associates at the peace table. He seems to have felt all along that in case of a deadlock all he had to do was to appeal over their selfish heads to the nobler impulses of their people. He seems to have felt that he represented, not merely an American, but a world constituency. In a very real sense he represented neither.

The second point of Wilson's address that needs emphasis appeared in his peroration. After urging his experts to keep constantly in touch with him and to bring to his attention any matters of critical importance, he pleaded: "Tell me what's right and I'll fight for it; give me a guaranteed position."

Here we see the workings of the careful academic mind. Trained as a specialist, Wilson respected specialists—academic specialists. They were "his kind"; they spoke the language he understood. He also respected facts. He did not want opinions from his specialists; he wanted only the facts. On the basis of the facts, he would form the opinions. And when he was assured that the position which he took was based on facts, he would fight for that position, "agreeably if we can, disagreeably if necessary."

We shall presently see how this pledge worked out.

4

The *George Washington* sighted Brest, France, on Friday the 13th, a date which bore no terrors for Wilson, for he had long regarded thirteen as his lucky number.

As the ship steamed slowly into the harbor, he was greeted with the strains of "The Star-Spangled Banner," with thunderous presidential salutes from the near-by warships, and with the huzzas of the populace. With high silk hat in his left hand, he bowed and smiled while acknowledging the plaudits of the people.

He did not tarry long at Brest. Through lines of cheering soldiers, flower-bearing children, and peasants in their picturesque Breton costumes, he pushed on to the train, and with waving hand began his triumphal trip to Paris. Lincoln Steffens records that here and there peasant families knelt beside the track in the dark to pray for him and his mission.

The capital gave Wilson an ovation that would have warmed the heart of a Caesar or a Napoleon. Proudly he rode down the beflagged Champs-Elysées with President Poincaré, while two million people, held back by tens of thousands of cheering soldiers, shouted "Vive l'Amérique!" "Vive le Président!" Countless bouquets of roses and violets were rained upon the open carriage. Wilson gracefully acknowledged the cheers, gray head bared, while the procession passed under a great banner bearing the words, "Honour to Wilson the Just."

This tremendous tribute was partly personal, partly an expression of gratitude to America for having helped rescue France from the heel of the Boche. It was also partly the manifestation of a belief that Wilson would carry through his ideals and bring a lasting and just peace—which meant, of course, that Germany would be ground down so far into the dust that she could never clench her mailed fist again.

After nearly two weeks in France, Wilson journeyed to England, where he was greeted by cheering throngs, reverberating salutes, and all the pomp and pageantry of a millennium of royalty. He dined at Buckingham Palace, and ate from gold services of plate valued at fifteen million dollars. At Carlisle he visited the church in which his grandfather had served as pastor, and delivered a few beautifully chosen extemporaneous words. His several formal addresses were all brief, dignified, and not especially revealing.

The six-day reception in England was noticeably cooler than that in France. Perhaps it was Gallic excitability; perhaps it was that England had already poured out her soul to Foch and Clemenceau only a few weeks before.

There is one other explanation. The British remembered how reluctant Wilson had been to bring his people into the fray on their side. Blood was not thicker than water; he had been "too proud to fight"; he had favored "peace without victory." In none of his speeches in England did he pay a graceful and eloquent tribute to the tremendous sacrifices of England in the war that had just ended, sacrifices far greater than those of late-coming America. British leaders, notably Lloyd George, were hurt and angry. But Wilson was probably thinking of the bright vistas of the future rather than the bloody sacrifices of the past.

One portentous development occurred while Wilson was in England. On December 29, 1918, Clemenceau appeared before the Chamber of Deputies, and with a sneering reference to Wilson's *noble candeur* ("noble simplicity") came out four-square for the old balance of power—with France the dominant end of the balance. He was resoundingly supported by a vote of confidence, 380 to 134, the greatest of his tempestuous career. Tactfully, the compositors of the official record of the debates changed *noble candeur* to *noble grandeur*.

The next day, speaking at Manchester, England, Wilson stated sharply that the United States was not in the slightest degree interested in supporting the old balance of power. We would join only a combination which was a combination of all.

The British press interpreted Wilson's statement as a rejoinder to Clemenceau, as doubtless it was, and printed the two speeches side by side. Clearly there was going to be a head-on collision between the leading spokesman for the Old Order, and the leading spokesman for the New.

5

Returning to rain-soaked Paris, Wilson made hasty preparations for a four-day journey to Italy. As his train snaked along under cloudless skies, thousands of peasants poured down from the hills to wave an enthusiastic Godspeed. At Rome, the hysterical masses, held back by the soldiery with great difficulty, cheered wildly, "Viva Wilson, god of peace," and poured a cascade of purple violets and golden mimosa upon him. At Milan, he stood on the balcony, led the band, and with both hands threw kisses to the delighted populace.

The Italian reception was nothing short of delirious. In Milan, wounded soldiers had attempted to kiss his clothes. Europe had seen nothing like it since the days of Peter the Hermit. Streets and public squares were renamed in Wilson's honor. Men thought of the millennium, of the second coming of Christ. A story—undoubtedly apocryphal—told of an Italian laborer who hoped that the Pope would not die, because "Voovro Veelson," as he was affectionately called, might appoint a Protestant.

One ugly incident marred the triumphal Italian tour. As George Creel tells the story—and he was there—some 50,000 people packed the Piazza Venezia in Rome, waiting for Wilson to speak to them as scheduled. They waited five hours, and then the Presidential procession swept by without stopping. A great groan rose up from the expectant multitude, and with Latin emotionalism women wept and men threw their hats upon the ground and tore wildly at their hair.

The explanation is that while Wilson wanted to meet the people, and expected to do so, the Italian leaders did not want him to. They were afraid that he would make such a moving appeal as to spoil the plans that they were secretly laying for imperialistic loot. So they took him in hand and saw to it that he was not permitted to make such an appeal, while officially announcing in the press that the President had never had any intention of speaking at the Piazza Venezia.

Mrs. Wilson vividly recalls in her memoirs the anger which both she and the President felt over these transparent attempts to keep him at arm's length from the masses. The common people would have heard him "gladly"—only they were not allowed to.

Returning to Paris after making a half-dozen fatiguing speeches, and after sightseeing in the Coliseum and elsewhere, Wilson on the whole had reason to be happy. He apparently believed that all the cheering meant that the peoples of Europe were enthusiastically in favor of the proposed League of Nations. But were they? Was it not relief from war; joy over the approaching peace; gratitude to the United States; appreciation of Wilson's leadership? Time would tell.

6

One cannot help feeling that these pre-Conference junkets were unfortunate, though it is difficult to see how they could have been avoided. But as long as Wilson decided to take them, it was well that he went before the Conference, rather than after. Had he gone later, he would have been the recipient of things less pleasant than flowers, especially in Italy.

There can be little doubt that the pressure to make these tours was great. The Conference would not meet for several weeks, and what valid excuse could be offered for disappointing all these worshipful people? We should also note that Wilson would have been less than human if he had failed in some measure to enjoy such unprecedented outpourings of devotion and good will. Besides, he did not believe that the statesmen represented their people, and here, he assumed, was a splendid opportunity to bring his message directly to the masses.

If Wilson had been looking for an excuse not to go on these presidential pilgrimages, he could have found an excellent one. All of his time and energy were needed in Paris for working out the preliminaries of the Conference. The trips consumed precious time, and sapped his slender store of energy. It is probable that at this early date he did not fully realize how valuable time was, and how much there was to be done. But if he could have applied the many days that were frittered away on trips to the tasks that came rushing to a head in April, the final story might have been different.

7

Wilson, in fact, did say "No" to one invitation—perhaps the one invitation he should have accepted.

The French and Belgians had made extensive preparations for taking him on a trip to the devastated areas and the graveyards, where the President could see with his own eyes the incredible damage inflicted by the Hun, and the countless acres of white crosses—mute testimony of the terrible sacrifices of France.

Wilson stubbornly declined these repeated invitations, and possibly was irked by them. He had come from America to make a peace of justice, and he did not want his mind beclouded with long rows of white crosses when he considered the fate of Germany. "The French want me to see red," he remarked. "I could not despise the Germans more than I do already." Wilson, the scholar, was going to make a determined effort to retain some of his scholarly objectivity. Wilson, the Southern boy brought up in devastated Georgia, already knew that war was what General Sherman actually made it and reputedly called it. He was too busy with more important things.

But from the political point of view Wilson made a serious error. France was eager to show the wounds of her still-bleeding body to him who would have much to do with binding them up. If the good physician had looked at them, he would have offended no one, and he would have given the patient a strong psychological "lift." Lloyd George went out to visit the devastated regions at the first possible moment, and made a speech about them at the first possible opportunity. But Lloyd George was a politician who overlooked few tricks.

"Pay for That!"

(From the New York *Evening World;* reprinted by permission)

The most curious thing about this entire episode is that Wilson finally did go out to the battlefields—when it was too late fully to appease the French. On January 26, 1919, he and Mrs. Wilson made a hurried, one-day excursion to Rheims. Lloyd George stresses the bad impression that was made when Wilson allegedly remarked that the damage to the priceless cathedral was not so great as he had been led to expect. One cannot be sure that Wilson said this, but in any case the trip was another instance of too little and too late. The Conference had already been in session for some two weeks, and the area visited was but a small sector, and not the most badly damaged one at that. It was not until late in March that Wilson made a hurried, one day trip to the more seriously devastated areas.

8

We have already observed that the trips to England and Italy were a waste of precious time. There are additional reasons why they were most unfortunate.

Wilson by his very presence exaggerated the hopes and aspirations of the masses of the people, and these hopes and aspirations, some of them territorial, were already sufficiently exaggerated. When the hour of disillusionment came, as it was bound to come, Wilson could not escape the wrath born of disappointment.

More important, perhaps, Wilson came away from these tumultuous ovations with mistaken ideas of his personal influence with foreign peoples. In all the hysterical cheering he saw convincing proof of his smug assertion on the *George Washington* that the masses favored the unselfish ideals that he stood for rather than the selfish principles that their rulers stood for. Possibly this would have been true—though one may doubt it—if the rulers had permitted him to present those ideals to the masses directly.

At the peace table the "dumb eyes of the people" continued to haunt Wilson. He knew that they were counting on him to give them a better world; he felt that they were so enthusiastically behind him that if it came to a showdown he could appeal directly to them over the heads of their rulers. Even the ordinarily levelheaded Colonel House believed that Wilson might "possibly" overthrow the governments of England, France, and Italy by exerting his influence among the liberals and laboring classes.

It is not surprising that Wilson should later have made one disastrous attempt to appeal over the heads of the rulers to their people. Perhaps he would not have done so if their uproarious vivas had not been still ringing in his ears.

CHAPTER EIGHT

BLUNDERING BEGINNINGS

*"Bolshevism is gaining ground everywhere. Hungary has just
succumbed. We are sitting upon an open powder magazine and
some day a spark may ignite it . . ."* COLONEL HOUSE,
March 22, 1919.

1

THE PARIS Peace Conference did not begin its formal deliberations until January 12, 1919, almost exactly one month
after Wilson landed at Brest. The first plenary session was not
held until January 18.

This delay is incomprehensible, particularly when we remember that the crying need of the hour was haste. The red
bacillus of Bolshevism was gradually spreading westward from
Russia, and anarchy was smoothing its path. Europe was bankrupt, starving, and sick, both mentally and physically. "The
wolf," said Herbert Hoover, "is at the door of the world."
Unless peace was made, and made quickly, Germany might
yield to Bolshevism, clasp hands with Russia, and reopen the
war. Or there might be no responsible government in Germany
to accept the peace when once it was drawn up.

The race was a breath-taking one between the makers of
peace and the makers of anarchy. Yet the makers of peace
dawdled away two months after the Armistice before putting
their feet together under the table. All the while their armies
melted away, their strength ebbed, and with it went the power
to enforce their decisions and garner the fruits of victory. In
what way was Wilson responsible for this perilous delay?

The answer is: he had little or nothing to do with it. This
judgment becomes all the more significant when we realize that
he was later criticized with great bitterness for delaying the
peace by forcing the League of Nations into the treaty. We

119

shall consider this point later, but for the moment we may observe that the time, if any, lost in making the League Covenant was as nothing when compared with the early weeks of thumb-twiddling, while Europe slowly crumbled to pieces.

Wilson could have settled down to serious work shortly after arriving in mid-December, and expected to do so on or about December 17. He had postponed his departure so that he could deliver his annual message to Congress in person, but if it had been imperatively necessary he could have sailed shortly after the Armistice, three weeks earlier. The President is not required by the Constitution to make personal appearances before Congress; in fact, Wilson was the first one in over a century to do so.

The common criticism that the Conference had to wait for Wilson may be met in still other ways. Far-away Japan, China, Siam, India, Australia, New Zealand, and South Africa were all entitled to send representatives, and under the best of circumstances they could hardly have been brought to Paris earlier than December 14, when Wilson arrived. And if, as alleged, the Conference was waiting breathlessly for him, why was there a delay of another month before it actually began its deliberations?

The true explanation of the delay must be sought in a number of different quarters. The victory had to be celebrated with processions and state visits. The fiery general election in England, which Lloyd George had called for December 14, the day of Wilson's arrival in Paris, had to be cleared out of the way. The Christmas holiday letdown had to be surmounted. It was also necessary to take stock of the situation; to let war-fevered emotions die down; to erect peace machinery on the foundations of war machinery. It was necessary to allow the revolutions in Russia and Germany to shake down, so that the Allied statesmen could see more clearly whom and what they had to deal with. It was necessary to give Wilson an opportunity to get the "feel" of the European situation; to visit the devastated regions; to absorb the Allied point of view. There is finally a not unfounded suspicion that the Allied leaders purposely delayed meeting earlier because they knew that delay would cool the enthusiasm of the populace for Wilson and his idealism. They would also have time to take the measure of their idealistic adversary, and find the weak joints in his armor. There is, in fact, some evidence that they deliberately set out to do so in advance of his coming.

Whatever the explanation, the results were highly unfortunate.

The nationalistic aspirations of France and especially of Italy were given time to develop in an overblown fashion. If the territorial terms could have been written earlier, they probably would have been more reasonable than they were later.

Public opinion began to lose faith in the negotiators—the "dawdlers of Paris." Everywhere there was a mounting impatience to get the thing over with and "bring the boys home," in spite of the fact that the war would not technically be over until the peace was signed.

During the weeks of delay, Wilson, having nothing pressing to do, consented to make his triumphal appearances in England and Italy, with the unfortunate results already described.

Finally, the frittering away of the costly weeks in December and January meant that the work of the Conference had to be rushed forward with frantic speed in April, when a number of hasty and regrettable decisions were made.

2

The selection of Paris as the site of the Conference was one of the cardinal misfortunes of the negotiation. The atmosphere of this shell-shocked city—"gashed to her very soul"—was the complete reverse of that serenity which should surround the making of great and lasting decisions.

Paris in the winter of 1918–1919 was underfed and under-heated. It swarmed with penniless refugees, soulless profiteers, and profligate women. Countless German cannon were piled up in the squares. Women in black walked the leafless boulevards, and mutilated veterans stumped through the streets, grim reminders of the Hun. The ruins left by the long-range Big Bertha were there for all to see. Excitable and gesticulating mobs sprang from the pavements, voicing their sentiments with Gallic intemperance.

One of the worst things about Paris was the clatter of the corrupt and corruptible French press. A dozen or so sheets responded to the commands of the government with servile precision. When Wilson opposed French claims in private conferences, denunciations of the pro-German President would immediately pour from the Parisian press, just as though Clemenceau had turned on a giant faucet. Some of this criticism was diabolically clever, and beyond a doubt vastly annoying to Wilson. At one time he declared that if the clamor kept up he would have to suggest moving the whole Conference to some quieter place.

Another reason why Paris was an unfortunate choice was that it gave to the nerve-racked French a disproportionate control of the program and machinery of the Conference. The able but domineering Clemenceau became chairman—a courtesy that could not be denied the host nation. This meant that the French had a disproportionate voice in the vastly important decision of what should be taken up, and when it should be taken up.

From the very outset the French favored Paris as the meeting place; the Belgians, Brussels. Colonel House cabled Wilson from France late in October that the only objection to Paris was that if sharp differences should arise between the French and their Allies, "it might be embarrassing." This was advice worth remembering.

Wilson promptly replied that he regarded a "neutral place of meeting" as "much wiser," and expressed a preference for the quiet of Lausanne, Switzerland, where pro-Ally influences were strong.

A few days later the representatives of the four powers in Paris came to a tentative decision to take Switzerland. Even Clemenceau voiced no objection at the time, though he clearly did not want Geneva.

But Wilson suddenly changed his mind and cabled House on November 7: "On second thought it occurs to me that Versailles may be the best place for the peace conference where friendly influences and authorities are in control rather than Switzerland which is saturated with every poisonous element and open to every hostile influence in Europe."

The "poisonous elements" to which Wilson referred were probably the Bolshevist and pro-German agents and the pro-German press, which were offset to a considerable degree by pro-Ally influences. In any event, it is doubtful if these "poisonous elements" would have proved as harmful as those of Paris.

The decision to shift from Switzerland to France seems clearly to have been made by Wilson. Although the hotel accommodations of Lausanne or Geneva were inadequate for the host that finally descended upon Paris, it is probable that the tentative decision to take Switzerland could have been made to stand if Wilson had thrown all of his enormous influence behind it. Lloyd George says that he favored Geneva, but had to give up the battle when Wilson shifted ground.

3

Wilson presumably changed to Versailles because he regarded it as much quieter than Paris and entirely without the pro-German influences of Switzerland. There can be no doubt that Versailles would have been better than Paris if it had been used, but it was not used except to present the draft treaty to the Germans, and later to provide the setting for the signing ceremony.

The explanation seems to be almost entirely a practical one. Versailles is virtually a suburb of Paris, and lacking in the spacious hotel accommodations of the metropolis. The delegates would have to live in Paris anyhow, and it would have been an indefensible waste of time, when time was at a premium, to commute to Versailles for the daily deliberations. So the Conference met in the sad and sick city of Paris.

There were other compelling reasons, both practical and sentimental, why the capital of France should have been honored. The hotels, as already noted, were large and numerous, but not too large or too numerous to accommodate without some strain the scores of delegates and their thousands of assistants. The city was centrally located, and the communications were excellent. The Allied leaders had met there for their principal war conferences, and it was logical that they should do so for the peace.

Finally, there was the honor due France. London, in many ways, would have been a more satisfactory meeting place; but if there was going to be a belligerent capital, that capital had to be Paris. France had sustained on her pulverized soil the bulk of the fighting; and she had given up more of her sons than any of her Allies. Arthur J. Balfour remarked to Clemenceau that one good reason for choosing Paris was the communications. Clemenceau, evidently thinking of France's ghastly sacrifices, sourly replied that he could think of other and better grounds.

One may suspect that the true explanation of Wilson's action is that in November, 1918, the question of locale seemed to be relatively trivial. The responsibility of creating a new world order was so overpowering, and the necessity for haste was so apparent, that the natural impulse was to choose a convenient place and get on with the task.

Yet, as it turned out, Paris was just about the last place that should have been chosen. Perhaps it is unfair to blame Wilson for not having recognized this in advance. There certainly was enormous pressure on the Allies to grant what seemed to be so modest and harmless a request. The French had fought the longest and had suffered the most. And who were the Americans—laggard converts to the Allied cause—to deny them this slight consolation?

Little courtesies may be fraught with big results. The green baize table cannot be dumped anywhere, and the negotiators told to go to work.

Even granting all this, one cannot be sure that the Treaty of Versailles would have been a substantially better peace if the Conference had met in Switzerland. Possibly it would have been somewhat better, but the fact remains that if the negotiators had met at the North Pole they would have carried with them the war hatred aroused by propaganda and passion. This is something that can be remedied only by time—not by place.

4

Ray Stannard Baker, who was director of the American Press Bureau at the Conference and who should have known, concludes that "the great failure" of the Americans was a "failure in constructive publicity."

This goes back to the first of the Fourteen Points, and to Wilson's disinclination to explain more precisely and more persistently what he had in mind.

Point I of the Fourteen was "Open covenants of peace, openly arrived at . . ." This easily slipped into the slogan, "Open covenants openly arrived at." Nothing could better illustrate the dangers of imprecision resulting from the over-simplification of a complex situation, and nothing could better illustrate the dangers of hastily phrasing statements that lend themselves to sloganizing.

Countless thousands of Americans mouthed this catchword, confidently believing that henceforth there would be no more hole-in-the-corner diplomacy, and that henceforth the whole world could gaze at every move at the peace table, much as masked doctors look down from the observation gallery upon a delicate operation.

This was not what Wilson meant at all. During the war the news had leaked out that various secret treaties had been made, treaties by which the signatories bound whole nations to dangerous courses. In all these cases the peoples concerned had not been told of their commitment, and in some cases large numbers of them would have opposed it if they had been. Wilson quite logically concluded that this was the very negation of the democratic process.

Wilson, of course, was not so naïve as to propose that there should be no confidential interchanges in the shaping of treaties. He knew perfectly well that the soul of negotiation is the principle of give and take: of asking for more than one expects, and then accepting less. If a negotiator took an extreme position, and then retreated from it, and the news came out in the press the next day, he would be driven from office with cries of: "Britain is betrayed!" "France is betrayed!" If all stages of negotiation proceeded under the full floodlight of publicity, the negotiators would have to move so slowly, if at all, that the whole procedure would be paralyzed. It would be either a farce or a free-for-all.

Wilson did not believe that the "birth pangs" of the peace should be exposed to the public gaze, or that newspaper readers all over the world should enjoy the spectacle of statesmen washing their soiled linen in public. What he meant was that, once a treaty was negotiated, the people concerned should know of its existence and be given a chance to discuss it. (One of the genuine contributions of the Covenant of the League of Nations was to make provision for the registering of treaties at Geneva.)

If this is what Wilson meant, why did he not say so in unambiguous terms—not once, but many times?

The answer seems to be that Wilson, unlike many college professors, hated to repeat himself; and he hated to have people repeat things to him. At the Conference, Ray Stannard Baker once urged him to explain something to the correspondents, but Wilson refused by saying, "But I've already said it." Yes, he had; *in a speech.*

The October appeal, we remember, had been savagely criticized and misrepresented. Yet Wilson issued no qualifying statement—no rebuttal. He had already said it, clearly, precisely, and finally. And that was that.

Wilson had stated his position with rigorous economy of words in the first of the Fourteen Points, and as it was clear to him, he thought it must be clear to everybody else. The good academic lecturer—and Wilson was an outstanding expositor—assumes that the students are all there, that they are awake, that they are interested, that they get the point, and that they will retain it. In a distressing number of cases none of these assumptions is valid.

The blunt truth is that the brilliant Princeton professor failed as a teacher. His classroom was the American public, and he overestimated their capacity to read his mind. Ray Stannard Baker, his understanding biographer, well says that many a "humbler politician could have told him" that an idea "had to be repeated a thousand times, published in every newspaper, put in the movies, set to music!"

The point to bear in mind is that the American people confidently expected to see an abolition of all secret conferences, and a perfect example of housetop diplomacy. They had been led to believe that there was no essential difference between delicate diplomatic discussions and dickering for a horse.

5

About five hundred of the world's ablest newsmen, expecting to capitalize on the new "open diplomacy," poured into Paris. American newspapers and news associations, at great expense, had sent some one hundred and fifty of their crack reporters. The Conference was one of the big news stories of all time, and these "ambassadors of public opinion" were there to see that nothing went unreported.

In mid-January the deliberations formally began. The delegates filed into the high-ceilinged halls of the French Foreign Office on the Quai d'Orsay, and the double doors were slammed in the faces of the expectant news hawks, and then carefully guarded. At the end of the day a secretary slipped out and read a juiceless, five-line summary of what had happened.

The disillusioned correspondents laid aside their freshly sharpened pencils and emitted an outcry of exasperation, disgust, and wrath. There was loud and angry talk about "gag rule," "diplomacy in the dark," and "the Congress of Vienna over again." So these were "open covenants openly arrived at"!

Wilson was strongly in favor of letting the reporters in. He hated censorship of any kind, for he believed that publicity was the lifeblood of public education in a democracy. The United States was the only great power that had no secret treaties, no territorial aspirations. Wilson had nothing to conceal, nothing to be afraid of. No matter what came out of the Conference, he would be President of the United States until March 4, 1921—barring death, resignation, or impeachment.

But, as we must constantly bear in mind, Wilson was the representative of but one of the five great powers, and he could not always have his own way. His position was secure for two more years; but Lloyd George and Clemenceau could be thrown out of office overnight if they made the wrong move, and the news leaked out. A disappointed public, backed by an unscrupulous press, would not hesitate to cry, "Off with his head!" Orlando, the Italian premier, was in fact politically decapitated before he even had an opportunity to sign the Treaty of Versailles.

We must also remember that the war had not ended; the armistice was technically a truce. The secrecy that had governed military councils during the war had also to govern diplomatic councils during the nominal peace. News of disagreement would encourage—and in fact did encourage—the enemy to resist the prospective terms.

The jostling nations of Central Europe, which had sprung from the ashes of revolution and defeat, were quarrelsome, suspicious, and greedy. Premature news as to the thwarting of their aspirations would evoke a tremendous outcry, and a consequent increase of pressure at Paris. There was enough clamor at the Conference as it was without encouraging any more from this source.

Altogether, complete publicity would have added immeasurably to the confusion and delay—and delay was deadly.

6

Wilson's determined fight for greater publicity was only partially successful. It was finally agreed that the correspondents might be admitted to the "staged shows" that were called the plenary sessions, but not to smaller private councils. The net result was that there were only six plenary conferences, and little of any consequence was ever done at these window-dressing affairs—dubbed "washouts" by the journalists—except to ratify decisions made in private. The necessity for even more secret discussions became evident as the Conference went on, and this is one of the main reasons why the Council of Four later established itself as the real power. When it became clear that little genuine news was to be given out while the Conference was in progress, a considerable number of the journalists disgustedly left for home, with little love in their hearts for Wilson.

It is interesting to note that certain of the French journals, which should have known better, blamed the American President for the lack of publicity. One of them satirized both Wilson and the "daily dope" of the official releases when it had the American President say: ". . . I have discovered that

Spring always follows Winter. That is the secret of my policy. I can also tell you another of my profound views, namely, that the weather will improve more quickly than will Europe. But this is a diplomatic confidence. Don't repeat it."

The correspondents were finally forced to fall back on the

When Truth Is Kept Within Doors
Lies Come Out at the Window
(Courtesy of the Brooklyn *Eagle*)

official, timetable communiqués, supplemented by "calculated indiscretions," "grapevine" rumors, and other "drippings" from the Conference, many of which were designed to conceal rather than reveal. Much of this "publicity by leak" came through the officially inspired French press, and this accounts for the French bias given a great deal of the news.

The more resourceful newspapermen were able to cultivate "leaks" and establish contacts with "inside" sources of information. On the whole they were able to penetrate the steel curtain of secrecy and send home a fairly satisfactory running account of what had happened. Lloyd George to this day insists that nothing was withheld which the public was entitled to know at the time. Certainly a vast amount of wordage was put on the wires; but unfortunately much of it was speculation of the most harmful kind.

7

This whole controversy over closed-door diplomacy got the Conference off to a bad start. To countless thousands of Americans it seemed as though the very first of the Fourteen Points had been flagrantly disregarded on the very first day of the Conference. Such disillusionment inspired no confidence as to what would happen to the remaining Points. It is small wonder that Wilson's private secretary, Joseph P. Tumulty, cabled in alarm from Washington that the country was up in arms; and that it would be better for the President to bolt the Conference than to submit to a "gag rule."

The rumor and speculation which were given wings at Paris by "calculated leakages" inspired a vast amount of suspicion and distrust. Hopes for a New Order began to take flight as the diplomats fell back upon the secrecy of the Old.

One cannot help feeling that much of this was avoidable.

First, Wilson should have publicly iterated and reiterated his views on open diplomacy until it was reasonably clear that American public opinion knew what he had in mind.

Second, the American press associations should have been emphatically warned about what to expect. If this had been done, they probably would not have sent over so many restless newsmen. This unfortunate situation was made infinitely worse by the month of delay in starting the Conference. There was little news to report, and where news does not exist the resourceful newspaperman makes it, whether through speculation or through imagination. Unfortunately also, many of the American correspondents had won their spurs in reporting domestic politics, and they knew little about the deep, underlying forces that were agitating Europe. The result was that their eyes were caught by the superficial, and their prognostications, often of the wildest sort, aroused unwarranted suspicions and expectations in America. The newsmen made up for the inadequacy of their information by the prodigality of their criticism.

Third, Wilson failed to tell the correspondents that he had put up a vigorous battle for them. As it was, they were resentful for the small favors they did receive, not knowing how energetically he had espoused their interests. Ray Stannard Baker urged Wilson to tell them everything, but Wilson more or less brushed the matter aside, evidently not thinking it important. The story finally did leak out in the press several months later, but at a time when it would do little good.

Wilson not only failed to cultivate the correspondents in this connection, but William Allen White, who was one of them, testifies that he was the only one of the Big Four who refused to meet the news representatives of his own country regularly and personally. He did so once in February; but someone betrayed a confidence, and he never appeared again. Perhaps he wanted to conserve his strength; probably he thought there were more important things to do. This was all most unfortunate. If he had kept up his fences with the correspondents, if he had told them of his battle for publicity, they would have been behind him foursquare. He did not, and they were not. The upshot was that he did not have the "good press" in America which he might have had, and which he so desperately needed when the real fight began.

Finally, this blundering beginning gave ammunition to Wilson's opponents in the Senate when they charged that he had gone to the Conference in order to "put something over on them." The Senate "irreconcilables" gave loud voice to their disappointment, and to the very end never ceased to complain that they did not know what was going on—and yet they were a part of the treaty-making power. Of course, Senators like Borah and Johnson and Brandegee would have found other grounds for complaint, but the inept rationing of news gave additional point and vigor to their denunciations.

CHAPTER NINE

THE PERILS OF IMPRECISION

"I am disquieted to see how hazy and vague our ideas are. We are going to be up against the wiliest politicians in Europe. There will be nothing hazy or vague about their ideas."

GENERAL TASKER H. BLISS, *December 18, 1918.*

1

IT IS difficult to find an eyewitness who was not impressed by the indescribable confusion and disorganization at Paris. Wickham Steed, the eminent British journalist, says that a true history of the Conference will never be written because mere words cannot re-create the atmosphere of Paris in 1919. Harold Nicolson speaks of "that sense of riot in a parrot house."

The explanation is not far to seek. There were twenty-seven Allied and Associated Powers, plus the five British Dominions, and each of the thirty-two was entitled to send delegates. The American contingent alone, counting various kinds of subordinates, totaled about 1,300. The British delegation occupied five hotels. And yet England, a century before, had sent only fourteen men to the great Congress of Vienna.

In addition to the official representatives, Paris swarmed with unofficial representatives of minority and other groups which had something to seek. Strange-looking men in strange-smelling garments walked the streets of Paris demanding recognition of some long-sought nationalistic aspiration.

There were Kirghizes, Circassians, Mingrelians, and Buryats, to say nothing of better known Koreans, Hindus, and Malays, from such far-away places as Tartary, Kurdistan, Samarkand and Bokhara—men with patriarchal beards and scimitar-shaped noses, clad in turbans and flowing mantles.

One of them, Emir Feisal from Arabia, bore a striking physical resemblance to the accepted likenesses of Jesus. But there the resemblance rather sharply ended.

Wilson gave ear to many of these people gladly, though he could in no case understand their language, and though he later confessed from the platform that he had not previously known of the existence of some of the places they represented. How he managed to work such suppliants into his already full day will remain one of the many minor mysteries of Paris.

The Conference set up more than sixty different commissions to deal with territorial, economic, and other problems. These groups, which held over 1,600 meetings, worked more or less in the dark, and often at cross purposes with other groups, whose functioning they were only dimly aware of. The reparations section labored long and hard on the question of exacting payments from Germany; the economic section labored long and hard to effect arrangements that would, as it turned out, make impossible the payment of expected reparations. The right hand seldom knew what the left hand was doing; sometimes the right hand did not even know what the right hand was doing.

Dr. James T. Shotwell, who was at Paris, remembers that the American experts were supposed to work on their respective specialties more or less in a vacuum. It was regarded as poor form to inquire what their colleagues in other fields were doing; only an exchange of gossip at luncheons or other casual meetings enabled them to glimpse faintly and imperfectly what was going on. The British, on the other hand, worked out a fairly satisfactory system of circularizing information among themselves as to the progress of the Conference.

Several years ago the present writer asked a distinguished American expert—one who had had a large hand in the drafting of the League Covenant—for some information about the Conference. "I do not know anything about it," he smiled. "I was only there." To the same question another distinguished American expert replied, "I do not know because I was there." "I would go further," he added, "and suggest that those who were there could not know."

What these men were saying, of course, was that while they knew something about what had happened in connection with their own narrow specialties, they did not have and could not have the over-all view of the Conference that was necessary for a well rounded picture. They were like soldiers in a campaign who know only their part of the trench on the battlefield; they are unable to glimpse the general plan of battle.

It would be unfair to suggest that the delegates at Paris did not work hard. Most of them did—perhaps too hard. At the Congress of Vienna, a hundred years before, they took nine months to dance their way to peace. Everyone seemingly danced except the club-footed Talleyrand: he had to content himself with playing whist. At Paris, in 1919, time was too short for much frivolity, at least among the leaders. Possibly the results would have been more lasting if there had been more relaxation.

The confusion was worse confounded by the complexity of the problem. The Allied statesmen were immediately concerned with making peace with the fallen enemy. They were also concerned with reordering the world in the interests of international stability. And finally, they found it necessary to keep their home governments functioning smoothly in their absence.

This last is very important. Every one of the heads of government at Paris had to spend a considerable part of his time looking after the home front. Wilson had to peck out his long message to Congress on his portable typewriter at odd moments before and after the regular meetings of the Council of Four. The sheer fatigue resulting from such numerous and oppressive duties undoubtedly contributed to some of the unfortunate decisions at Paris. This, it will be noted, is another argument for having the work done by representatives, rather than by a head of government.

2

The machinery of the Conference was gradually perfected by trial-and-error methods. A great body of several hundred delegates was too unwieldy, too dilatory, too loquacious, and too leaky for the efficient dispatch of business. So the plenary sessions became rubber stamps for the smaller groups.

The Supreme Council, or the Council of Ten, which evolved from the Allied Supreme War Council, at first did the most important work. It consisted of the two ranking delegates from each of the five great powers: Great Britain, France, Italy, Japan, and the United States. President Wilson and Secretary Lansing represented the United States.

The Council of Ten in turn proved to be too cumbersome and too leaky, but it was not until March, 1919, when the Conference came squarely to grips with the problem of Germany, that it gave way to the Council of Four—the Big Four—which more or less usurped authority. We shall consider the personnel of this remarkable body later, but for the moment we may note that it consisted of Wilson for the United States, Lloyd George for Great Britain, Clemenceau for France, and Orlando for Italy. Some of the time it was the Council of Three, for Orlando was not infrequently absent. At the early meetings there were neither secretaries nor written records. Three lone men in a room deciding the destiny of the world! An ironically undemocratic ending indeed for a war that had been proclaimed as a crusade to make the world safe for democracy.

After the Council of Ten resolved itself into the Big Four, the Foreign Secretaries met separately as the Council of Five (Council of Foreign Ministers). Although their work was not of the first importance, they nevertheless served a useful function.

Once the machinery of the Conference was set up, the next question was: what should be the plan of procedure? What subjects should be taken up, and in what order?

This was a question of supreme importance. All experienced negotiators recognize that the man who has written down a well thought-out plan has an advantage over those who have none. He can seize the initiative and propose positive measures; they can only criticize, object, or amend. The man with a plan will seldom secure the adoption of all his proposals, but he will almost invariably retain a considerable residuum of them.

Much better than having one man come to a conference with a plan is the procedure by which the conference agrees in advance what the plan shall be.

Harold Nicolson attributes many of the woes of the Paris Conference to the "marsh of imprecision"—and properly so. If ever a conference needed a carefully worked-out program, as well as a precise definition of terms, this one did. Let it not be forgotten that the basis of the pre-Armistice contract was the Fourteen Points, which were only vaguely defined and hesitatingly accepted. The isolationist Washington *Post* not inaptly remarked that "the trouble is not so much with the fourteen points as it is with the fourteen interpretations."

Yet the amazing fact is that the ever-logical French, alone among the great powers, had a carefully outlined plan for the agenda. The British had none. The United States not only had none, but Wilson had quashed all attempts to frame one or to agree upon one. It may well be argued that his great error was not in going to Paris but in going without a plan.

This almost unbelievable blindness to the elementary facts of negotiation by conference requires some explanation.

3

While it is true that the Americans went to Paris without a detailed plan of procedure, it is not true that they went without information. There were cartloads of information; the great problem was to coordinate it and give it meaning.

One basic explanation of the lack of coordination is that the war came to an end unexpectedly soon. The military men had been looking forward to administering the finishing blow in 1919, and the unexpected crumbling of German resistance caught both the warmakers and the peacemakers off balance and unprepared. In the summer of 1918, when the Allied

The Race
(Courtesy of the St. Louis *Post-Dispatch*)

drives were progressing favorably, Winston S. Churchill, then First Lord of the Admiralty, remarked that if these victories continued peace might "come upon us like a thief in the night." It did. Churchill later wrote that, for the British, the transition to peace "was more violent than the entry into war . . ." It is worth repeating that in time of war one must prepare for peace.

Yet we cannot be sure that the result, as far as Wilson was concerned, would have been different if the conflict had lasted another six months. He was strongly opposed to any carefully worked-out plan, though he was firmly wedded to a few basic principles. It was easy enough, says Ray Stannard Baker, for the representatives of the Old Order (the Powers of Darkness) to draw up a precise program based upon the procedure of the Congress of Vienna. But Wilson represented the New Order (the Powers of Light), and he had no precedents to work on. When one is venturing out into an unknown sea, it is both useless and dangerous to make charts in advance. One must feel one's way slowly, inch by inch, and chart the rocks and shoals as one finds them. One's only compass must be sound general principles.

So Wilson, the amateur diplomat, would go to Paris and work out his program on a day-to-day, catch-as-catch-can basis. Lloyd George would do likewise; but the tough, resourceful, and opportunistic Welshman loved rough-and-tumble grappling, with no holds barred, and Wilson did not. This, of course, would make for informality and flexibility; but flexibility gave a distinct advantage to the hand that held the lever which moved the machinery of the Conference. That hand was the gray-gloved hand of "The Tiger"—Georges Clemenceau.

Ray Stannard Baker rather indignantly rejects the charge that the Americans had no program. He says that Wilson's program was first the principles of justice as laid down in his public utterances, and secondly the application of these principles by his experts. This, one must confess, is not a program but a nebulous statement of general principles.

After reaching Paris, Wilson presented to the Council of Ten five general topics that he wanted to have discussed. This, one must concede, was not a program but a skeleton list of subjects.

Before leaving Washington, Secretary Lansing took it upon himself to inform Wilson that the experts in the Department of State had already worked out a tentative draft of a skeleton treaty. According to Lansing, Wilson resented this usurpation of authority, and rebuked him stingingly with the remark that "he did not propose to have lawyers drafting the Treaty."

The French evolved several detailed programs, and one of them, dated November 29, 1918, was presented by the French Ambassador in Washington, and put into Wilson's hands on December 2, two days before his departure for Paris. He took it along with him, but there is no evidence that he ever bothered to reply to it, much less indicate acceptance. He may have discussed it orally upon reaching Paris, but it is clear that he made no determined effort to secure its adoption.

Wilson's failure to seize upon this program and use his enormous prestige to push it through, with modifications, is regarded by certain critics as a blunder of the first magnitude.

4

We need not analyze the French program in detail, but merely consider certain features that have an important bearing on the failures of the Conference—failures which will be discussed later at length.

First, preliminary terms were to be imposed upon the Germans without discussion. (The Conference began as a preliminary conference, got into a hurry, and hastily made the preliminary terms the final ones.)

Second, provision was made for the representation of both enemy and neutral states at the Conference. (Neither was permitted to take part in the final oral discussions.)

Third, reparations were to be levied only for direct damage resulting from German aggression. (The Conference most unfortunately added pensions and other charges.)

Fourth, all secret treaties were to be suspended. (We shall presently consider the disastrous effect of these agreements.)

Fifth, a detailed schedule was set forth under which the most important problems would be considered first, and the less important ones postponed for subsequent discussion. (The less pressing problems were actually considered first, and the fundamental task of making peace with Germany was postponed for about two months.)

This French program, one must grant, was far from perfect, but it was reasonably comprehensive and precise, and it embodied several supremely important features that were conspicuously lacking in the final terms. It also gave a prominent place to the League of Nations, and it referred repeatedly to specific Fourteen Points. Some writers have said that Wilson was offended because the French proposal tactlessly mentioned the vagueness of the Points, but this probably had no important effect on his thinking. More important, one may suspect, were the references to the peace congresses of the past. Wilson simply did not want to be shackled by the precisions of the Old Order.

If Wilson had adopted with enthusiasm the better parts of this program, if he had thrown the weight of his then enormous prestige behind it, could he have secured its adoption at the outset?

Any answer would be pure speculation. It may well be doubted whether he could have forced Japan, Italy, and Great Britain to "suspend" the secret treaties under which they were to receive the spoils of war. But there seems to be no good reason why Wilson could not have secured substantially all of the other more desirable parts of the French program, and this would have been an immense gain for precision and sanity.

As it was, the discussions began with no agreed-upon agenda. The Conference drifted along from day to day like a rudderless ship, with the powers combating one another's proposals, and forming combinations against one another. Then, when it became clear that the race between chaos and peace would be perilously close, the Conference buckled down and in a spasm of work gave birth to a treaty that was as ill coordinated as its parent. Heredity will tell.

It is all well enough to have new ideas and to propose New Orders. But one cannot cut loose completely from the lessons of the past. Even the Old Order can tell the New Order some valuable things learned in the rough school of experience.

5

We must come back once more to the secret treaties, for our indifference to and ignorance of them must take rank as one of the inexcusable blunders of American diplomacy.

During the course of the war the various Allied powers had made a dozen or so secret bargains with one another for parceling out the skin of the yet unskinned bear. We need single out only two, the two that caused Wilson the most sleepless nights.

In 1915, Italy was for sale to the higher bidder, prepared to enter the war on the side that could make her the more attractive offer. The territory that she most wanted belonged to the Central Powers, so the Allies were able to outbid their enemy. Put brutally, Italy's assistance was bought with liberal promises of territory in the secret Treaty of London of 1915.

In 1917, enemy submarines were taking an alarming toll of British shipping in the Mediterranean, and the British and French were desperately anxious to induce the Japanese to provide destroyer escort. The Japanese drove a hard bargain when they extorted a secret pledge from Great Britain (and later from France) that Japan should have German rights in Shantung (China), and all of Germany's Pacific islands north of the equator. The British on their part were to obtain all of Germany's islands south of the equator.

Some of these secret deals were being made after the Allies had proclaimed unselfish war aims, after they had accepted the Fourteen Points, and after the Conference had actually convened. No one could tell behind whose back some kind of trade was being cooked up. Certain promises, for example, were made to the Rumanians which conflicted with the aspirations of the Serbs, who were fighting on the side of the Allies, and on the whole more valiantly. The slimy trail of the serpent of secret diplomacy led into strange places.

Such Machiavellian machinations were shocking to moralists and non-professional diplomatists like Wilson, and the tendency was to dismiss all these agreements as evidence of the incurable wickedness of the Old Diplomacy.

This is entirely too narrow a view. Diplomacy had been carried on this way for untold centuries, and the leopard was not going to change his spots overnight. Secret treaties were not immoral until Wilson made them so.

Nor can we ignore the fact that the Allies probably would have lost the war if they had not made these clandestine bargains. We should not forget that Germany and her allies were bargaining also, and that if the proposals of the enemy had proved more seductive, Italy would doubtless have gone over into the other camp, with disastrous results to the Allied cause. The more liberal British diplomats held their noses as they negotiated these malodorous pacts; but military necessity condones many acts that would not pass muster in the days of peacetime morality. The enemy was using such methods, and it was necessary to fight the devil with fire.

6

During the course of the war, rumors had leaked out from time to time as to the existence of the secret treaties. But the real exposure came with the Bolshevist revolution of late 1917. Rummaging through the archives of the Russian Foreign Office, the Bolsheviks found these dynamite-charged pacts, and seeking to discredit the imperialism of the Tsarist regime, forthwith published them.

The surprising thing is that these sensational revelations, which came to light in November, 1917, made scarcely a ripple

in the United States. Only a few newspapers gave them any notice whatsoever; only one seems to have published them all; and only six of some two thousand journals published them in part.

One would think that the American people should have been profoundly concerned about the secret and selfish aims of their Allies, with whom they were associated. Why were they not?

One answer—and one that disposed of much unpleasant truth during the war—was that this was pure enemy propaganda, and as such beneath notice. Besides, the publication of the treaties coincided with the collapse of the Italian front, and this served to focus attention on the fact that we were in a desperate war, and that we had better concern ourselves with really important things. It would be folly at this critical period to weaken Allied morale and prestige by deigning to notice such wicked deals.

There was also the feeling—and this probably accounts in part for Wilson's indifference—that even if these commitments existed, they did not bind the United States. It must be re-emphasized that we were not allies of the Allies, merely Associates—a thing apart; and their unsavory bargains seemingly were of no direct concern of ours. Upon reaching Paris and learning of the Sykes-Picot secret treaty for the partitioning of Turkey, Wilson remarked disgustedly that it sounded like the name of a tea.

Finally, the secret treaties were complicated, and they involved the disposition of strange-sounding places about which we knew nothing, cared less, and had no desire to learn anything. A real comprehension of the foreign affairs of Europe involves a background which the average American did not have then, does not have now, and is unwilling to go to the effort to obtain. This means hard intellectual labor, and the American voter is not distinguished for a capacity to inform himself on domestic problems which are on his very doorstep, let alone three thousand miles away on the other side of a very wide ocean. So the tendency was to skip the finely printed texts of these complicated treaties, when they were printed, and get on to the more important world of sports heroes or comic-supplement villains. Everything would work out all right once we had "licked the Kaiser."

We can find some excuse for the indifference of the average American, whose business is not primarily foreign affairs, but how about the Department of State, whose business is foreign affairs? Incredible though it may seem, Secretary Lansing told the Senate Foreign Relations Committee in the summer of 1919 that before going to Paris he had learned something of the Treaty of London with Italy, but as for the others, he did not even know that they existed. He registered considerable surprise when he was told that they had been published in the New York press.

This does not mean that there were not officials in the State Department who were taking cognizance of these treaties. But Lansing's attitude is dumbfounding. He was Secretary of State; he was the prospective head of the American peace delegation; he could not approach the Conference problems intelligently without a fairly exact knowledge of such secret agreements as had been published. Unlike Wilson, he was a stern realist; he had little faith in the League of Nations; he was well aware of the implications of balance-of-power politics. He could not have been so simple-minded as to believe that the acceptance of Point I of the Fourteen Points—that regarding open covenants—would invalidate all preexisting secret treaties.

Of course, Lansing might have dismissed the published treaties as German propaganda, just as the man in the street did. But, unlike the man in the street, it was his business to look into these revelations, and he had at his command the long tentacles of the State Department. If we may take his word at its face value, he evidently did not regard these things as important.

It seems reasonably clear—if it is not clear already—that we should exercise more care in selecting our Secretaries of State. If they will not concern themselves with important aspects of our foreign affairs, then who will?

7

One approaches the subject of Wilson and the secret pacts with considerable hesitancy, because it involves the odious question: "Was he a liar?"

After returning from Paris with the completed treaty, Wilson allowed himself to be catechized by the members of the Senate Committee on Foreign Relations, and he apparently answered all the questions fired at him with the greatest of candor.

Senator Borah asked him if, before arriving in Europe, he had known about the secret deal with Japan regarding Shantung. Wilson replied in the negative, and went on to say that upon reaching Paris "the *whole series*" of secret treaties was revealed to him for the first time. This is doubtless true, because the "*whole series*" was extremely complicated, and to some extent was being reshaped after the Conference assembled.

If the questioning had ended here, Wilson would appear to better advantage. But after other subjects had been reviewed, Senator Johnson, with the zeal of a prosecuting attorney, came back to the embarrassing question of the secret treaties. The Senator categorically listed the various pacts, including the Treaty of London. Wilson flatly asserted that none of these had been brought to his attention before reaching Paris, and he denied having had any previous knowledge of any of them.

This, we know, was not the truth. Numerous references in Wilson's private papers, large excerpts from which have been published recently by his biographer, relate to the provisions of some of the secret pacts. We know also that the original Fourteen Points, especially the first point about open covenants, were deliberately designed in part to offset the disastrous effect on world opinion caused by the Bolshevist revelation of the secret treaties.

Why Wilson told a different story to the Senators is still a major mystery. He could hardly have been guilty of a mere slip of the tongue, as sometimes alleged, because two different Senators at two different points approached the same question from different angles and repeatedly got the same reply. The true explanation may be confusion of dates or mental fatigue, as sometimes stated. But this excuse is open to the objection that during the course of the questioning Wilson freely and accurately gave intimate details of no less important subjects.

It is not altogether improbable that Wilson was in the position of a doctor who finds that he must tell the patient something that is not true. We must not forget that the whole Treaty of Versailles was under heavy fire at this time, and the arrangement giving German rights in Shantung to Japan under a secret treaty was being bitterly condemned. Wilson must have realized by this time that the fight might be close, and it is altogether likely that he did not want to introduce any new and confusing elements into the struggle. Certainly it would have been embarrassing to explain why, knowing in advance about the secret treaties, he did not do more at Paris to head them off.

8

But the question of Wilson's truthfulness is relatively minor. It seems clear that while he knew the general terms of these secret bargains, he did not know enough. It also seems clear that he did not recognize their importance, for if he had, he would have made it a point to find out more about them. At Paris he flatly refused to be bound by secret treaties, except in so far as their provisions were just, and this determination may explain why he declined to give them more careful study. But the mere refusal to recognize disagreeable realities does not dispose of those realities.

One other explanation may account for Wilson's indifference. In the summer of 1917 he wrote Colonel House that the peace aims of the Allies were not the same as those of the United States, but he was confident that by wielding the enormous economic power of the United States he could force our associates to his way of thinking. So why become concerned too much about the specific terms of secret pacts?

The proverb tells us that he who is forewarned is twice armed. If Wilson had known as much about the secret treaties as he should have known, and as he subsequently learned, he could hardly have refrained from showing more interest when the French, in the program which he spurned, suggested that they be scrapped.

In this connection some critics reasonably argue that Wilson made another costly mistake. If, early in the Conference, when his prestige and influence were still overshadowing, he had insisted that all of the secret treaties be officially disavowed, he might well have carried the day. Instead, he took the purely negative and defeatist attitude of refusing to recognize them at all.

Later, when his influence had waned, they were brought out of their secret pigeonholes, and then they could not be waved aside. Their beneficiaries even argued that one reason why the Allies had fought was to make Germany recognize "scraps of paper," and the victors would merely be aping the Hun if they refused to recognize their own treaties.

Even if Wilson had been unwilling to sweep all these pacts from the table with one bold gesture, he should have studied them. If he had known of their full import, he could have made plans in advance for coping with them, and these plans could have been made quietly, after mature reflection, and with adequate counsel. As it was, new and totally unforeseen situations were sprung upon him at Paris, while he was worn down with overwork and while the Conference was moving into its final hectic stages. With his head in a daze, and his feet tangled in the web of secret treaties, he battled his adversaries at a serious disadvantage.

CHAPTER TEN

THE OLYMPIANS

"It is going to be a rough-and-tumble affair, this Peace Con-
ference." ARTHUR J. BALFOUR, *November 28, 1918.*

1

WE MUST now consider briefly each of the great protago-
nists in the Council of Four—"The Olympians"—before turning to the actual work of the Conference.

Woodrow Wilson was both the best known and the most influential, for he represented the bursting energy of the wealth-
iest and most powerful of the nations. At heart a Scotch-
Presbyterian clergyman but trained as an academician, he was,
up to this time, the darling of the gods. Within the two short
years from 1911 to 1913, and by a series of incredible political
accidents, he had been catapulted from the President's house
in Princeton to the White House in Washington.

Though gracious in a rather stiff manner, he was innately
shy and sensitive; and unlike Clemenceau his skin had not been
toughened by prolonged years of exposure in the rough and
tumble of the political arena. An idealist, a philosopher, a
moralist, a religionist, he was born, as someone has well said,
halfway between the Bible and the dictionary, and he never
lost his faith in the power of words. There have been philos-
ophers who were more profound, there have been politicians
who were more powerful, but the world had never before seen
a philosopher-politician who combined with his ideals such
tremendous physical power to carry them into effect.

At the Conference table Wilson made an excellent impression, and he certainly belied Roosevelt's barb that he "looked
like an apothecary's clerk." Immaculately if soberly dressed, he
was alert, dignified, modest, soft-spoken, patient, conciliatory,
and pleasantly stubborn, with Scotch stubbornness. Thirsting

150

for and respecting facts, he largely ignored his fellow commissioners, except Colonel House, but sought information from
his experts, who frequently sat on a cushion behind him and
whispered promptings into his ear. Professor Douglas W.
Johnson, an American expert on the Adriatic, remembers that
on one occasion, late at night, the telephone rang in his bedroom, and Wilson asked for some papers which Johnson had
promised but which had not arrived with sufficient promptness.

Wilson at the Conference was by no means the inflexible,
know-it-all professor of popular fancy. When the Commission
on the League of Nations assembled, he expressed the hope that
no minutes would be kept. He wanted to feel free to change
his mind, and he felt that a written record would handicap him
in doing so. Changing his mind was one of Wilson's most dis-
tinguishing characteristics.

Clemenceau knew more about French interests than Wilson,
but Wilson probably saw the over-all picture better than any
of the other members of the Big Four. He was one of the
hardest-working men at the Conference, unwilling to delegate
important responsibilities, and laboring late at night over
much paper work that should have been left to subordinates.
Lord Riddell relates that Wilson once asked for his typewriter
(a word then used for "stenographer"). Riddell conjured up a
picture of a beautiful blonde secretary, but the messenger
brought in a portable typewriter, on which the President proceeded to tap out a long memorandum.

Wilson's fine brain rapidly grasped a great deal in the few
weeks at Paris, but no one man could have mastered in a lifetime all of the subjects that were dumped onto the sagging
peace table. Sir Henry Wilson recalls that the American President deliberately absented himself from one session, to the
anger of some of those present, because he had not had time to
study thoroughly the question under debate.

Wilson tried hard—too hard—to do the impossible. Being an
academician, he was reluctant to make important decisions
until he had all the facts and all the points of view; but the

world would not stand still while he carried on his researches. He would squat down over a gigantic map, listen to his experts, pencil the boundary where he thought it ought to go—in Asia Minor or some other place he had never seen—while all the others were made to squat around him. Mrs. Wilson once came upon them thus, and perhaps thinking of the parlor pastime of hunt the thimble, remarked that they looked as though they were playing a game. "Alas," replied Wilson, "it is the most serious game ever undertaken"—a game involving the lives and happiness of millions living and millions yet unborn.

The European statesmen resented Wilson's attempt to master their problems in a few short weeks, and to choke a ready-made solution down their throats. Europe had been the battle-ground; Europe had sacrificed millions of her sons. And now this closet-philosopher, who had held off to the last moment before entering what he now admitted had been America's fight—whose holding off had prolonged the war—was here to tell France what she might or might not do. As Lord Riddell put it: "What sort of peace would the Americans have imposed if a German army had been encamped for four years within fifty miles of New York?"

We have already seen that Wilson was not led around by the nose by his colleagues of the Big Four. At one stage, Dr. Isaiah Bowman, Chief Territorial Specialist of the American Commission, suggested to some of the British experts, following a debate between Lloyd George and the President, that they should keep tabs on their respective chiefs to see which one scored the more points. The British replied, "Up to now, at least, your chief has won them all!"

2

Clemenceau was in many ways the dominating figure of the Conference, though less well known and less influential than Wilson in the world theater. As head of the French govern-

ment, he controlled the press; as head of the Conference, he controlled the agenda; as presiding officer, he controlled debate.

The stormy petrel of French politics, Clemenceau was then seventy-seven years of age—"the grand young man of France," as Lloyd George graciously described him. He was nicknamed "The Tiger," obviously because of the unrelenting ferocity and savage energy with which he had attacked his enemies over a long and checkered career. Known as a destroyer rather than a builder, he had sunk his fangs into the jugular veins of more than a dozen ministries, and had brought about their downfall. He feared nobody and nothing.

In personal appearance, Clemenceau suggested the gorilla rather than the tiger. Short, squat, and stooped, but powerfully built, he presented a striking figure with his black skullcap protecting a white-fringed bald spot on a massive head; drooping white mustaches that curved downward as if to shield a powerful jaw that needed no shielding; bushy, interrogatory, and skeptical eyebrows; glittering brown eyes, half masked in repose by ivory eyelids; and the eternal gray suède gloves, which covered eczema-cursed hands and which gave him the formal air of an undertaker.

The Tiger had one great love—France; and one great hate—Germany. As a young man of twenty-nine he had seen Paris under the heel of the Hun invader, and the smoke billowing up from the brutal burning of the palace at St. Cloud. As an old man of seventy-two, he had seen the gray German hosts pour into his beloved France. He was determined that it should not happen again. Motivated though he was by this great hate, he was not so vindictive as Marshal Foch or President Poincaré.

Clemenceau had a commanding presence, and he was one of the great orators of his day, with fine voice, logical mind, and forceful delivery, though sparing of Gallic gesticulation. As presiding officer of the Council of Ten he was on the whole patient and deferential, and most of the time he slumped back in his chair, apparently half asleep, with an expression of bored tolerance. But as presiding officer of the plenary sessions he drove a steam roller through the opposition. *"Y a-t-il des objections? Non?* . . . *Adopté,"* he would rattle off with machinegun rapidity, and despotically rush on to rubber-stamp something else before a voice could be raised in protest.

Trained as a doctor, Clemenceau had early forsaken the scalpel for journalism and politics. He visited America for several years shortly after the Civil War, and wrote a number of stories for a French newspaper. This American sojourn had helped him perfect his English, which he spoke fluently, though he had experienced early difficulties. He used to amuse his hearers by telling how he had once ordered "smashed potatoes" in an American restaurant.

In November, 1917, during one of the darkest hours of the war, he was called to the premiership of France. Grim, dogged, and courageous, Dr. Clemenceau did not shrink from prescribing heroic medicines. Infusing new spirit into the drooping nation, by sheer power of will he snatched victory from the furnace of defeat. It was not for nothing that he was called "le Père la Victoire" (Father Victory).

3

Clemenceau was deeply puzzled by his Calvinist colleague, the American President. He had lived a long time, and he had seen the seamy side of mankind. Realistic, cynical, logical, he had no faith in the League of Nations. France had been saved by bayonets, not ideals. If she were invaded again, America would perhaps come rushing to her assistance—after three long years—with two million words. Words were all right; but first there must be bayonets.

The Tiger was the incarnation of the Old Order—of Europe as it had been. Wilson was the incarnation of the New Order—of Europe as he hoped it would be. Clemenceau could not understand all this. He believed that mankind should be taken as it is, and not as it was unlikely to be. He called Wilson "Jupiter," sneered at his "elevated simplicity," and made cutting remarks about the "Fourteen Commandments." He told Colonel House: "I can get on with you. You are practical. I understand you, but talking to Wilson is something like talking to Jesus Christ!"

Occasionally, but only occasionally, there were sharp words

"Great Expectations"

(Courtesy of the Louisville *Times;* the cartoonist, Paul A. Plaschke, is now editorial cartoonist on the Chicago *Herald-American*)

between Clemenceau and Wilson. Once the Tiger hotly accused Wilson of being a pro-German, and bolted from the room, eyes flashing, voice vibrating. From long experience in debate he knew the trick of simulating passion, and perhaps he was doing so at this time. When the Conference was over, Clemenceau was reported to have said of Wilson: "He is a nice man and means well." Later, in 1925, the Tiger wrote: "Wilson was a noble figure, but he did not appreciate the facts or the significance of European history."

There were few who did not fear Clemenceau's withering tongue. His *bons mots* were the talk of France, and there are few enduring epigrams from the Conference that are not attributed to him, whether correctly or not. He loved the racy phrase, the biting epigram, the sarcastic sally, and when one came to him, whether at the expense of friend or foe, he seemed powerless to hold it back. His voice was penetrating, and his terrible audibility frequently brought blushes to the cheeks of all his hearers. At one session of the Council of Four, a Japanese delegate made some remark. Clemenceau understood English, but not Japanese-English, so he turned and said in a loud stage whisper, *"Qu'est-ce qu'il dit, le petit?"* (What's the little fellow saying?)—as if a small child had spoken out of turn at the dinner table.

Dogged, domineering, honest, courageous, realistic, and narrow—this was the Tiger. Wilson respected him because one could tell where he stood—back in 1871. There was no deceit or equivocation about the man: he had the courage to meet his problems head on. If he seemed to be dozing at some of the sessions, there could be no doubt as to his vigilance when the interests of France were concerned. And here, as the record reveals, he yielded remarkably little.

4

David Lloyd George, the British Prime Minister, was short and stocky, like Clemenceau, and he had a white mustache, like Clemenceau, and he had had a checkered political career, like Clemenceau. But here the comparisons, physical and political, end. Unlike the bald Clemenceau, Lloyd George had a bristling shock of white hair, which he brushed straight back. Unlike the grim and stolid Tiger, the "Welsh wizard" was amiable and charming, with a genial smile and twinkling eyes;

at times jovial and cheery with bluff heartiness. Bursting with personal magnetism and sleepless energy, he was vivacious and impulsive, given to sudden enthusiasms and panics, and always a torrential talker. He brought with him to Paris the habits of a British lifetime. He insisted on having his afternoon tea, and got it—much to the consternation of French formalism. He also had the British passion for fresh air. Ray Stannard Baker once saw him burst out of the stuffy French foreign office, exclaiming, "I don't believe the air in that room has been changed since the time of Louis Philippe!"

One always knew where the dour Tiger stood; one never could be sure where Lloyd George stood. He was the master opportunist of his time; expediency was his guiding principle. He had a sixth sense for the changes in the pulse of public opinion, and like the chameleon he changed with them. If they wanted vengeance, he promised vengeance; if they wanted leniency, he worked for leniency. Whatever his catapultic public wanted was right. Though gifted with vision and ideals, he could never completely rise above the arts of the demagogue. His opportunism bordered on shiftiness.

The magnetic Welshman had a scintillating mind, the quickest of the Big Four, and like many another man with a scintillating mind, he used it as a substitute for hard work. One of the greatest debaters of his generation, he relied on intuition, imagination, nimble wit, and a ready tongue to confound and discomfit his adversaries.

His ignorance of some things was astounding. As already noted, he had never heard of Teschen before the Conference; he confused Silesia with Cilicia—places that were more than a thousand miles apart. But his skin was tough. When he stubbed his toe, he would brush himself off with a laugh and plunge off in some other direction. When he found that he had taken a position that was untenable because his facts were incorrect, he would blithely or blusteringly shift to the other side and carry on with equal brilliance. To him consistency was the mark of a small mind, and strict truth an insuperable handicap to political preferment. He once quoted to Lord Riddell the cynical adage: "If you want to succeed in politics, you must keep your conscience well under control."

Lloyd George was as reliable as quicksilver, as direct as a zigzag, as unwavering as a weathercock. One day he was immovably for a certain position, the next he was as immovably for another. Sometimes he changed his mind overnight; at others the electorate changed, so he changed with it. Yet with all his wobbliness, shiftiness, and superficiality, such was the man's personality that one could hardly help liking him.

Wilson was for the New Order; Clemenceau was for the Old Order. Lloyd George was for whatever order would promote the best interests of Great Britain and endear him to the electorate. His general strategy was to whittle down Clemenceau's extreme demands on Germany, and for this reason he seemed more moderate at times than Wilson. But there was a reason for Lloyd George's leniency. Clemenceau must not be allowed to create any new Alsace-Lorraines, for that would mean a new world war, and Britain would inevitably be dragged into it. Clemenceau must not be allowed to prostrate Germany, for that would mean no reparations for England, and above all the loss of a valuable customer, one essential for postwar economic recovery. Lloyd George was willing to leave Germany with enough strength to trade and to pay reparations, but not enough to fight with. And France must not be allowed to dominate Europe too completely; that was contrary to traditional British policy.

Wilson and not Lloyd George was Clemenceau's principal antagonist. The Welsh weathercock generally stood on the side lines and threw his weight on the side of moderation, except where Britain's reparations and colonial spoils were concerned, while Wilson carried the burden and heat of the day. On a few occasions Lloyd George aroused the Tiger, and Wickham Steed relates that after Clemenceau had once repeatedly charged inaccuracy of statement, Lloyd George seized him by the collar, and there was mumbled talk about challenges to a duel. But the storm quickly blew over. "Lloyd George," the Tiger growled, "believes himself to be Napoleon, but President Wilson believes himself to be Jesus Christ."

5

Vittorio Emanuele Orlando, the Italian premier, was the least influential of the Big Four. Italy was the weakest of the four powers, and Orlando was the weakest of the four representatives, both in personal and in political force. He had relatively little to say during the discussions, because Italy was concerned primarily with the fate of Austria-Hungary, rather than Germany, and the other three men were primarily concerned with Germany. And when the showdown came over Italian claims, Orlando bolted the Conference, under circumstances which will be described later.

The Italian premier was short and rotund, with a thick white pompadour, white mustache, and full lips. When he smiled, which was often, he revealed dimpled cheeks. Amiable and attractive, he was a learned and cultured gentleman of the south Italian school. Though florid in manner, he was eloquent in speech—a skilled debater and a really gifted orator. Lansing, a fellow lawyer, admired his fine legal mind, and regretted that there were not more lawyers on the Big Four. Generally genial, Orlando would occasionally reveal a volatile temper and burst into tumultuous speech. At other times he would give way to the emotionalism of the Latin, and shed copious tears.

Orlando labored under a serious linguistic handicap. He was the only one of the Big Four who could not speak English, and everything he said had to be resaid by an interpreter. David Hunter Miller relates that Orlando was once asked at the Conference if he knew any English. "Nothing," Orlando replied, "except these words, 'eleven o'clock, I don't agree, good-bye.' "

Apparently these were useful and easily learned words in the Paris of 1919.

Of his three colleagues, Orlando had the most in common with Wilson. Both had studied law, though Orlando had become a distinguished barrister, and both had been professors, Orlando of law, Wilson of government. Both had progressive ideas, and Orlando gave Wilson loyal and unwavering support in the framing of the League of Nations. The Italian premier no doubt expected Wilson to return the favor when Italian claims came up for consideration.

In some respects Orlando was overshadowed by Baron Sidney Sonnino, his foreign minister. The son of an Italian Jew and an English mother, the Baron revealed the native shrewdness in bargaining characteristic of his father's race. With white mustaches, florid complexion, eagle features, powerful nose, and viselike jaw, he was cold, intractable, taciturn, and scheming.

Sonnino, unlike Orlando, had no weakness for the New Order. With cold logic he favored the Old Order, the balance of power, naked imperialism, and all Italy could grab—and then some. Wilson did not get on well with this son of Machiavelli, who had arranged to keep him away from the people in Rome; and Wickham Steed relates how Wilson, when mentioning his name, once clenched his fist and used unparliamentary language.

Orlando, though somewhat slippery, was progressive; Sonnino, reactionary. Each tended to cancel the efforts of the other. Orlando's political position was precarious, and he could not go far with the ball and chain of his foreign minister on his leg. At times the two men were not even on speaking terms. Near the end of the Conference, Wilson told his experts: "I can get along with Orlando, and could quickly arrange matters with him, if he was not scared to death of Sonnino."

6

Each one of the Big Four, save Wilson, had come into his
high office during a war crisis—Lloyd George late in 1916,
and Clemenceau and Orlando in 1917. Clemenceau and Lloyd
George in particular had distinguished themselves for the
unrelenting zeal with which they brought hostilities to a victorious conclusion. Each was naturally continued on in office
for the making of the peace, yet neither had ever given careful,
first-hand attention to the direction of foreign affairs. Not the
least among the handicaps of the Conference was that the warmakers became the peacemakers, as was inevitable; but unfortunately the two tasks require different talents and tempera-
ments.

Each one of the Big Four without exception was in some
measure, and with varying success, a politician. Yet the arts of
the politician are on the whole the very arts that are not
wanted in the negotiator. Lloyd George was a brilliant politician, but his gifts handicapped him at the peace table. He
could overwhelm his enemies with invective; but there is no
place for invective in peacemaking. He could rout his enemies
with brilliant sallies; but the peace table needs the judge and
not the prosecuting attorney. The situation called for statesmen, not politicians.

Each one of the Big Four without exception had to spend a
distressing amount of time in keeping up his political fences
at home. Lloyd George had to absent himself from the Conference for protracted periods; Wilson had to make a return
trip to America to explain the Covenant of the League; Clemenceau did not have far to go, but he had Foch, Poincaré, and
others constantly yipping at his heels. If Wilson had his Senate,
Clemenceau had his Chambers, and Lloyd George his House.

Each one of the Big Four had to get out beyond his depth in
passing upon the problems that pressed for settlement. Lloyd
George lightheartedly confessed his ignorance; but Wilson

made a supreme effort to grasp too much. Only the individual experts were competent to rule upon their specialties, and even they often disagreed among themselves. When they agreed, they could not in a number of cases grasp the larger political implications of the recommendations they were making.

The decisions had to be made by the Big Four, because they alone could assume political responsibility for what they were doing. The result was that these four lone men, who were experts in nothing, had to be experts in everything. Giants in the political sphere at home, they were cut down to the size of mortal men in the international theater.

As one reads how the Big Four, out of the depths of their ignorance, divided portions of the world as if they had been parts of a gigantic cake, one can but regret that man has so ordered his affairs that the peacemaking of 1919 had almost inevitably to be a kind of blindman's buff

CHAPTER ELEVEN

THE WHITE MAN'S BURDEN

*"The German colonies were to be disposed of. They had not
been governed; they had been exploited merely, without thought
of the interest or even the ordinary human rights of their inhabitants."* WOODROW WILSON, *July 10, 1919.*

1

WILSON ATTENDED the formal sessions of the Conference
for about five weeks before returning to America for a brief
interlude. During this period he fought two great and successful battles: one for the mandate principle, the other for rivet-
ing the League of Nations into the treaty of peace. If his reputation as a negotiator rested on these two achievements, it
would be much higher than it was at the end of the Conference.
Henry White believed that Wilson's mistake was not in going
to Paris but in returning after he had won these two initial
engagements. This may be doubted, but even if true Wilson
was not one to put his personal reputation above the responsibility of making an enduring peace.

We have already observed that peacemaking was essentially
a desperate race against the rising tide of anarchy and Bolshevism sweeping in from the east. Yet it is significant that the
negotiators became involved at once and for many weeks to
come over two problems that had only indirect relevance to
the immediate task of restoring peace to Central Europe.

The natural tendency, of course, is to do the easy and pleasant things first, especially when overwhelming problems loom
in the offing. The pleasantest job of all, and the one which
seemed to present no great problem, was dividing the booty.
The expectant delegates were there with whetted knives and
whetted appetites, and the first cry was, "When do we eat?"

Upon one thing they all agreed, and this was very important, for agreement was at a premium. They all agreed—even Wilson—that the former German colonies, with their approximately 15,000,000 helpless natives, should not be returned to

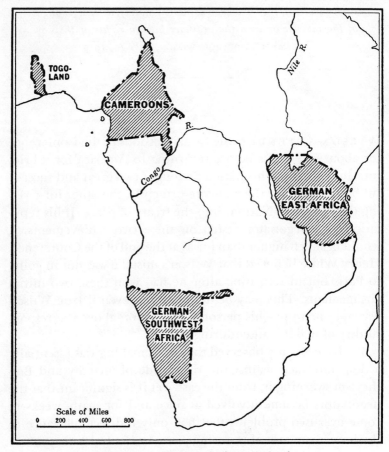

Germany's Prewar African Colonies

Germany. But here agreement ended. The apple of discord proved to be the first fruit of victory.

The British of South Africa had fought desperately, and with heroic sacrifices, to conquer German Southwest Africa, and they had no intention whatever of allowing the Germans to come back and reestablish military and naval bases from which to threaten them in the future. The British of New Zealand and Australia had captured Samoa, New Guinea, and other South Pacific islands, and they had no intention of allowing the Germans to return and jeopardize their security.

These reasons were sound enough, but they did not apply so forcibly to regions like German East Africa and particularly the Cameroons and Togoland, which were so far distant from large areas of British and French population as hardly to constitute a menace. It is true that they could have been used as bases from which to threaten British shipping lines, and this was pointed out by the submarine-conscious Allies in their written interchanges with the Germans. As things turned out, such bases would have been pinched off rather quickly in 1939 by the British and French; but in 1919 the threat seemed very real. So to cover all possible contingencies, and to reinforce the strategic argument, the allegation was made and generally accepted by the Allies that the Germans were not fit to be entrusted with the guardianship of cannibals and other backward peoples.

This convenient article of faith was not difficult to accept in view of the exaggerated but far from groundless atrocity stories which had come out of Belgium. The Hun was a brute, and there the argument ended. It was unfortunately true that while German colonial administration had many bright chapters, which were conveniently overlooked, it also had some dark chapters. These had been repeatedly aired in Germany by opponents of imperialism, who charged that the soil of the colonies had been "manured by the blood of natives"; and the words of these critics were now put into the mouths of the enemies of the Fatherland. Not only did the Allies overlook the bright chapters of German colonialism, but they kept tightly closeted some of the horrible skeletons of their own, including those from the Belgian Congo.

Wilson completely and sincerely agreed with the Allies that the Huns were not fit to be entrusted with the White Man's burden, and he further agreed that they should not have so much as one coral atoll of their former vast colonial empire.

We cannot fairly criticize Wilson for not having been wiser than all of his contemporaries, for suffering from the shell-shocked psychosis of the Allied statesmen, and for not having seen at this early stage the meteoric rise of the paper-hanging corporal who had recently fought in the German army. But the fact is that two far-reaching mistakes were made, and Wilson seems to have made no attempt to head off either.

2

With the wisdom of hindsight, we can see that it was probably an error to take away every single one of Germany's colonies. We can understand why New Zealand and Australia and the Union of South Africa were adamant on the principle of security; but, as we have seen, places like the Cameroons and German East Africa were in a somewhat different category. Neither was a real strategic threat; neither was a vitally important economic asset; and both covered large and satisfactorily delusive areas on the map.

The complete loss of all the colonies was a bitter enough pill in itself, but the bitterness was increased by the fact that Germany expected to retain most of them, or at least a share in some of them. Point V of the Fourteen promised "a free, open-minded, and absolutely impartial adjustment of all colonial claims," with due regard for "the interests of the populations concerned . . ." The Germans felt that they had done a good job of colonial administration, at least comparatively, and there was nothing in this Point to indicate that they would not get their overseas possessions back. It is true that the publicly expressed war aims of the Allies gave no basis for such a hope; but the Fourteen Points (the heart of the pre-Armistice contract) did. One may again point to the perils of imprecision.

We all know that one of Hitler's most telling arguments in

his rise to power, and one with which he lashed huge audiences to near frenzy, was his condemnation of the robbing of Germany. There can be no doubt that, if the Germans had been allowed to retain some of their least profitable and harmless colonies, the Führer would have found other grounds for complaint; but certainly the wind would have been partially taken out of his sails.

To take all the colonies was a harsh enough blow; but partially to justify the taking on the pretext that the Germans were brutes was to turn the knife in the wound. As a student of history, Wilson should have remembered that all colonial powers have their black chapters, and that not even the United States, with its "water cure" scandals in the Philippines, was in a position to cast stones. If all the colonies had to be taken, it would have been much more candid to write them off as reparations, and credit them to the total bill. The distinguished German liberal, Matthias Erzberger, estimated that they were worth nine billion dollars. Granted that this is an exaggerated figure, it is clear that any reasonable allowance would have helped to reduce reparations payments to manageable proportions, and would have been a powerful contribution toward a lasting settlement. It would also have spared Germany the additional humiliation of losing all her overseas possessions, under the hypocritical guise of humanitarian motives, much as we dispossess a feeble-minded person of his property.

Perhaps one should be more careful in using the word "hypocritical." To us in a different age and in a different atmosphere, this may seem like hypocrisy. To men of that age—men who had seen the devastation of France and Belgium, who knew of Big Berthas and Zeppelin raids—there was no room for argument as to Hunnish barbarity. Among a few men there may have been some conscious dissimulation. If so, it was hypocrisy; if not, it was not.

But whatever the motive, the net result was the same. The Treaty of Versailles, with its long train of humiliations, created a vast inferiority complex in the German people which ultimately found expression in the insane leadership of Adolf Hitler. Some of these humiliations were inevitable, no matter how wise the treaty, for defeat in itself was a bitter enough draught for this proud and military-minded people. But we who live in a later generation can but wonder that the colonial question was handled so shortsightedly.

The great problem before the Peace Conference was to work out some order under which Germany would be peaceable and reasonably contented. If the negotiators had sat up nights devising ways and means of rekindling German nationalism and developing a spirit of revenge preparatory to a new war, they could hardly have done better than in their handling of the colonies.

The victors finally saw their mistake in the 1930's, when it was too late. By then they could not make restitution because that would merely be throwing scraps of fresh meat into the mouth of a hungry lion.

Wilson's errors, as we have seen, were negative rather than positive. When he might have protested, he was silent; when he might have been drawing parallels from history, he was apparently thinking of something else. This something else was the mandate system.

3

The mandate idea, though not entirely original with Wilson, apparently came to him independently. Its chief feature was that the German colonies should not be ceded outright to any one power, but should be handed over to certain nations for administration under the general supervision of the League of Nations. Wilson's original plan was for certain of the neutrals, such as Holland and the Scandinavian countries, to act as mandatories.

The scheme was unquestionably ingenious. On paper, it would please Germany, because the League and not her enemies would get the colonies. In the course of time, she

would presumably be admitted to the League and have a voice in the control of her former possessions. The mandate scheme would please liberals everywhere, because it would fulfill Wilson's "no annexations" pledge; it would redeem Point V regarding the colonies; and it would hold out to subject peoples the hope of self-determination. It would also please the imperialistic powers, because they could make off with the substance while leaving the League with the shadow.

The mandate idea was also thoroughly in keeping with the American tradition of trusteeship or temporary tutelage, under which our territories had become states. In places like Cuba and the Philippines, we had pursued or were pursuing a policy of temporarily shouldering the White Man's burden, and then, when the natives were strong enough to carry it themselves, or when we were tired of carrying it ourselves, handing it over to them.

Wilson was further attracted to the mandate idea because it would give the League of Nations something specific and important to do from the very start. Perhaps he remembered that the American Union had been held together from 1781 to 1789 in part because the weak government under the Articles of Confederation was charged with the trusteeship of a vast area of public lands. Similarly, the mandate system might insure the success of the League.

The interested British Dominions battled bitterly for the outright annexation of the German colonies, and the intractable and cynical Premier Hughes of Australia led the fight. "And you mean, Mr. Hughes," queried Wilson, "that in certain circumstances Australia would place herself in opposition to the opinion of the whole civilized world?" Hughes, who was deaf but heard all that he wanted to hear through a machine-gun-like contraption, replied bluntly, "That's about it, Mr. President."

But Wilson kept up the fight. The Conference was already under fire, and he felt that it would be doomed if the powers began with a snarling division of the booty contrary to the

Fourteen Points but in keeping with the imperialism of the Old Order.

The French press began a vitriolic attack upon the "impracticable ideals" of the American doctrinaire, evidently securing their information secretly through French official channels. Wilson protested strongly against this misrepresentation, and even went so far as to threaten to publish his own side of the controversy. The direct attacks of the French press immediately ceased.

With the support of Lloyd George, Wilson finally won a partial victory when he secured the mandate system in modified form. But not until he had threatened to break up the Conference and go home.

4

The mandate system as finally worked out was a compromise with Wilson's original ideas—a compromise between lofty idealism and naked imperialism.

No neutral nation was given a mandate over any former German territory, although Wilson had originally planned to invite these small countries to participate.

The great powers, except Italy, all got substantially the areas that they had claimed. These, to be sure, were mandates, and they were hedged about with certain rather illusory restrictions. But possession is nine points of the law.

The mandates for Constantinople and Armenia were left up in the air. The tribulations sure to arise in these two areas were certain to exceed the profits to be taken from them— there were no rich oil fields there—so it was assumed that rich Uncle Sam would play the role of the Good Samaritan. On one occasion, when Constantinople was under discussion, Clemenceau turned to Wilson and said jokingly: "When you cease to be President we will make you Grand Turk." The gibe was not appreciated.

Wilson, though at first expressing some misgivings, gave un-

accountably strong encouragement to the belief that the
United States would assume a mandate over at least Armenia.
That he should have done so, even to the extent of later recom-
mending an Armenian mandate to Congress, is further evidence of his blindness to realities. American public opinion
was virtually unanimous on one thing: it would have no mandates, especially outside this hemisphere. The trusteeship over
Armenia would involve an estimated 50,000 troops and millions of dollars. The American people sympathized abstractly
with the sufferings of the Armenians at the hands of the "terrible Turk," but they had no intention of going over there and
suffering along with them.

Various critics, like Nicolson and Keynes, have condemned
the "appalling hypocrisy" and "Jesuitical exegesis" of the
Treaty of Versailles. Certainly the division of Germany's colonies seems to give them some support.

We have seen that the fifth of the Fourteen Points provided
for "a free, open-minded, and absolutely impartial adjustment
of all colonial claims" based on the principal that the "interests of the populations concerned must have equal weight with
the equitable claims of the government whose title is to be
determined."

When the Germans formally protested at Versailles against
the unfairness of the mandate system, the Allies replied that
they had "placed *before every other consideration* the interests
of the native populations . . ." Perhaps, in that poisoned atmosphere, they sincerely thought so. Yet it later developed that
France was privileged to conscript the natives of the former
German colonies into her army, where they could be used, if
need be, to fight a defensive war against Germany.

In 1919 it was embarrassing to explain how it came about
that the parceling out of the mandates bore so close a relation to the secret treaties negotiated during the war. The great
powers made off with oil fields and other incalculably rich
resources, while looking after the "interests of the native popu-

lation," though, thanks to Wilson, they did not secure as complete control as they desired.

In February, 1919, a week after Wilson's departure from Paris for a hurried trip to the United States, Lloyd George privately remarked to Lord Riddell that while America had obtained a bundle of dubious paper money in the form of the League of Nations, he had "returned with a pocket full of sovereigns in the shape of German Colonies, Mesopotamia, etc. Everyone to his taste."

Ideally, perhaps, the mandates should have been under the complete control of the League of Nations. But the powers would have none of this. They had fought a grueling and exhausting war of self-defense for over four years, and they had to have something to show on the credit side of the ledger. They had not entered the conflict to seize German colonies, but they could hardly be blamed for wanting to salvage something from the economic ruin that Germany had seemingly forced upon them. The alternative to outright annexation was the modified form of Wilson's mandate plan that was finally adopted.

From the larger point of view, the system as finally worked out was preferable to undisguised imperialism. It provided for a species of control, and it gave promise of getting the League off to a good start. Certainly the mandate system proved to be one of the more successful and creditable enterprises of the League of Nations. It was, as someone has said, "an angel conceived in sin."

On the debit side of the ledger, we must weigh the effect of this whole arrangement on the German mind. It was disillusioning to be deprived of all colonies; it was humiliating to be informed that Germans were unfit to govern natives; and it was insulting to be told that all this was being done largely in the interests of backward peoples. To the great body of Germans—and to many liberals elsewhere—the mandate scheme seemed like a clumsy camouflage for outright annexation. Even the Socialist press in France damned the arrangement as "a

bastard compromise between Wilsonian idealism and imperialism." There were many liberals who were still convinced that
the White Man's Burden was nothing but the loot sack.

5

One of the most persistent latter-day criticisms of Wilson is
that he stupidly permitted the German islands of the North
Pacific to fall into Japanese hands. The assumption is general
that if he had been gifted with any foresight at all, he would
have wrested them away from Japan, and that in 1941 we
should have held them as fortified outposts.

Yet what else could Wilson have done? Neither he nor his
countrymen had any more than the dimmest conception of the
value of these islands in the waging of naval and aerial warfare
in the Western Pacific. And why become alarmed about Japan?
She was one of our Associates; and while we had some suspicions of her motives, we were certainly not at that time seriously
contemplating war with her even in the remote future. There
were many other problems at the Conference of really pressing
importance. Why worry about global flyspecks when one is busy
reshaping the world?

Even before Pearl Harbor, some Americans began to see a
new light; and certainly after Pearl Harbor an increasing number of our citizenry came to appreciate the value of these numerous stationary and unsinkable aircraft carriers in the hands
of a resourceful and tenacious foe. Here we have a striking
example of after-the-event wisdom, for it has not been until
relatively recent times that the American people have come to
see what they assume Wilson should have seen at Paris.

If we are going to blame anyone for not having been able to
part the veil of the future, why not pick on President Mc-
Kinley? Presumably he could have gathered in the Carolines
and the other islands from vanquished Spain without the
slightest difficulty if he had only had the wit to do so.

As a matter of fact, there is much excuse for McKinley. Germany had begun negotiations to purchase these islands in the 1880's, and in 1898–1899 she exerted very strong pressure

Disposition of Germany's Pacific Colonies

both at Paris and at Washington to induce us to keep our hands off. Our relations with Germany were then rather embittered, and when it was discovered that our missionary and cable interests were adequately safeguarded we stepped aside and let the Germans buy the islands from Spain.

It seems hardly fair to blame McKinley for this oversight, if it was an oversight. He had no way of knowing that Japan would one day get the islands and attack Pearl Harbor. He had no way of foreseeing the coming of aerial warfare. If he had been a soothsayer, he perhaps would have done differently. But we cannot expect our statesmen to be crystal gazers; the best we can expect them to do is to weigh possibilities and probabilities, and make their decisions accordingly. In an age which knew neither the airplane nor the long-range submarine, it did not seem reasonable to suppose that these islands could ever be used effectively against us.

If our statesmen adopt the policy of acquiring everything that can be purchased or seized, from the Antarctic to the Arctic, for fear that at some distant day and in some unforeseen manner it may be used to our disadvantage, then we shall surely embark upon a sea fraught with more than ordinary peril.

6

The American naval experts in 1919 thought that it would be desirable to have the German islands, but they recognized that the best they could hope for was some form of international control. Wilson later recalled before the Senate committee that there had been one memorandum presented in behalf of "some base" in the German group, but he did not seem to think the matter of any vital importance. His only real concern seems to have been for American cable rights on the island of Yap, and he vaguely entered a reservation which later returned to plague our relations with Japan. Incidentally, this was the only request even remotely resembling a territorial claim that the United States presented at Paris.

On technical grounds, the American negotiators in 1919 had much less excuse than McKinley's negotiators in 1898. The submarine had been recently used with devastating effect, and the aircraft had clearly foreshadowed enormous destructiveness. While it is true that our relations with Japan were superficially amicable, there were many points of friction, and there had been occasional war scares on both sides since 1906. It would be difficult enough to defend the Philippine Islands and Guam, in the event of war with Japan, without having our communications flanked by innumerable Japanese bases.

The inescapable fact is that even if Wilson had fully recognized the value of these tiny islands, which he did not, he could not have pried them away from Japan, no matter how desperately he tried. He had a difficult enough time as it was with our cable rights on Yap, and this controversy was not settled until after he had left the Presidency.

When the Conference met at Paris in 1919, the Japanese had already occupied the islands for over four years. They had been guaranteed permanent possession of them by the secret agreement with London and Paris early in 1917, under which Britain was to get the German islands south of the Equator, and Japan was to provide antisubmarine reinforcements for Mediterranean waters. The Japanese had faithfully carried out their end of the bargain, and the British and French were in honor bound to carry out theirs. More than honor was indeed involved, for if the British had repudiated their agreement at this late date, they could hardly have claimed the German islands south of the equator which New Zealand and Australia were demanding.

Early in the Conference, Wilson flatly announced that he would not recognize the secret understanding with Japan. But he eventually had to, in connection both with the Pacific islands and with Shantung. We must not forget that he was only one of the Big Four; and that the United States was only one of the Big Five Powers at Paris. He was quite willing to tear up this secret agreement, but how about the Japanese, the British, and the French?

As a result of the war the British Empire was to pick up over

950,000 square miles of former German territory as mandates;
the Japanese were asking for only 830 square miles of North
Pacific islands—an area less than that of Yosemite National
Park. This was all the territory they were claiming as a reward
for their participation in the war, and they would lose face
intolerably if they did not get it. They were in possession of the
islands; they were determined to stay; the only way they could
have been thrown off was by force of arms. And since the
United States, which was the only nation interested in dis-
lodging them, was not willing to go to war for this purpose, the
Japanese were there to stay.

Thus Wilson was able to win a partial victory when, on the
advice of his own experts, he secured the adoption of the mandate system. We did not get the islands; neither did Japan—in
fee simple. She was made a mandatory of the League, and
pledged herself never to fortify the places entrusted to her
care. If she could be depended upon to keep her word, these
tiny atolls would seemingly present no menace to our Pacific
communications.

7

It now seems clear that the alternatives were not: would the
Japanese or the Americans get these islands? We went to Paris
not wanting or asking for a square foot of territory, and we
could hardly have reversed our position at this late hour. The
alternatives were: would Japan get these outposts in fee
simple, or as mandatories of the League? If Japan had got them
in fee simple, she would have been free to fortify them. If she
got them as a League mandate, as she did, she *might not* fortify
them. So, granting honor on the part of Nippon, we should
gain by this arrangement. If she should prove false to her
promises, the United States would be no farther behind than
it would have been in the first instance.

When Japan left the League in 1933 she did not return the
islands. Whether she fortified them before Pearl Harbor or

not is a disputed question; the important point is that she certainly did after Pearl Harbor.

Those who blame Wilson for not having brought these islands back from Paris assume that, if he had, we should have had them in 1941. No assumption could be farther from reality. Following Pearl Harbor we lost everything west of the Hawaiian group, including Wake, Guam, and the Philippines. We had pursued a policy of not fortifying these outposts for fear of annoying Japan. There is not the slightest reason to believe that we would not have followed the same policy regarding the Japanese mandated islands, if we had then held them. In fact, with these potential bases in hand, our false sense of security probably would have been increased, and we probably should have been even less disposed to take vigorous defensive measures.

It seems reasonably clear that Wilson made the best of a bad bargain, and that the picture would not be appreciably different if he had done the impossible and got the islands. The basic blunder was not in letting Japan have these places, or in setting up the mandate system, even in modified form, but in handling the problem of Germany's colonies so shortsightedly as to provide combustibles for future Adolf Hitlers.

CHAPTER TWELVE

A LIVING THING IS BORN

"It is the spirit back of the Covenant that counts more than the text." COLONEL HOUSE, *February 7, 1919.*

1

A GREAT many people still think of the Covenant of the League of Nations and the Treaty of Versailles as two separate instruments. This, of course, is incorrect. The League of Nations Covenant was incorporated in the Treaty of Versailles as Section I. Not only was it placed at the very first, but considerable portions of the rest of the pact were so interwoven with it that the United States Senate could not cut out the Covenant without unraveling the whole fabric.

This is of vast importance, for it is clear that the League of Nations, with its vulnerable Article X, was what defeated the Treaty of Versailles in the United States. To put it another way, if the Covenant had been a separate instrument the treaty would almost certainly have been approved by the Senate.

We have already seen that Wilson won two great diplomatic victories during his first month in Paris. The first was wringing from the Conference an acceptance of the mandate principle. The second was forcing the detailed Covenant of the League of Nations into the text of the treaty. This represented a triumph over those who wanted to postpone consideration of the League to the indefinite future, notably the French, and those who wanted merely to outline the general principles of a League in the Treaty. This latter view initially commanded much support from the British.

Wilson regarded the League as the "key to the whole settlement," and from the start he favored the bodily incorporation of the Covenant in the Treaty. He encountered some opposition, chiefly from the French, but in the end he was able to have his way. It was a great personal triumph for him when, on January 22, 1919, the Council of Ten went on record as favoring his plan, and three days later the plenary session formally and unanimously gave its approval to the integral idea in the very first resolution of the Conference.

This unanimity does not mean that there was tremendous enthusiasm for the League. Wilson had made it clear, notably in his Manchester reply to Clemenceau's balance-of-power

Two Votes for the League of Nations
(Knott in the Dallas *News;* courtesy of the Dallas *News*)

speech, that acceptance of the League was the price that Europe would have to pay for America's cooperation in the peace settlement. The price seemed small indeed for the benefits that the wealthy United States could confer on a sick and impoverished Europe. One usually humors a rich uncle.

The efforts of Wilson to secure an acceptance of the League as an integral part of the treaty have erroneously been pictured as a last-ditch struggle against the wicked powers of the Old

Order. While it is clear that Clemenceau had little desire to put the League first, it is true that Wilson received considerable support from the British, who actually drafted the resolution adopted by the Council of Ten and strongly supported it in the plenary session. But it is significant that the original resolution read that the League should be a "part of the peace." Wilson objected. This might mean that his pet project would in some vague manner be associated at a later time with the entire peace settlement, and this in turn might mean that the League would be sidetracked. He promptly proposed an amendment to read that the League should be "an *integral* part of the general treaty of peace." The amendment carried without difficulty.

One need not overdramatize Wilson's part in this episode to conclude that he must bear the major part of the responsibility for forcing the Covenant bodily into the Treaty of Versailles.

2

We must note at the outset that there were powerful arguments for Wilson's position. The League was the Fourteenth Point—the capstone point—and he could conceive of neither a satisfactory treaty nor a lasting peace without the Covenant's being the heart of the whole arrangement. He believed that liberal opinion throughout the world, which had rallied to his stirring war aims, would be profoundly disappointed if he should bring home from Paris the corpse of a treaty which did not include the League—a League that would smooth out the inevitable imperfections of the entire pact.

Not only would the League be the keystone of the edifice but, if adopted in principle at the outset, it would strike the keynote of the Conference—a clarion call for the new order. It would also facilitate the making of the rest of the treaty, for— to take only one example—if a puissant League existed to maintain order, there would be less need of haggling over such problems as strategic frontiers.

A great many of the European leaders, especially those of lesser rank, rather mildly favored the League of Nations; but they generally regarded it as of secondary importance when compared with the urgent necessity of making peace with Germany. Once this was done, and the spoils were divided, and the enemy was enchained, it would be in order to draw up a League in a leisurely fashion—a powerful League which would make sure that the Allies could keep what they had taken away from their fallen foe. The problem was merely one of first things first. "Why," it was currently asked, "should the roof be put on before the foundations are solidly laid?"

This argument was unanswerable—if Wilson could take it for granted that when the loot was parceled out, and the treaty signed, the weary delegates would not pigeonhole the League and go home. Yet this was precisely what he could not take for granted. He knew that neither Lloyd George nor Clemenceau really believed in the League. Clemenceau not only had sneered at it quite openly, but had, as we have noted, come out unabashedly for the old balance of power. The French delegation at the Conference had the League last on their agenda.

It is true that the security-obsessed French would have been enthusiastic about the League if they could have had the kind of arrangements they wanted: a League of Allies rather than a League of Nations. From first to last they fought for an international army under League jurisdiction, preferably with a French general in command, or at least an international general staff, which could take vigorous action against Germany at the slightest sign of assertiveness. In other words, a powerful military machine for freezing the status quo, and keeping the heel of the victor permanently on the neck of the vanquished.

From first to last, Wilson fought this proposal. There were various objections to it, but one need only point to the fact that the Constitution of the United States puts the war-declaring power in the hands of Congress, not in that of an international body in Geneva. Wilson was amply warned by his advisers—and this must have been evident to him without such advice—that a treaty providing for an international police force would not have a ghost of a chance in the Senate. To paraphrase William Allen White, a superstate with a superarmy and a superstaff might even be tempted to knock the superdaylights out of the United States.

In short, the French conceived of the League as an instrument for perpetuating the military alliance of the victors, and they were quite willing to call it a League of Nations or a Society of Nations or any other name that would please Wilson. When Clemenceau found that the League might be forged into such an instrument, he ceased to sneer at it. But when it turned out to be a milk-and-water League, he had no enthusiasm for it. He felt that it was not totally useless, because it might add something to French defenses when taken in connection with other guarantees; but he placed no reliance on it, and would not accept it as a substitute for real security. One Gallic wit reflected a common view when he said that the League was "impossible" but "indispensable."

It is clear from all this that Wilson had unassailable grounds for believing that if the Covenant was not forced into the Treaty, it might easily be sidetracked for all time

3

On the whole it seems as though Wilson's instincts and strategy were sound, though, as will become evident, the same cannot be said for his tactics. Like a great gambler, he was staking everything on a new world order and a new era of perpetual peace. If such a new world order were to be established, there would have to be a League; and the only way to be sure of a League, Wilson felt, was to have it in the treaty.

Public opinion throughout the world seemed ripe for such an innovation. The time to strike was when the iron was hot.

When the iron cooled off, and public opinion began to lose sight of the horrors of war and become absorbed in domestic reconstruction, enthusiasm for the League would undoubtedly wane, if not evaporate. The world in 1919 was hot and malleable; the time to reshape it was before it grew cold and hard.

We do not know what would have happened—we can only guess—if Wilson had been willing to postpone the League to a subsequent pact. We do know that he waged a determined fight to force it into the Treaty of Versailles, and that the whole Treaty was defeated by a narrow margin in the United States, largely if not primarily because it contained the League. But so many other factors contributed to this narrow defeat—a number of them much more foreseeable than this particular one—that it is hardly just to censure Wilson for it. One must repeat: Wilson was gambling for enormous stakes; the odds seemed to be not altogether unfavorable. If he won, he might win enormous benefits; if he lost, the world could hardly be worse off than it had been under the bankrupt old system of power politics.

But it does not seem to have entered Wilson's head at this stage of the game—and perhaps never—that he could lose. He simply took it for granted that the Senate would approve what he brought home, and he ill advisedly assured his British and French colleagues at the Conference that this was so. He was confident that the American people would rise up in righteous wrath and not permit their representatives to defeat his treaty. He did not believe that the Senate would dare incur the odium of committing so dastardly a crime against humanity.

His strategy was obvious to the Senators, and they were infuriated by it. Before he reached Paris, some of them had served public notice on him not to put the League into the treaty. But he had gone right ahead and done so. The only way the Senators could kill his League was to kill the whole treaty: throw out the baby with the bath. Would they dare incur this terrible responsibility? Time alone would tell.

4

The Senators fought desperately to head off the frightening dilemma which Wilson was preparing to present them, and one of their strongest arguments was that the making of the League at that time would delay the making of the peace. The urgent task, they said, was to stop the war, halt Bolshevism, and "bring the boys back." The time that Wilson wasted on the League might be the very margin by which anarchy would triumph over stability. There would be plenty of time to frame and discuss a League when the dangers of the moment were surmounted.

This was a potent argument, and Wilson recognized its force. He finally went so far as to issue a public statement, explaining that work on the drafting of the League was invariably carried on during odd hours, after regular sessions of the Council of Ten. This was true, for the Commission on the League of Nations, of which Wilson was made chairman, met after the day's tasks were done, in Colonel House's spacious headquarters, Room 315 of the Hotel Crillon. Some of these sessions ran to midnight, and at least one until after one o'clock. It is therefore utterly fantastic to allege, as Lansing did, that the framing of the League prolonged the Conference by a matter of weeks.

Even granted that the League delayed the Conference by a few days, had not the Allies already held up the sessions for a month after Wilson's arrival? And was not the Senate of the United States to dally with the treaty for more than eight months, three months longer than the Conference took to frame it?

It may even be argued that the League Covenant actually expedited the drafting of the treaty. Article XIX was the great expediter. It provided that the Assembly might advise from time to time the "consideration of international conditions whose continuance might endanger the peace of the world."

After the delegates had wrangled fruitlessly over a problem without prospect of agreement, an unsatisfactory solution was not infrequently adopted in the hope that Article XIX would ultimately take care of it. Harold Nicolson speaks of the many errors and obstructions that were passed over "under the aegis of that blessed Article XIX."

If one were asked to guess, it probably would be safe to say that the existence of the League Covenant with its "blessed" Article XIX saved much more time than was lost by the actual drafting of the Covenant. This catch-all article proved to be a convenient kind of attic into which the Conference could thrust all unfinished furniture. We need not discuss at this point the question whether time saved in this way was time profitably saved. It will suffice to observe that some of the problems which the Conference could not solve and which it left to the League, notably disarmament, the League could not solve either. And the failure to do so contributed directly to the League's final collapse, and to that of the whole postwar settlement.

5

While we may argue that the drafting of the Covenant did not seriously delay the making of the Treaty, it is clear that Wilson's preoccupation with his brain child led to serious, not to say disastrous, consequences. Time is not necessarily important in itself; the important thing is what is done with it.

During the month before the Conference met, Wilson was much wrapped up in the League. As it turned out, some of the attention that he then devoted to this subject might better have been given to other problems of more pressing importance.

Specifically, there was the vexatious question of the secret treaties. We have already suggested that if Wilson, at the opening of the Conference, had taken a bold stand against these pacts, he might have been able to sweep them from the green baize board. Instead, he spent his initial momentum in behalf of the League, and when he had to grapple with the secret treaties he was forced to fight on much less advantageous ground.

The Commission on the League of Nations was a distinguished body, which at times eclipsed the Council of Ten, and which for the entire Conference was exceeded in importance only by the Council of Ten and the Council of Four. The prolonged after-hour sessions on the League, superimposed upon an exacting day's labor with the Council of Ten, doubtless preoccupied Wilson's mind, possibly dulled it, and certainly lessened his efficiency for the important sessions of the next morning, when he had to contend with the fresh Lloyd George and Clemenceau, neither of whom was carrying such an overtime burden.

These midnight meetings were undoubtedly a severe drain on Wilson's meager stock of nervous and physical energy, and this would certainly have been true of a younger or more robust man. He had no time for his customary golf or other systematic recreation, and it is altogether probable that this onerous double duty had a real bearing upon his final tragic collapse.

6

But the question of delay and preoccupation seems to be less important in some ways than that of the hasty and imperfect drafting of the Covenant.

The Constitutional Convention, meeting in Philadelphia in 1787, took twelve weeks of exacting labor to complete a constitution for thirteen thinly populated provincial states.

The Commission on the League of Nations, working at night and after a grueling day's work, took only ten meetings, totaling about thirty hours, to strike off a constitution for the entire world. Laboring under such pressure, and confronted with such an enormous responsibility, it could hardly have brought forth a perfect instrument. And it did not. The Covenant bristled with imperfections, many of which, it now seems, were avoidable.

This picture, of course, is oversimplified, and it is necessary to correct a series of common misconceptions.

Many people still believe that Wilson thought up the idea of the League of Nations all by himself, that the British and the European peoples were not much interested in it, that he rammed the general principles of a League down their throats, and that as Chairman of the League of Nations Commission he sat down and dashed off the Covenant in a few days.

The League idea was not original with Wilson; it may be traced at least as far back as Dante. Many Americans had been much more forward and enthusiastic than he in accepting it, and this group includes Senator Henry Cabot Lodge. Wilson in truth was a belated if zealous convert.

In England, a distinguished group of liberals had been actively at work for many months on the League principle, and the famous Phillimore Report was in a very real sense the backbone of the final Covenant. Ray Stannard Baker is free to admit that there were many men at Paris as well prepared for the task of covenant-making as Wilson. The League could hardly have been brought into being without the cordial teamwork of Frenchmen like Léon Bourgeois, and Britons like General Jan C. Smuts and notably Lord Robert Cecil.

No, Wilson did not force the idea of the League upon the powers at Paris against their vigorous opposition. There was more apathy and indifference than actual hostility; more of a feeling that the League should come last rather than first. In brief, the question was not: Shall there be a League? It was: Shall the League be a part of the Treaty or a separate instrument?

Several months before reaching Paris, Wilson had worked out with House a rather careful draft of the proposed League. This explains why the Covenant could be struck off so rapidly. The problem was basically an editorial one of comparing and composing the differences in the several drafts that already existed. If Wilson had sat down to the task with empty hands, he simply could not have brought out of the committee an instrument so nearly complete as this one.

7

Reference to Wilson's early draft of the League Covenant leads us to what may be regarded as one of his most costly errors in the handling of public opinion.

If, as we have seen, he had rather carefully worked out the specific outlines of the League of Nations several months before leaving America, why did he not make his general principles public? He could then have studied the comments of the press, the criticisms of the opposition, and above all the reactions of the Senate. If he had done this, he would have been able to anticipate and meet many of the objections that were finally raised against the draft which was so hurriedly pasted together in Paris.

Wilson was at pains to keep his draft secret, and he also desired that the British withhold theirs from the press. The explanation is obvious. He did not want to arouse premature controversy.

We cannot deny that there was much force in Wilson's objections. But the same objections would not have been so weighty if he had been willing to publish the general outlines of his scheme, rather than specific details. And even if he had balked at publishing general outlines, he could have let them come out anonymously as trial balloons, and then have watched the reaction. Certainly he could have taken the leading Senators into his confidence, Democrats if not Republicans, and got their criticisms. But one finds no record that he did so. Here, as elsewhere, he simply failed to keep up his fences. He was evidently supremely confident that the Senate would not dare reject his handiwork.

The net result was that serious imperfections cropped out in the first draft of the League, imperfections which Wilson could have ironed out much more easily during the drafting than later. As it turned out, he had to go back to Paris, hat in hand, and beg the powers to insert certain amendments that would appease the angry Senate. This weakened his position, and opened the door for embarrassing counter favors, which were advanced either sincerely or as bargaining levers. We shall have to come back to this later, but for the moment we may note that the whole process of securing amendments increased the strain on Wilson, added to the general confusion at Paris, and introduced a not inconsiderable amount of genuine delay.

8

The decision to force the Covenant into the Treaty led to a train of tragic consequences. It necessitated a hasty and imperfect drafting; it introduced an element of distraction and confusion which diverted energy from the primary business of making peace with Germany. It tarred the Covenant with the black brush of Versailles, and caused neutrals to feel uncomfortable about going into a League which was embedded in a punitive treaty of peace. And finally, as already noted, the Covenant brought about the complete defeat of the Treaty in the United States, and in this way contributed powerfully to the collapse of the whole postwar settlement. All this, it seems, might have been avoided if Wilson had not stubbornly refused to accept a compromise between his point of view and that of his critics.

Certain leaders at Paris, including Secretary Lansing, Lord Robert Cecil, Colonel House, Arthur J. Balfour, and others, believed that the ideal solution was neither to postpone consideration of the League until after the Conference, nor to insert the Covenant bodily into the Treaty. Rather, there should be a general statement in the Treaty committing the signatories to the broad principles of a League, and making specific provision for the formation of a commission to erect the machinery in a saner and less hurried atmosphere.

Once the Senate had approved the Treaty, with the general outlines of the Covenant in it, and had sanctioned the creation of a commission to draw up the final instrument, the resulting League Covenant possibly could have been adopted by a simple executive agreement. In this case the Senate would have been by-passed, and Senators Lodge and Borah and Brandegee would not have had a chance to attach a long list of qualifying reservations.

In other words, the negotiators at Paris might have planted an acorn in the Treaty, with the expectation that it would grow into a lusty young oak in the sunshine of experience. As it was, they planted an oak and finally got only a sickly acorn.

The acorn-planting method undoubtedly had much to commend it. It would have prevented that sidetracking of the League which Wilson very properly feared. It would have avoided any serious delay, because the drafting of a few general principles would have taken little time and would have commanded general assent. It would have enabled neutral representatives to take part in the subsequent discussions. It would have given time for passions to cool, and would have made possible the deliberate working out of the specific problems in a more wholesome atmosphere.

Above all, a general statement of principles in the Treaty would have choked off hostile criticism in America. It would have given ample opportunity to the opponents and proponents of such a plan to advance their ideas—as co-authors if you will—for the guidance of those who were later to be charged with the task of drafting the League Covenant.

This is vastly important. General principles, as a rule, do not offer much for critics to attack. Everyone—or almost everyone—favors peace and good will toward men, and some measure of international collaboration toward that end. But when anyone advances specific and detailed plans for achieving those ends, the critic has something definite to sink his teeth into. He will raise questions and doubts; and questions and doubts tend to multiply in the minds of the public. Details were what ruined the League in America.

This does not mean that the Covenant was an unnecessarily wordy instrument. It was an admirably succinct and simple statement, in the tradition of the United States Constitution. Wilson was opposed to elaborate machinery, and insisted that it was the spirit of the thing that counted. Yet, even so, the Covenant was too detailed for its enemies. Some found it too strong, some too weak; some too vague, some too specific. A determined and jaundiced critic could find lurking in it all the hobgoblins he was looking for.

Why Wilson did not listen to Lansing and the others when they advanced the acorn-planting idea, one cannot say. He was a stubborn man, and did not compromise readily. He had made up his mind that the Covenant—a detailed Covenant—should go into the Treaty. And it did.

9

On a snowing and raining St. Valentine's day, February 14, 1919, Wilson stood before the plenary conference, cool and self-possessed, to present the still-warm draft of the League Covenant. It was a day of great personal triumph for him—perhaps his last great day of triumph—for he had forced his will upon those who were bent on postponement. The document which he held in his hand bore the unanimous approval of the fourteen nations represented on the drafting committee.

Without heroics or histrionics, but in quiet and measured tones, he began reading this charter for a new world order. The occasion in itself was so impressive, and the atmosphere was so heavy with big events, that Wilson's almost studied casualness was extraordinarily effective.

Upon completing the reading, he added a few explanatory

words. Quietly yet exultantly he announced: "A living thing is born . . ." Mrs. Wilson smiled proudly. There was not even a flutter of applause; one does not applaud after a prayer.

Others spoke. Significantly a French delegate said that France reserved the right to present further suggestions, and a Japanese delegate announced that Japan would later offer a proposition, presumably on the racial equality question. These remarks merely underscored the fact that the Conference had not yet approved the League; only the drafting committee had. A number of rough edges remained to be filed off.

Wilson was far too optimistic when he proclaimed that a living thing was born. The living thing was stillborn. The Senate, which Wilson did not think would dare take such liberties, was yet to have its say. It had in fact been doing some preliminary saying before and during the birth of the Covenant—enough to alarm a less preoccupied and confident man.

Following the presentation of the Covenant, the President and Mrs. Wilson left hurriedly in a torrential downpour to take the train for Brest, whence they would sail for a brief visit to America. An epoch in their lives and in the life of the League had ended, and another had begun.

CHAPTER THIRTEEN

A PROPHET IS NOT
WITHOUT HONOR

"No matter what I do, they will continue the attack."
WOODROW WILSON, *March, 1919.*

1

ON A wintry February 15, 1919, the *George Washington* glided out of Brest harbor, bearing the weary Wilson homeward for a brief sojourn. The guns from the forts boomed a noisy farewell, while lines of French marines stood rigidly at salute along the walls.

Wilson had every reason to feel jubilant. He had won his first two battles: the first, against a brazen division of the spoils; the second, for the incorporation of the League in the Treaty. More than that, he had in his pocket the draft of a Covenant which he had driven through a committee of fourteen nations, and which he had triumphantly read to the assembled Conference.

Then why go home? Why not stay on, and without loss of momentum push on to other victories? Why delay the Conference further by a junket back to the United States?

Mrs. Wilson relates that her husband had hoped to have the Treaty far enough toward completion by mid-February so that he could leave Paris and not have to return. But the delays of December and January, combined with difficulties both expected and unexpected, had retarded progress to such an extent that this was a vain hope. The treaty with Germany had not yet even begun to take shape.

Wilson had now been absent from America for two and one-half months. The Sixty-fifth Congress was about to adjourn, and it seemed imperatively necessary that he return, sign the essential bills, and take care of other important administrative matters. Above all, he must explain in detail the nature and purposes of the newly born Covenant, for it was already being grossly misrepresented.

It is difficult to see how this return trip, or a similar return trip, could have been avoided. Without it, Wilson would have been absent from the United States for more than seven months; and we may well doubt whether the pressure of domestic business or the temper of public opinion would have permitted such a prolonged absence.

Nor is it at all clear that this return trip appreciably delayed the work of the Conference. During Wilson's absence, the various committees were assiduously at work, and they made remarkable progress in the direction of the real task at hand— peace with Germany. Lloyd George had to be absent in England looking after his political fences; while Clemenceau was convalescing from an assassin's bullet in the lung. "My enemies never could shoot straight," he was reported to have muttered as he pitched forward.

2

Probably, as already remarked, the most important reason in Wilson's mind for returning home was to explain and defend his League before the American public. Even before the publication of the draft there had been growing criticism of his yet unborn child; now that the child, crooked limbs and all, was exposed to the public gaze, the Senatorial and other flaw pickers could get down to cases.

Before sailing from France, Wilson had cabled an invitation to the members of the House and Senate committees that deal with foreign affairs, asking them to dine with him shortly after his arrival in Washington for the purpose of discussing the Covenant. He also requested that in the meantime they refrain from debating the subject in Congress.

This was a gracious gesture, and on the face of it indicates that Wilson was recognizing the importance, even though belatedly, of enlisting Senatorial support.

The fact is that Wilson did not favor this move at all. When Colonel House first suggested it to him, he insisted that the most he would do would be to make an address to Congress. Upon House's pointing out that Congress would resent being

Anxious Moments—Will He Give Me His Boot or His Blessing?

(Courtesy of the Spokane *Spokesman-Review*)

called together and lectured to as the professor lectures his class before handing them an assignment, Wilson reluctantly gave in.

This is a classic example of locking the barn door after the theft. The time to have deferred to the Senate was when Wilson was making up the personnel of the Commission, and considering what his program would be. When he finally got around to making conciliatory gestures, the Senate was in an angry mood, and too many bitter things had already been said, both publicly and privately.

On the day of the sailing from Brest, it was announced that Wilson would land at Boston and there deliver a speech. The Senators thereupon declared that it was unfair of Wilson to ask them to keep silent while he was making public addresses, so they paid no attention to his request for postponing a discussion of the League. Perhaps they would have spoken anyhow, but this was a plausible pretext. While the *George Washington* was steaming swiftly toward Senator Lodge's bailiwick, Senators Poindexter, Borah, and Reed were thundering against the League. Senator Reed's scorching attack received an unprecedented five-minute ovation, in which the Senators and the gallery joined, while the presiding officer made no effort to check the demonstration. The Newark *News* acidly observed that "in the Senate it's the League of Fulminations."

3

The *George Washington* almost ran ashore, on the mid-afternoon of February 23, 1919, while trying to make Boston harbor in a dense fog. "I don't care if it is the beach," exclaimed one returning soldier. "It's the good old U.S.A., whatever it is, and I say hurray for it!" Nothing could better epitomize the growing isolationist sentiment.

The next morning an estimated 200,000 Bostonians cheered the conquering hero en route from the pier to his hotel, while business houses and schools declared a holiday.

That afternoon some 7,000 persons elbowed their way into Mechanics' Hall to hear Wilson speak, while thousands more milled around outside. The first part of his address was pitched on a plane of high and nebulous idealism—the customary "prose poem." Wilson's supporters gazed glumly at their abstruse gladiator. But toward the end he aroused tremendous cheers when he came down to earth and revealed a determination to strike back at his Senatorial critics. "I have fighting blood in me," he boasted, "and it is sometimes a delight to let it have scope . . ."

Was the speech in Boston a mistake? Was it tactically wise to stop off in the largest city of Senator Lodge's state and make a provocative address? Would not the Senator resent this apparent insult, and sharpen his knife to razor edge?

There is little reason to suppose that the Boston speech made any difference one way or another. Lodge was out to "knife" Wilson anyhow, and it is difficult to see how this incident had any relation to his subsequent course. As for the other hostile Senators, they had already thrown down the gauntlet while Wilson was on the Atlantic, if not before.

On the evening of February 26, 1919, two days after landing in Boston, Wilson kept his dinner rendezvous at the White House with the Senate and House foreign relations committees. The atmosphere was tense. The attacks on the League had been continuing in the Senate. Senator Borah refused to attend on the ground that he would be honor bound not to reveal confidential information, and he wanted to reveal all the information he could. Senator Fall, of later Teapot Dome infamy, also stayed away.

Wilson discussed the League with the Congressional representatives until nearly midnight. He explained various provisions at length, and expressed the hope that the Covenant would be accepted without fundamental change.

The President's friends testified that he appeared to very good advantage, answering questions with completeness and candor. His critics came away with a different story. Senator Brandegee of Connecticut, an intense man who later committed suicide, subjected the President to the cross-examination of a prosecuting attorney. Lodge wrote in his diary that Wilson's performance was "anything but good." The next day Senator Brandegee was quoted as saying: "I feel as if I had been wandering with Alice in Wonderland and had tea with the Mad Hatter."

The conference was clearly a failure. Certainly no new converts had been made. Those who were hostile to the League had evidently come for the purpose of finding confirmation of their suspicions.

Wilson was much irritated by the whole affair, and when he returned to Paris he told Colonel House that "*your* dinner" was a "failure as far as getting together was concerned." Senators Lodge and Knox, he said, had sat in sullen silence, refusing to enter into the spirit of the discussion. Colonel House replied that Wilson had done something to mollify public opinion, for he had refuted the charge that he was so dictatorial that he could not consult Senators. Wilson supposed that this was so, but he still felt that little or nothing had been gained with the Senate.

Apparently nothing had. One cannot recapture one's horse by locking the door after it is stolen.

4

Many people still labor under the delusion that criticisms of the hastily drafted League Covenant were voiced only or primarily by Senators. As a matter of fact men in public and private life, both at home and abroad, as well as newspapers throughout the country, were all airing their opinions. The Covenant was not yet in final form, and the possibility of amendment doubtless encouraged many persons to express their views.

It is not fair to suggest, either, that all those who criticized the Covenant were motivated by partisan or malicious motives. Earnest friends of the League of Nations are prone to give the impression that the Covenant was attacked only by those who were stupid, depraved, or ill intentioned.

This is far from the mark. Many of the suggestions that were

made, notably those by men like Taft and Root, were designed
to be helpful, and genuinely to improve the Covenant. Many
other persons sincerely believed that this was too sharp a break
with the past to be taken all at one leap. They argued that the
policy of Washington—nonentanglement in the purely political affairs of Europe—had served the Republic well, and that
it would be folly to throw it into the ash can, and then dash
madly after Wilson's will-o'-the-wisp. Although this point of
view did not take properly into account the nature of our
shrinking world, the names of the Founding Fathers could be
used with great effect to give it support.

But it is undoubtedly true that partisan and other less worthy
motives were also present. It is a noteworthy fact that the great
bulk of support for the League of Nations came from the
Democratic press of the country, while the great bulk of the
opposition was voiced by the Republican and Hearst press.
Relatively few Democratic newspapers of importance opposed
the League; though a considerable number of Republican
journals were to be found in the same camp with the Covenant.

This is a curious situation. The League was designed to
benefit all the nations, including ourselves; and if peace came
to the world as a result of the League, the benefits would accrue
not only to Democrats but to the entire country as well. Surely
if any issue in foreign policy should have been completely di-
vested of partisanship, it was this one.

But American politics move in a mysterious way. We have
a two-party system, and it is the business of the party out of
power to criticize the proposals of the party in power. Wilson
happened to be President. He happened also to be a Democrat.
If he drove through his tremendous program and brought
lasting peace to the world, he would add new and greener
laurels to his already laurel-wreathed brow. He might, on the
strength of his great diplomatic victory, consent to run for a
third term, and if he did, he might well win. There was in fact
considerable third-term agitation already.

Yet even if Wilson did not choose to run again, his success

with the League would shed a brilliant luster on his party. The Democratic platform would point with pride to his transcendent achievement; Democratic spellbinders would gloat from a thousand stumps. Their great cry would be that only the Democratic party, on the basis of its accomplishments, could be entrusted with the national administration, and particularly with the launching of the League which Wilson had fathered.

The Democrats, of course, insisted that the League was not a partisan issue, but an organization for the good of the entire country. Yet if it had been finally accepted, they would have made partisan capital out of it. On these narrow grounds, at least, the Republicans were justified in anticipating such partisan praise by interposing partisan obstruction. Such are the vagaries of politics. Such are the difficulties when delicate problems involving foreign affairs are thrown into the dusty arena of partisanship.

So it was that political motives became intermixed with sincere ones. The true partisan will put the good of his party above the good of his country. If he is also conscientious and resourceful, he will not find it difficult to discover reasons for believing that the good of the party is also the good of the country.

The supreme goal of a political party is to attain power, and then to stay in power. If, in so doing, it is necessary to throw overboard all plans for a new international order, those plans will be thrown overboard—or at least the attempt will be made.

5

Some of the criticisms of the League Covenant were of a general nature. It was a war-breeding, entangling alliance—an unjustifiable and dangerous departure from the precepts of Washington. It involved yielding a substantial part of our sovereign rights. It was a superstate which would jeopardize

and overbear its constituent members. It was a manifestation
of Wilson's "Messiah complex"—of his desire to become the
"drum-major of civilization."

Most of these arguments were advanced with greater vehe-
mence at a later date, when the Covenant was put into final
form and the real fight began. But in February and March of

*It's So Sudden—We'd Like a Little
Time to Think It Over*
(Courtesy of the Columbus *Dispatch*)

1919, when the Covenant was still in a formative state, certain
specific objections were raised so insistently and persistently
that something obviously had to be done about them.

First, public opinion demanded a reservation regarding our
sacred Monroe Doctrine, which few Americans understood but
which most of them would defend unto death. Suppose that
the members of this new superstate should come over and
threaten us or interfere with us, just as the Holy Alliance had
seemed about to do in 1823?

Second, the Covenant contained no provision for withdrawal from the League. After we had stuck our heads into the lion's mouth, and did not like the prospects, there we should have to stay.

Third, there was no provision for exempting purely domestic disputes from the purview of the League. Suppose that this superbody should lay unhallowed hands on the sacred ark of our tariff? Suppose that the Japanese, or the Chinese, or the Hindus should try to flood our fair land, and the League prevented us from excluding them?

Fourth, the Covenant did not specifically permit a nation to refuse an unwelcome mandate. Suppose that the League should assign us Armenia, or some other place that would involve a large army of American boys and vexatious entanglements in the Old World?

Wilson did not believe that any of these four proposed changes was either necessary or desirable. Most of the things to which the American people were objecting had been fully discussed in the League Commission, and finally rejected for what seemed to be good reason.

But so evident was the determination of the public not to accept the Covenant without these four changes that Wilson was finally convinced of the necessity of going back to Paris and reopening the whole issue. Of his success, more will be said later.

6

The various objections to the Covenant have here been discussed at such length as perhaps to give the erroneous impression that public opinion was generally in opposition. On the contrary, the indications are that in March, 1919, the American people were on the whole strongly if not overwhelmingly favorable to the League.

At best, public opinion is a phantom thing, difficult to measure. This was before the age of the various public opinion "sampling" polls, which on the whole have proved surprisingly accurate. Fortunately the *Literary Digest* had already begun to pioneer in the field by polling newspaper editors throughout the country, and its only general poll on the League, published on April 5, 1919, is highly significant.

The *Literary Digest* had sent an inquiry to all daily newspapers in the United States, asking: "Do you favor the proposed League of Nations?" The replies were tabulated as follows: Yes, 718; No, 181; Conditional, 478. From the standpoint of circulation, the figures were: Yes, 9,886,449; No, 4,326,882 (2,488,976 represented the circulation of Hearst newspapers); Conditional, 6,792,461.

On the basis of these statistics, those who had definite opinions on the League were favorable to it by a margin of two to one. The Democratic press, especially in the solid South, was almost unanimous for the League, while the great body of conditional votes was Republican. The most formidable opposition came from Hearst, who was bitterly anti-British, and who resented any League of Nations in which the British Empire would have six votes. His position was vociferously applauded by Irish-Americans.

At this point one highly important fact must be particularly emphasized. If, as seems clear, a strong majority of those who had made up their minds were for the League, their support must have been very strong indeed, because they were asked to pass judgment on the unrevised draft. If, without the proposed amendments, the League could command this much popular support, it would presumably enlist even more if and when the suggested changes were written into the Covenant.

The figures compiled by the *Literary Digest* are not satisfactory, but they are all we have. The newspaper editors were asked to give not merely their own views but those of the section in which they lived, and their replies square with such other fragmentary evidence as we have. Even Senator Lodge was then conceding in private that a majority of the American people favored the League.

Wilson boasted publicly and said privately that an "over-whelming" sentiment supported the Covenant. He doubtless saw the *Literary Digest* figures, and they may have given him a false confidence in his dealings with the Senate. A majority of the country may have favored the League, but a two-thirds majority was necessary in the Senate. It was in fact theoretically possible for Senators representing about 10 per cent of the nation's population to kill the Treaty.

One other point. Doubts are often slow in germinating. Given a little time, and assiduous cultivating and watering, the minority might blossom forth into a majority.

7

Early in March, 1919, shortly before Wilson's return to Paris, the opposition in the Senate bared its teeth in an ugly fashion.

The Republican minority deliberately filibustered vital appropriation bills to death before the short session ended on March 4, 1919. Ordinarily, Congress would not meet again until December, 1919, some nine months later, at which time the Republican majority would take control of the Senate. But with the appropriation bills killed, Wilson would have to summon Congress in extraordinary session if the government was to carry on. This meant that the Republicans could organize the Senate some six months in advance of the normal time, and keep a more careful watch on the President. More important, they could use the floor of Congress as a sounding board for echoing criticisms against the League, and thus weaken his position in Paris.

The stratagem worked perfectly. Wilson was forced to call Congress in special session for May 19, 1919, and it stayed in session until November 19, 1919, the day the Treaty was first laid to rest.

Much more spectacular was a bold move by the opponents of

the League. At two minutes after midnight on the morning of March 4th, Senator Lodge presented to the Senate an extraordinary document that has come to be known as the Round Robin. This was a pronunciamento, drawn up by the Republican leaders at the instance of Senator Brandegee, which announced to the world that the signatories did not find the Covenant of the League acceptable "in the form now proposed." The Round Robin further urged that the Conference address itself to the urgent task of making peace with Germany, while deferring such proposals as the League for later "careful consideration." The document was signed, or soon signed, by thirty-nine Republican Senators or Senators elect. Only thirty-three votes were needed to defeat a treaty.

The New York *Sun* loudly rejoiced: "Woodrow Wilson's League of Nations died in the Senate to-night." George Harvey, a vitriolic editor and a venomous foe of Wilson, who had been castigating "the President's League of Nations Claptrap" and "the League of Denationalized Nations," cried "Honor and Praise" to Lodge and the others who had fathered the Round Robin.

The Round Robin was promptly put on the wires and published in the European press, as the authors intended it to be. Clemenceau, Lloyd George, and the other statesmen in Paris took due notice, as the authors intended they should. When Wilson returned, his voice would ring with much less authority.

Yet the Round Robin, as Senator Hitchcock wrote the President, was not necessarily a sure guarantee of failure. The saving clause regarding the League was "in the form now proposed." This meant that Wilson would have to go back and secure amendments to his Covenant; and this meant that the other powers would seek to extort corresponding concessions before giving in. His position was definitely weaker than it had been when he sailed from Brest.

It is possible that the Round Robin, among other things, was designed to sting the President into some rash declaration or act which could be used against him. If so, it was strikingly successful. Wilson had come home extending the olive branch, belatedly, to the Senate. For his pains he had got a sullen reception at the White House dinner; then a vicious Senate filibuster; then an unprecedented Round Robin. Wilson's vaunted fighting blood was now boiling; henceforth it was war to the death with the Senate.

8

Wilson was scheduled to deliver a farewell speech at the Metropolitan Opera House, in New York City, on the evening of the day the Round Robin was presented, and the day before his sailing for France. From the Pennsylvania Station, in the nation's metropolis, all the way to the meeting place, he received a prolonged ovation, comparable only with the demonstrations on Armistice Day.

Five thousand people jammed the Opera House. Enrico Caruso, immortal tenor, sang "The Star-Spangled Banner." Wilson and ex-President Taft walked onto the platform arm in arm, together with Governor Alfred E. Smith, who introduced them. Taft, who had been engaging in a strenuous barnstorming campaign for the League, and whose portly frame was so fatigued that he came against the advice of physicians, spoke forcefully and effectively.

When Taft sat down amid warm applause, the band played George M. Cohan's stirring "Over There." Wilson rose and, after waiting for a mass handkerchief salute to subside, announced that he accepted the implications of the stirring song. "I will not come back," he pledged, "till it's over, over there." Then he launched into a fighting speech, during the course of which he said:

". . . When that treaty comes back gentlemen on this side will find the Covenant not only in it, but so many threads of the treaty tied to the covenant that you cannot dissect the covenant from the treaty without destroying the whole vital structure. The structure of peace will not be vital without the League of Nations, and no man is going to bring back a cadaver with him."

This revealed a fighting but indiscreet Wilson. Granted that his strategy was sound, it was poor tactics to boast about it. The "irreconcilables" in the Senate were out to unhorse him anyhow, but this ill-tempered outburst publicly revealed an angered, self-centered, headstrong Wilson, who was determined to have his own way at any cost, and who was apparently unwilling to listen to the sweet reasonableness of compromise.

Many persons in our democracy react unfavorably to such a leader, and there can be no doubt that this flare-up gained Wilson little or nothing. The Indianapolis *Star* found that "it is hard to escape the impression that President Wilson is riding for a fall."

That evening the *George Washington* drew slowly away from the pier at Hoboken on the return trip to France. There was no pomp or display comparable to that of the first departure, though a few hundred of the faithful were there to cheer their President. To the newspaper reporters Wilson remarked that the people were with him, even if the politicians were not.

The auguries were not nearly so bright as they had been when the hope-freighted *George Washington* had sailed in December. The Senate was up in arms. The country was beginning to mutter about the stubborn President. And the real fight at Paris for a treaty with Germany had not yet begun.

CHAPTER FOURTEEN

THE BATTLE BEGINS

*"The difficulties here would have been incredible to me before
I got here."* WOODROW WILSON, *April 25, 1919.*

───────────

1

IN THE early evening of March 13, 1919, the good ship *George
Washington* again steamed into the harbor of Brest. Although
a few banners were hastily hung out proclaiming "Welcome
to Wilson," and although the shouted greetings were spon-
taneous and cordial, this reception naturally lacked the magnitude and exuberance of the first one. Messiahs tend to arouse
less enthusiasm the more they show themselves: the role requires aloofness and the spell of mystery. And the French
people were beginning to have grave doubts as to the ability
of this particular Messiah from the West to deliver the Promised Land of Perpetual Peace.

Wilson was anxious to discover precisely what had happened
in his absence, for no general can leave the battlefield for a
month and find things just as he had left them. Colonel House
met Wilson at the dock, and hastened to tell him in detail how
the battle had gone. The two men were closeted together for
several hours, and when Wilson emerged from the conference
his wife was shocked by his appearance. Seemingly he had
"aged ten years." He smiled bitterly and said: "House has given
away everything I had won before we left Paris. He has
compromised on every side, and so I have to start all over
again . . ." In this incident Mrs. Wilson sees the beginning of
her husband's tragic collapse.

The testimony of a loving spouse must always be accepted
with caution, and in this case it is clear that Mrs. Wilson enter-
tained a strong distrust of the quiet Colonel. But it is also clear
that Wilson, with good reason or not, was displeased with what

he heard, and his growing coolness toward House seemingly dates from this time.

Briefly, the story is this. Before the Conference assembled it was generally though hazily taken for granted that there would be two treaties, a preliminary and a final one. The preliminary peace would impose military, naval, and aerial terms on Germany. Then the Conference could move on in a leisurely fashion to the larger problem of making the final economic, territorial, and other terms; and in these discussions the German delegates could take part.

The plan for two treaties had a great deal to commend it. The immediate military situation would be taken care of, and then there would be no need for frantic haste in the making of the definitive peace. Perspective would sharpen; passions would cool off; and sanity would return. The Allies would also have an opportunity to discuss terms among themselves, and then present a solid front to the enemy. This would prevent the Germans from playing one Ally against another, much as Talleyrand had done at the Congress of Vienna in 1814–1815.

Wilson was quite favorable at first to the idea of a preliminary military peace. Upon sailing for America, he left Colonel House to work for it, and even to discuss the inclusion of territorial and economic adjustments, but these were to be withheld from final decision pending his return.

During Wilson's absence the Conference for the first time rolled up its sleeves and came squarely to grips with the problem of making a treaty with Germany. The French did not want the preliminary peace to contain military and naval terms only, as Wilson had originally planned and as was generally intended. If this were done, the Allied armies would feel free to demobilize, and the victors might be unable to club the Germans into an acceptance of the final treaty. Steps were therefore taken to include in the preliminary peace certain territorial and other terms that had not been originally contemplated. The League would be postponed until the final treaty, because much work remained to be done on it, and because it seemed imperative to rush through the preliminary pact at once.

When Wilson returned to Paris he found the Conference pushing through a preliminary treaty which would dispose of the most pressing military, economic, and other problems, while leaving the League for later consideration. This might mean that in the last-minute scramble the Conference would forget all about Wilson's pet scheme. Everywhere people were saying, "The League is dead."

Alarmed by this prospect, Wilson hastened to issue an emphatic statement to the press on March 15, 1919, the day after his return to Paris. He announced that the Conference had formally voted to make the Covenant an integral part of the Treaty, and that he would stand on that decision. This verbal bombshell caused a sensation, and aroused strong resentment among the anti-League newspapers of England, France, and particularly of the United States.

2

Certain writers of the more dramatic school, notably Ray Stannard Baker, have seen in this episode a gigantic and sinister conspiracy on the part of the British and the French, aided and abetted by Colonel House, to "sidetrack" the League of Nations.

There apparently was no such conspiracy. Colonel House kept closely in touch with Wilson by wire, and faithfully informed him of all important developments. It does not appear that in any important particular House deviated from the parting instructions of his chief, although he was by nature a compromiser, and he may have misunderstood the President's views. Nor is there evidence that the British and French officials had any intention of backing down on their agreement to include the League in the final treaty.

But Wilson evidently feared that this might happen; otherwise it is difficult to explain why he should have issued his proclamation out of a clear sky. It is possible, of course, that he had no deep-seated suspicions, but was merely trying to make assurance doubly sure. In any event, he must have suspected, whether rightly or not, that something was afoot.

This reverberating declaration was the epitaph of the preliminary peace. Wilson had gone home favoring such a scheme; he returned opposing it. There is some direct evidence, and a great deal of circumstantial evidence, that he was thinking of the Senate, about which he had forgotten, but which he had now seen at first hand. And he did not like the looks of what he had seen.

If there were to be two treaties, one preliminary and one final, they would both have to be approved by the Senate. If the preliminary peace covered only military and naval terms, but not a League, as originally planned, the Senate almost certainly would consent to it. But if the final peace contained the League, as contemplated, the perverse Senators, having approved the preliminary peace, might balk. If there was only one treaty, with the League firmly riveted in, then the Senate would have to accept it, and the League would come into being.

So it was that all plans for framing a preliminary peace were thrown out the window, and, incredible though it may seem, the Conference realized for the first time that what had started out in January to be a preliminary peace was now to be the definitive peace. By inserting the League, by adding here and patching there, the final draft could be thrown together.

3

Wilson's torpedoing of the preliminary-peace plan led to far-reaching and momentous consequences.

The ultimate result—and the supreme irony—was that the Peace Conference never really met. The official title of the gathering was, and remained, the Preliminary Conference of the Allied and Associated Powers. The original plan, as already noted, was for the Preliminary Conference to draw up the preliminary peace, decide on the final terms to be presented to the Germans, and then discuss those terms orally with the German representatives. Now, with the preliminary conference telescoped into a final conference, and the preliminary

"Look Out, or I Won't Consider Myself Defeated."

(From the New York *World*; reprinted by permission)

peace into a final peace, there was no place for face-to-face conferences with the enemy. This, as we shall see, was a development of the greatest importance in arousing German bitterness against the Treaty of Versailles.

We should also observe that when the negotiators in Paris began drafting what they supposed was a preliminary treaty, they included a number of "maximum demands." They naturally expected that when the German delegates arrived, and the bargaining began, the "maximum demands" would be whittled down by the usual compromises.

When the decision was made to rush the preliminary peace through as a final peace, many of these "maximum demands" remained as final terms. This, as Harold Nicolson says, accounts in considerable measure for the severity of the Treaty of Versailles.

It is not fair to suggest that all this was Wilson's fault. He was only partially responsible—and largely in a negative way —for the disorganization and planlessness at Paris. One may indeed say in his defense that there would have been ample time to draw up a preliminary treaty if the Conference had met in mid-December, when he had expected it to meet.

In the final analysis, two important factors apparently killed the preliminary peace. One was French fear of a general demobilization before Germany was brought to heel. The other was Wilson's determination that the League of Nations—which he put ahead of everything else—should run no unnecessary risks, either at the hands of the Conference or at those of the Senate.

4

Wilson was now in an extremely embarrassing position, for the Covenant of the League—that "living thing" which had been "born" at the last plenary session—was in need of surgery.

Not only the Senate, but American public opinion as well, was demanding amendments. Sincere friends of the League in the United States, men like William Howard Taft and A. Lawrence Lowell, were telling Wilson bluntly that without these amendments the Senate probably would reject the treaty; with them, it could not avoid approving the treaty.

Wilson's own impulse was to stand pat, for he still did not think that the Senate would dare to incur the odium of putting the axe to the whole treaty in order to chop out the League. To him the proposed amendments were irrelevant or repetitious. Why, for example, insert any special mention of the Monroe Doctrine when the Covenant of the League merely extended the security principle of the Monroe Doctrine to the entire world?

Colonel House exerted strong pressure to budge the stubborn Wilson from his position, and in this he had the loyal support of Lord Robert Cecil, the most distinguished British advocate of the Covenant. Cecil was anxious that the League should not fail, and he recognized the necessity of meeting Senatorial opposition. This is an ironical situation indeed: a British statesman more keenly aware of the necessity of placating the Senate than the American President himself! Significantly and ominously, Cecil found that Wilson was receptive to amendments on their own merits, but when any suggestion was made of appeasing the Senate, he was "up in arms in a moment."

But Wilson's reluctance to propose amendments was by no means pure stubbornness. For one thing he would have to re convene the League of Nations Commission. If he brought in new amendments, then the other powers would be privileged to bring in theirs. The European premiers, hardly less than Wilson, had Senates of their own to appease. Old amendments which had been voted down would be dusted off and brought back; new and even more offensive ones would doubtless be presented. Some of these would be introduced in good faith; others, for their bargaining power in securing additional concessions from the United States.

Wilson was finally convinced that there was no other way out, and the League of Nations Commission was again convened. Colonel House records a revealing incident which further disposes of the charge that the President was a dull-witted professor. On March 26, Wilson announced to the League Commission that he intended to appoint the "old drafting committee." At this point House slipped him a memoran-

dum containing the names of a new drafting committee, so
Wilson, without a halt, continued, "but I think it would be an
imposition to ask them to serve again, therefore I name the
following."

To gain time, the League of Nations Commission met in the
evening, as before; and it debated the various amendments in
five exhausting sessions, two of which lasted until after midnight.

5

Two of the amendments that American public opinion was
demanding went through the League Commission without undue difficulty. These were the right to refuse a mandate, and
the exemption of domestic questions such as immigration and
tariffs from League jurisdiction.

But two other American demands—the right to withdraw
from the League and a reservation safeguarding the Monroe
Doctrine—encountered stormy weather. Even Lloyd George
tried to bludgeon the United States into abandoning its current naval program in return for British support of the Monroe
Doctrine. He seems to have succeeded to the extent of securing
from Wilson an informal pledge to suspend the second three
year building program then before Congress.

The strongest opposition, as might be expected, came from
the French, who vehemently argued that the two American
amendments would further weaken a League which was already well-nigh toothless. If the Americans could walk out
whenever they wanted to, what would become of French security? If the great powers should recognize the Monroe Doctrine, did this not mean that the United States would not have
to intervene in the Old World to honor its commitments?
Then where again was French security?

The French were shrewd bargainers, and they played their
cards for all they were worth. They knew that they had the
Americans at a serious disadvantage, because newspapers on

both sides of the Atlantic contained emphatic statements from United States Senators and other leading Americans to the effect that no League could be approved without these amendments.

Privately, the French admitted that they did not attach much importance to the Monroe Doctrine, and that they were making all this outcry for bargaining purposes. But their obstruction, whether serious or not, was a great trial to those who sincerely wanted to make progress. At one session the quiet but exasperated Colonel House growled that the French "could go to Hell seven thousand miles deep."

Wilson put up a brilliant fight for a reservation on the Monroe Doctrine, and one of his extemporaneous speeches before the League Commission was of such "witching eloquence" that even the hardened secretaries forgot to take notes. In the end the French yielded, but the circumstantial evidence indicates that they utilized their "nuisance value" by forcing Wilson to accord them a limited military occupation of the Rhine. Whatever the price, the Monroe Doctrine was specifically safeguarded, which in itself was a signal victory, for Europe until then had persistently refused to give formal recognition to the American dogma.

But the victory was Pyrrhic. American demands encouraged the French, the Italians, and the Japanese to press for concessions, including the bothersome "racial equality" amendment of Japan. France's confidence in the League, already at a low point, was further undermined, and this partly explains the French acceptance of the Security Treaty, which, as we shall see, opened a new Pandora's box of woe.

It seems reasonable to conclude that Wilson could have secured all these amendments with less effort and at less cost if he had written them into the first draft of the League. He probably would have done so if he had paid more attention to what the American people were saying, and especially if he had given them an opportunity to criticize his general ideas before the League Commission began its work.

Wilson nevertheless had reason to be pleased when the plenary session of the Conference, on April 28, 1919, unanimously approved the final draft of the Covenant with its twenty-six articles. Although one of the French delegates put in the usual word for security, Clemenceau peremptorily cut him short, and presumably in accord with the Rhineland-Monroe Doctrine deal, gavelled the pact through.

The stillborn infant, after a good deal of surgery at the hands of the doctors, had been given a patched-up and not too satisfactory birth certificate—yet it was a birth certificate, and it was unanimously approved.

6

The last week of March and the first three weeks of April were the crisis of the Conference—what Ray Stannard Baker calls "the Dark Period." To expedite business and plug up leaks (Lloyd George was angry over newspaper attacks), the Big Four began meeting together officially for the first time as the Council of Four, thus superseding the Council of Ten. The convalescing Clemenceau, not fully recovered from the assassin's bullet, was much less alert than before; and the walls re-echoed his violent paroxysms of coughing.

The world weighed heavily on Wilson's shoulders, as events tumbled over one another with breath-taking rapidity. Hungary and Bavaria were going Bolshevik; the "succession states" of Jugoslavia, Czechoslovakia, and Poland were keeping up a constant clamor for their claims. At night, Wilson spent his energies fighting for amendments with the League of Nations Commission; during the day he wrestled with reparations, the Saar Basin, a Rhineland buffer state, French occupation of the Rhine; security for France, Fiume for Italy, Shantung for Japan. The past, the present, and the future were locked in death grapple.

All these problems ran concurrently with one another, and a decision on one frequently had a good deal to do with helping to solve another. The Saar Basin was one of the key logs in the jam—if not the key log itself—and we shall turn to it first.

This area adjoined Lorraine on the north and east, and derived its importance from immensely rich deposits of coal, which, taken in conjunction with the iron ore of Lorraine, furnished the key to an industrial empire. In prewar days, the Saar Basin had annually produced some 17,000,000 tons of coal, or about 8 per cent of the entire output of the German Empire. The reserves of the Saar alone were estimated to exceed those

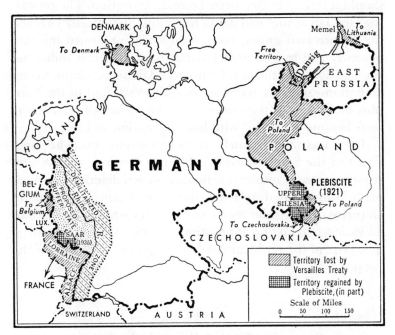

Germany's Territorial Losses

of all France, which was a country relatively poor in coal.

The French wanted the Saar at all costs. They realized that war with Germany was probable in the future, and whatever they took away from their hereditary foe would weaken him by that much, and make aggression less likely. Whatever they subtracted would add to their own industrial potential; and they were well aware that modern wars are fought as much with smokestacks as with guns. They also knew that the German Reich had been built not so much by blood and iron as by coal and iron. Finally, the Saar Basin was in itself an important strategic link in France's proposed eastern defenses.

The French claimed the Saar coal on two grounds. First, restitution. From 1793 to 1815 roughly one-half of the area had been in the possession of France, and as the historical argument was being used in Poland and Alsace-Lorraine, why should it be overlooked here? Second, reparation. The retreating German armies had deliberately and diabolically wrecked the French coal mines, both as an act of presumed military necessity and as a means of hamstringing French industrial competition after the war. France could therefore claim as compensation—and reasonably so—her historical half of the Saar, plus ownership of the mines in the German half. Hence the issue became entangled with both reparation and security.

There was only one catch—and a very serious one. The population of the Saar was overwhelmingly German, and Wilson regarded it as an intolerable flouting of self-determination, already badly flouted, to hand over several hundred thousand Germans to the tender mercies of French rule. This would also do violence to his "no annexations" pledge of February, 1918. The crux of the problem was how to get the coal without the people.

7

On the *George Washington*, Wilson had urged his experts to tell him what was right and he would fight for it. But in this case "right" was not a simple matter of black and white. The Point on self-determination cried out against French annexation; yet Point VIII promised France restoration and reparation. What was to be done when the Points clashed with one another?

The American experts, it is important to note, were impressed by the historical and economic arguments. Some of the ruined French mines would not come into production for an estimated five years, and it seemed only fair that France should have the coal of the Saar. This certainly was in keeping with both the spirit and the letter of the Fourteen Points.

But Wilson was more moved by self-determination, and completely unmoved by the argument that France had held a part of the territory for a brief period under Napoleon more than a century ago. He rightly contended that much injustice could be perpetuated by citing previous acts of injustice. Besides, as he told Clemenceau, "That was a hundred years ago—a hundred years is a very long time." "Yes," replied the Tiger cuttingly, "a very long time in the history of the United States."

The atmosphere between Clemenceau and Wilson became more and more tense. The Tiger made the utterly preposterous statement that there were 150,000 Frenchmen in the Saar; Wilson branded this as a deliberate misstatement. Clemenceau hotly accused Wilson of being a pro-German. Wilson thereupon asked whether he should go home to America if France did not get what she wanted. "I do not wish you to go home," said Clemenceau, "but I intend to do so myself." With that, he flung himself out of the room.

Interested intermediaries smoothed the Tiger's fur, and asked him to have a talk with Wilson. "Talk with Wilson!" he snorted. "How can I talk to a fellow who thinks himself the first man in two thousand years to know anything about peace on earth?"

8

At the very height of the crisis over the Saar and other pressing problems, Wilson's health gave way, and it may be doubted whether he ever fully recovered. Herbert Hoover found that during the period of convalescence Wilson had lost his former alertness and flexibility of mind, and had to be pushed into decisions.

Wilson had never been robust. Nervous, high-strung, and suffering from indigestion and neuritis, he had entered the White House in 1913 with a stomach pump and a generous supply of headache pills. The distinguished Dr. S. Weir Mitchell, of Philadelphia, had predicted that he would not finish out his first term without a physical collapse. The first years of Wilson's administration had been unusually turbulent on the domestic front; then came the outbreak of the European war, the death of the dearly beloved wife of his youth, the vexations of neutrality, the gigantic task of mobilizing an unready America for war; and then piled on top of all that, the inferno of a peace conference abroad and venomous political opposition at home. We can believe Mrs. Wilson when she says that her husband grew thin and visibly grayer during the hectic weeks at Paris.

Why Wilson did not collapse sooner will always remain something of a mystery. The explanation is perhaps to be found in his indomitable spirit, his iron self-discipline, the four restful trips across the Atlantic on the *George Washington*, and the unrelenting vigilance of his personal physician, Dr. Cary T. Grayson.

At Paris, Wilson worked too hard, and delegated too little authority. Only occasionally would he go for a hurried automobile ride or a brief walk. Between conferences he would step quickly to the window, and hastily inhale a few breaths of fresh air, as if to seek a few additional ounces of energy to revive the sputtering machine.

Much of the time he was running on sheer nerve. Ray Stannard Baker would go up to his room at night after the meetings of the Big Four, and find him "utterly beaten, worn out, his face quite haggard and one side of it and the eye twitching painfully . . ." But the next morning he seemed refreshed and eager to get on with the fight.

On April 3, 1919, Wilson took to his bed, with what the press said was a "cold." The befuddled newsmen had no real inkling either of the seriousness of the crisis over the Saar or the seriousness of Wilson's condition. The attack was very sudden; he was seized with violent coughing; and his fever shot up to 103 degrees. Dr. Grayson was deeply worried, fearing at first that poison had been placed in Wilson's food, but he quickly diagnosed the malady as an attack of the deadly influenza then sweeping the Continent.

But the show had to go on. In the book-lined outer room, beyond Wilson's bedroom, Lloyd George, Clemenceau, and Orlando continued to sit, with the faithful Colonel House representing the ailing President. From time to time House would bring into the bedroom some new French proposal, or a revamped old one. To every demand for surrender the feverish Wilson sent back a firm "No."

By April 7, Wilson's patience was at an end. On that day he dispatched a dramatic cablegram to Washington inquiring how soon the *George Washington* could be put in readiness for the return trip to France. To those on the "inside," the implication was plain that Wilson was going home if he could not have his way. Either that, or he was bluffing.

This sensational telegram was headline news in America. It was interpreted as meaning one of two things: either the Conference was hopelessly deadlocked, or the work was so nearly completed that Wilson could plan to go home. Nothing could better illustrate the fog in which the newsmen had to grope.

The precise effect of this bluff—if it was a bluff—is a matter of dispute. From Washington, Joseph P. Tumulty cabled in alarm that American opinion was reacting unfavorably to what seemed an act of petulance: it looked as though Wilson would not play with the other boys unless they played his way. The French press took up the refrain and jeered that he was going home to mother. The Tiger muttered privately, "I am disgusted . . . Wilson acts like a cook who keeps her trunk ready in the hallway. Every day he threatens to leave."

The Tiger could go home when things went badly; he had only to step around the corner. But Wilson could not run away without creating an international sensation.

The French knew that Wilson could not afford to leave the Conference in the lurch. If he did so, it would probably collapse, Europe would go Bolshevik, there would be no treaty, above all there would be no all-important League of Nations, and Wilson's prestige would hit bottom. His departure would be a public and spectacular confession of failure.

Yet the French realized that they could not afford to take too many chances: Wilson was a stubborn man, and he might just possibly bolt the Conference. If this blind Samson should pull down the temple, they, as dwellers within the temple, would suffer the most. And by now they were beginning to count on a strong defensive military alliance with both Great Britain and the United States.

9

Whether as a result of the *George Washington* incident, or in spite of it, the French at this time began to reveal a less obdurate spirit. This was due partly if not primarily to Wilson's willingness to meet them at least halfway, and during the period of the President's convalescence a compromise was worked out.

The French would not get the Saar in fee simple, but they would secure ownership of the coal mines for a period of fifteen years, during which time the entire area would be governed by a Commission representing the League of Nations. This aspect of the solution undoubtedly appealed to Wilson, for it would further dignify his League by giving it something important to do.

At the end of fifteen years, there would be a plebiscite to determine whether Germany or France should retain the coveted basin. This meant that unless the French in the meantime could convert the German population to French allegiance, the Saar would go permanently to the Reich.

The compromise solution on the Saar had much to commend it. Self-determination would be respected—after fifteen years; and full reparation would be exacted, because the French coal mines certainly could be repaired within that period. Thus the principal claim of both Wilson and the French could be met. As for the historical argument, if the French lost the Saar, they would merely lose what they had lost a hundred years before. And a hundred years is a long time, even in the history of France.

Wilson's bold stand for self-determination in the Saar was not without far-reaching aftereffects. The French press sneered at the settlement as "neither fish, flesh, fowl, nor good red herring." Deprived of this additional economic and military security, France sought compensation elsewhere, and this in part accounts for her insistence upon the Rhineland and for her acceptance of the Security Treaty, to which we shall turn shortly.

The temporary solution of the Saar problem set the stage for a tremendous boost to German nationalism, and a public humiliation of France. With so much depending on the vote of each inhabitant of the basin, a protracted electioneering campaign began, which came to a climax in 1935, when Adolf Hitler was in the saddle. Over 90 per cent of those who marched to the polls voted a vigorous "Ja" for Hitler and the Reich. It was a bloodless yet impressive triumph for the paranoiac paperhanger.

On the other hand, if the Saar had been ceded outright to France, it would have become another Alsace-Lorraine. As much as Danzig or the Sudetenland it would have figured in Hitler's program of reconquest.

On the basis of abstract justice, as seen through the lenses of the Fourteen Points, Wilson was probably right in opposing the French claims. On the basis of history, economics, and reparation, France had a strong case—a case that appealed to the American experts. On the basis of security, the French had perhaps an even stronger case; the partial loss of the Saar, later a complete loss, removed an important cornerstone from the edifice of security which they planned to erect. We shall see later what the French feeling of insecurity had to do with the wrecking of the peace settlement.

A cynic, especially a French cynic, would say that Wilson should have listened to his experts and kept quiet. If he had done so, France almost certainly would have won the Saar. This would have meant an act of injustice, but there were already injustices in the Treaty. And since there were already enough to infuriate an enchained Germany, why not let the French have the Saar, so that they could fight more effectively when the giant burst his chains? If this was done, the inevitable war might not come so soon, and Germany would wage it with less prospect of success.

But Wilson was gambling for greater stakes. If there were injustices in the Treaty—the full number could not yet be counted—the League would iron them out. And there surely would be enough without deliberately putting them in

CHAPTER FIFTEEN

THE PHANTOM OF
FRENCH SECURITY

*"I quite admit that the French cannot see beyond their noses;
but after all they are their noses: and, my word, what they do
see, they see damned clearly."* HAROLD NICOLSON, *May 1, 1919.*

1

SCRATCH THE surface of any problem at the Conference, a
recent critic has written, and you get French security. The
League, German colonies, the Saar, the Rhineland, Poland,
Upper Silesia, reparations, and other questions were all tied in
with security, and with one another.

The British were not especially concerned about security.
Their principal worry, the German naval arm, had been
neatly amputated, and it would take many years to grow another.

But with the French it was different. They were an exhausted
nation of 40,000,000, with a declining birth rate, wedged
against a neighbor of 60,000,000, with a prolific birth rate and
a warlike tradition. And that neighbor did not take kindly to
defeat.

France, quite understandably, was suffering from national
shell-shock. The mark of the German beast was on her northern
departments; upon every empty chair in a widowed or orphaned cottage. After a war which had seared both her soil
and her soul, and which had turned on a hair, France was now
on top, and she was determined to stay there. Men still living,
including Clemenceau, had seen the hated invader twice pour
over the French frontier. "My house was in the hands of the
Germans in 1814, again in 1870, and again in 1914," sadly remarked Abbé Dimnet. "I pray God that He will make it impossible that it shall ever be in their hands again."

The memory of German incursions deeply colored the attitude of the French. "Each of us lives encased in his own past," observed Clemenceau. "Auguste Comte said that we live dead men's lives and it is true." Everywhere and at all times the constant refrain of the French press was, "Guarantees, guarantees, guarantees." The hated invader must not be permitted to come again.

The crux of the French security problem was the strategic

In Memory of Wilhelm II
(Courtesy of the Chicago *Tribune*)

Rhineland. If the Germans should retain a foothold on the west or French side of the Rhine River, they would have a dangerous springboard for future invasion. But if they were kept on the east side of the Rhine, the French would have the springboard.

The most important French demands in this connection were two. First, the German area west of the Rhine (excluding

Alsace, Lorraine, and the Saar) must be erected into a buffer state, which would be demilitarized and put under the tutelage of France. While it is true that there was a rather vocal pro-annexationist group in France, the Paris government did not demand outright ownership of this region. Clemenceau was content to keep the area a satellite state, though satellite states have a way of gravitating permanently into the embrace of the controlling body. But whether annexed outright or not, the loss of the Rhineland to Germany would mean the loss of some ten thousand square miles of territory, containing vitally important industries, and some five million German people. If this area were shorn away, Germany would be correspondingly weakened, and France correspondingly strengthened. (See map on p. 219.)

The second French demand in connection with the Rhine-land was that Allied troops must occupy bridgeheads on the east bank of the Rhine for thirty years. From these strategic springboards, it would be possible to point a pistol at the heart of a disarmed Germany, and demand the full pound of flesh under the Treaty of Versailles.

2

Both Lloyd George and Woodrow Wilson emphatically opposed tearing the west bank of the Rhine from the side of the Reich. Lloyd George's stock argument was that there must be no new Alsace-Lorraines to agitate Germany for the next generation and threaten Britain with a new world war. Wilson, in addition, objected to the scheme on the ground of self-determination. It would be immoral to detach some five million loyal Germans from the Fatherland in which they had been born, and to which they ardently desired to belong.

After many prolonged sessions in the Council of Four, Clemenceau finally and reluctantly consented to a compromise in which he made two important concessions. First, Germany was to keep her territory *west* of the Rhine. But she was never to fortify it, nor an area fifty kilometers *east* of the Rhine. Second, Allied troops were to occupy strategic bridgeheads on the *east* bank of the Rhine for a maximum of fifteen years, as compared with the thirty that the French had been demanding.

The unreliable Lloyd George sadly relates in his *Memoirs* that one part of the "deal" by which Wilson consented to a limited French occupancy of the Rhine was that Clemenceau would call off his journalistic dogs, which were then yawping at the American President with indecent ferocity. It is possible, however, that Lloyd George was misled by some rather interesting circumstantial evidence. We do know that at this very time Colonel House went to Clemenceau and expressed the hope that the violent attacks on Wilson would cease. The Tiger summoned his secretary and told him emphatically that all these intemperate criticisms must be stopped. The next day the Parisian papers broke out in enthusiastic praise of the President.

While this part of the story is probably correct, we may doubt if it was part of a "deal" with Wilson on the Rhine issue. Wilson was not one to yield great principles for purely personal reasons. When he compromised on principle, it was to yield a lesser principle to save a greater one. The evidence is not conclusive, but it seems that one of the reasons why he gave way on the Rhine occupancy was to save his League of Nations by inducing France to accept a reservation on the Monroe Doctrine.

In any event, the French did consent to give up the Rhineland buffer state, and they did consent to an occupancy of the Rhine for fifteen rather than thirty years. These were apparenly great concessions, and they were naturally opposed with extreme bitterness by President Poincaré, Marshal Foch, and the other French generals. What did Clemenceau receive in return for his seeming surrender?

The answer is: a hard and fast military alliance with Great Britain and the United States, under the terms of which both nations would come to the aid of France in the event of another German invasion.

3

The extraordinary proposal of a security treaty seems to have originated in the fertile brain of Lloyd George. Two days before Wilson's return to Paris in March, 1919, the British Prime Minister told Colonel House that Great Britain was willing to come immediately to the assistance of France should the Germans launch another attack.

Lloyd George discussed the scheme with Wilson upon the latter's arrival in Paris, and out of these discussions came the proposal of the new Triple Alliance. Both Great Britain and the United States would sign separate treaties with France, pledging themselves to come to the aid of their ally in the event of an "unprovoked movement of aggression . . ." But there was one highly significant "escape clause." If either Great Britain or the United States failed to ratify the alliance, then the other signatory power would be released from its commitments.

Clemenceau was bitterly criticized in France for his alleged surrender, but it is highly significant that the Security Treaty was approved by both the Chamber and the Senate without a dissenting vote.

The British House of Commons, which had never before thus pledged its military support in advance to another nation, promptly approved the Security Treaty without a single negative vote and without serious debate. The House of Lords did likewise. It was self-evident in both London and Paris that if the two great Anglo-Saxon powers were to pool their might in support of France, a resurgent Germany would never dare risk war against such an overpowering combination. There could be no surer guarantee of peace in Europe.

What happened in America? The Security Treaty died of inanition in a pigeonhole of the Senate Committee on Foreign

Relations. It was not even accorded the honor of a formal and loquacious rejection by the Senate. There was so little sentiment in favor of it, and so much against it, that it was not even reported out of the committee.

When the United States failed to live up to its part of the bargain—or rather the bargain that Wilson had made for it—the whole structure of the Security Treaty crashed to the ground.

4

Wilson's acceptance of the Security Treaty turned out to be one of his most far-reaching blunders, and one of the least excusable, because he should have been able to foresee the result. He knew—or at times did know—that one of the most pervasive and potent American prejudices was that against military alliances. Ironically, this tradition had grown out of an earlier entanglement with the very same nation with which Wilson was now proposing to entangle us again. Already, as Wilson knew—or did he forget?—the Senatorial big guns were thundering against the weak, permissive entanglement in Article X of the League of Nations. What would they do to a hard and fast military alliance?

Not only did such an entanglement run counter to American tradition but it also ran counter to Wilson's own pronouncements. One of the most telling of his supplementary Fourteen Points had struck hard at military alliances. Not only would he contradict himself but he would seemingly undermine the whole structure of the League if he opened the door for separate military engagements. He would merely be confessing to the world that he had no faith in the new order which he was bringing into being.

All these objections and others were forcefully raised by Wilson's advisers, notably Bliss, Lansing, and White. Such criticisms were promptly seized upon and reechoed by the opposition press at home, just as soon as the rumor leaked out that such a pact was in prospect.

The argument about undermining the League seemed plausible, but on this point at least Wilson could defend himself with vigor. It is true that the Security Treaty was a military alliance, but it was a purely defensive alliance (not contrary to the spirit of the Covenant), and it was to last only during the interim when the League was being established on such strong foundations that it could guarantee French security. Surely if the Senate would swallow the League, it should have no difficulty in swallowing this preliminary and tentative military pact. Wilson seems to have completely rejected the ugly thought that the Senators might refuse to swallow both.

But Wilson did recognize the necessity for compromise and concession. The French would not yield the Rhineland without a Security Treaty—at least, so it seemed—and the deadlock could not continue forever. If he gave them the Rhineland, he would merely be sowing the seeds of a war that would undo all he was doing. The Security Treaty seemed to be much the more desirable alternative.

But was this the only alternative? Lloyd George had suggested a Franco-British treaty of assurance; and it is possible that the French would have accepted this instead of the tripartite treaty, particularly in view of the uncertainties of American ratification. A strong Anglo-French alliance would have been infinitely better than an Anglo-American-French alliance which never came into being, and which had scant prospects of ever coming into being.

Whether Lloyd George would have gone ahead with a purely bilateral treaty, and whether the French would have accepted it, we cannot say. But it seems clear that Wilson's willingness to share the responsibility ended whatever chance there may have been for a dual pact. If he had told Lloyd George and Clemenceau the brutal truth—namely, that a military alliance of any kind was completely out of the question—they probably would have made other arrangements or perhaps no military arrangements whatever. As it turned out—and this eventuality Wilson should have foreseen—the treaty which was drawn up was vastly worse than no treaty at all.

5

We come now to an interesting problem in ethics. What shall we say in defense of statesmen who put their names to treaties which they have good reason to believe will not be approved by the Senate?

If Wilson did not have such doubts, his mental condition must have been deplorable indeed. Even if he had been blind to what was then going on in the Senate, he could hardly have been deaf to the warnings of his own advisers. Colonel House was fearful of the Senate; Henry White dismissed the treaty as simply impossible; Lansing thought it preposterous.

Wilson may have been guilty of self-deception, but one may doubt that he deliberately tried to deceive Clemenceau. Wilson knew—as the worldly-wise Clemenceau knew—that no executive can guarantee in advance what a legislative body will do. Wilson was aware, certainly in his less preoccupied moments, that every treaty which enters the Senate arena runs some risk—often serious risk—of mutilation or death.

It seems fair to assume that Wilson, misreading both history and the signs of the times, entered into this pact in good faith. He doubtless knew that there would be opposition, as there almost always is, but he probably concluded that there was a better than even chance to secure senatorial approval, particularly after he had explained that the treaty merely supplemented and implemented the League, which he took for granted would be approved.

Above all, Wilson had supreme confidence in his expository powers, and especially in his ability to build a fire of public opinion under the recalcitrant Senate. Clemenceau records that when he expressed doubts Wilson "invariably replied with an imperturbable confidence." "America," he said in another connection, "has taken much from me. She will take this also."

But if Wilson was naïve, what shall we say about Clemenceau? The wily old Tiger was giving up French claims to a Rhineland buffer state, and reducing Allied occupation of the Rhine from thirty to fifteen years, in return for a guarantee that rested on the whims of a fickle and already hostile United States Senate. Had the assassin's bullet affected his head as well as his lung?

The answer is that Clemenceau knew all about the uncertainties of Wilson's position—possibly better than Wilson did himself—and made what seemed to be ample provision to meet them.

By the specific terms of the Treaty of Versailles (Article 429), the Allied (including French) troops were not required to leave the Rhineland at the end of fifteen years *if France deemed that her position was not secure*—that is, if the Security Treaty had not been ratified. Provision was also made for the Allies to stay if the reparations clauses were not fully lived up to (Article 430). It is clear that a resourceful French government could have so read the treaty as to keep the Rhineland for generations.

So all that France really gave up was the buffer state, which would be of little military value to Germany, because this area would be demilitarized and French troops would be keeping the watch on the Rhine. France would have preferred the Rhineland, for it would have given her definite economic and military advantages; but before surrendering it she made doubly sure of her eastern frontier. As early as April, 1919, she was also busy forging the network of alliances with the nations of the Little Entente on Germany's eastern flank. France believed in forming all the leagues and pacts she could, while keeping her powder dry.

In return for the Rhineland concession, Clemenceau had a fair chance—so it seemed—of effecting a military alliance of transcendent importance to French security. If he won his gamble, he would win a tremendous advantage. If he lost, French soldiers could camp on the Rhine indefinitely. So what could France lose?

6

What else should Clemenceau have done? What else could he have done?

As we have seen, his critics in France assailed him mercilessly for letting the Rhineland go, and for turning up with nothing better than the Security Treaty. But they voted for it.

This was a colossal opportunity. Never before had the British been willing to commit themselves in advance to a guarantee of France's eastern border. Never before had the United States been willing to commit itself in advance to protect the borders of any European nation. The two overseas giants, taken together, could form a combination that would frighten Germany into perpetual submission. This would in effect be a continuation of the core of the alliance of the victors. What more could France ask for?

Clemenceau did not solicit the alliance. It was freely offered by Lloyd George and Wilson. Should The Tiger have spurned it? Could he have said that a tiny Rhineland buffer state was worth more than an alliance with the irresistible Anglo-Saxon combination?

All things considered, Wilson is more to be censured for having offered the alliance than Clemenceau for having accepted it. Where the stakes are enormous, a gamble is often worth while, or at least excusable. But this was not even a gamble. The treaty simply did not have as much as a fighting chance in the Senate of the United States, and Wilson should have recognized this. If he had taken Senators to Paris, they doubtless would have told him. Whether he would have listened, after disregarding the advice of House, White, and Lansing, one cannot say.

Even where the odds are a thousand to one, a gamble may be justified if one does not sacrifice too much when the dice fall wrong. On paper, France did not stand to lose a great deal if the Security Treaty did fall through. On paper, she had taken ample steps to protect herself. But there were certain disastrous psychological results that were neither foreseen nor entirely foreseeable.

After the signing of the Treaty of Guarantee, the people of France naturally began to paint roseate pictures of the thousands of ships and millions of men that would come to their aid. When the bottom fell out of the pact, the French were actually not appreciably worse off than they would have been without any treaty. But their expectations had been so great, and their disillusionment was so keen, that they felt betrayed and deserted. They had given up the Rhineland state for false promises of security; now security was denied them; they would have to seek it themselves. "There is nothing in the long run," said the French, "to stand between us and invasion, but the bayonets and breasts of our soldiers."

Bitterness rapidly developed among the erstwhile Allies. The security-obsessed French felt that they had to take stringent, lone-hand measures to guarantee their security, measures for which they now felt they had complete moral if not legal justification. And some of these measures recoiled disastrously upon their authors and played an important part in the undoing of France in 1940.

CHAPTER SIXTEEN

MAKING THE PIPS SQUEAK

"We have been attacked; we want security. We have been despoiled; we demand restitution. We have been devastated; we want reparation." STEPHEN PICHON, *French Minister for Foreign Affairs, December 30, 1918.*

1

WE MUST continue to bear in mind that the problems of the Rhineland occupation, the Rhineland buffer state, and the Treaty of Guarantee, as well as the Saar, were all related to security and to one another, and that they were all solved more or less concurrently. Precisely the same thing may be said of reparations.

The first great battle over reparations was waged by the American delegation in connection with the Allied demand that Germany should pay the entire cost of the war. This, of course, was directly contrary to the pre-Armistice contract, which stipulated that Germany should pay only for civilian damages.

But as the Allies viewed their staggering bills, and observed that the enemy was now completely at their mercy, they began to repent of their bargain. Why should they pay the cost of Germany's aggression, and especially why should France pay— France, whose only crime, in the words of Clemenceau, "is to have taken up arms against the invader!"

Under the pre-Armistice agreement, a French peasant should obviously be compensated for the loss of his ruined farm. But, demanded Prime Minister Hughes of Australia, how about the Australian shepherd who had lost his farm through a mortgage foreclosure resulting from the war? When the American experts objected to this line of reasoning, Hughes accused them of being pro-German, and shouted, shaking his finger in their faces: "Some people in this war have not been so near the fire as we British have, and, therefore, being unburned, they have a cold, detached view of the situation."

The cold Americans stood their ground, and the Allies gave up the fight for total war costs (except for Belgium) in March, 1919. The American delegation received strong support from Wilson, who was then returning to Paris on the *George Washington,* and who wirelessed that he would have to dissent, publicly if necessary, because total war costs were "clearly inconsistent with what we deliberately led the enemy to expect and cannot now honorably alter simply because we have the power."

In the whole struggle over reparations the Americans could preserve a high degree of detachment, in large part because they were asking nothing for themselves. Perhaps they should have asked for something. Ex-President Herbert Hoover thinks that Wilson might well have demanded a share of both territorial spoils and reparations, and then have yielded them in return for concessions to his views. But Wilson was neither a good horse trader nor a poker player. Advancing insincere proposals for bargaining purposes was foreign to his nature and rasping to his Calvinist conscience. Under the new order of things, one laid one's cards on the table as completely as possible.

2

The second great battle over reparations raged about the Allied demand that Allied pension bills should be added to civilian damages. After unaccountably weak resistance, Wilson hoisted the white flag, and in doing so committed what was perhaps his most disastrous and far-reaching blunder at the Conference. This was all the more regrettable because he could almost certainly have held his ground if he had shown the stubbornness on this issue that he did on others.

The economic results of Wilson's capitulation may be

quickly described. The reparations bill, as finally presented to Germany in 1921, totaled approximately $33,000,000,000, of which roughly one-third represented damage to Allied property, and one-half to two-thirds, pensions and similar allowances. In short, Wilson's decision doubled and perhaps tripled the bill. It spelled the difference between a sum that Germany could reasonably be expected to pay—say $10,000,000,000—and one that she could not or would not pay.

But what was wrong with the decision morally? If we accept the proposition that Germany had deliberately and wantonly forced the war on the Allies—and this was an article of faith in the Allied camp—then why should she not be forced to pay for the support of maimed Allied soldiers, and of the widows and orphans whose breadwinners had fallen on the Somme and a dozen other fronts?

There are several answers. First, Wilson had announced in one of his supplementary Fourteen Points speeches, on February 11, 1918, that there should be "no annexations, no contributions, no punitive damages." The inclusion of pensions with actual damages would swell reparations to a point where they probably would be punitive. The word "reparation" itself suggests the repairing of damage done. To multiply this sum by two or three would cause the reparations payments to take on the character of indemnities.

Germany had accepted the Fourteen Points, and they were solemnly written into the pre-Armistice contract. According to both the letter and the spirit of that contract, it would be illegal and immoral to ask for anything beyond actual reparations for civilian damages, the more so since the Germans were now partially disarmed and virtually at the mercy of the Allies.

3

How can we account for Wilson's flagrant flouting of his own principles?

England, unlike France, had no great devastated area, though her merchant marine had suffered heavily. If the British were to receive a substantial share of German reparations, they would have to establish the validity of pension charges. Lloyd George recognized this, and, consummate politician that he was, evolved an argument which appealed to the heart. If France was to be compensated for the loss of a peasant's hut, then why not for the crippled soldier who had once occupied that hut? Was not life more precious than property?

Shortly after Wilson's return to Paris in March, the British financial experts drew up a lengthy memorandum in support of pensions. Wilson, still disliking lawyers, especially verbose lawyers, rather contemptuously threw it out as "very legalistic."

Then Lloyd George had General Smuts, the great South African liberal, try his hand at virtually the same argument, which in this case was concisely and beautifully written. Wilson greatly admired Smuts, and was undoubtedly grateful to him for unwavering support on the League of Nations Commission. So where the legalists had failed, Smuts succeeded. Wilson was persuaded that pensions might be included with reparations.

This unfortunate decision, though supported by some of the American financial experts, was contrary to the unanimous opinion of the American legal experts, whom Wilson had previously asked to tell him what was right. It was contrary to the Fourteen Points. It was contrary to the spirit, if not the letter, of the pre-Armistice contract. It was contrary to every tenet of good faith and honorable dealing.

But Wilson was a stubborn man. He had given his word, and a man of honor must keep his word. The legal experts—these lawyers were most annoying—objected that the decision was

illogical. "Logic! Logic!" Wilson burst out somewhat petu-
lantly. "I don't give a damn for logic. I am going to include
pensions!"

Wilson had also given his word of honor—and the word of
honor of the Allies—to the entire German nation. Then why
should a statesman who set such great store by honorable international dealing have wavered at this critical time? Should not
a pledge given to some 60,000,000 people take precedence over
one later given to a single individual?

The most plausible explanation comes from Wilson's official
biographer, Ray Stannard Baker. At this time the American
financial experts were contending for a reasonable lump-sum
payment, based upon Germany's capacity to pay over a specified number of years. This figure would presumably not cover
more than actual damages, and if the Allies, in apportioning
the money among themselves, chose to set aside a certain
amount for pensions, rather than for reconstruction, this
would obviously have no effect upon Germany.

The tragedy is, as we shall presently see, that the total sum
was not fixed in the treaty, and it was not based upon a reasonable estimate of Germany's capacity to pay. Why Wilson or his
economic experts should have been so confident at this time
that they could carry their point is another unsolved mystery.
It seems clear that Wilson did not understand the full implications of what he was doing. Certainly, as he said on his first
trip to France, he was "not much interested in the economic
subjects" which were to be debated at Paris. This was most
unfortunate, for about half the treaty was devoted to economic
arrangements.

There is one other aspect of the problem. The French
wanted pensions included in reparations, if for no better reason
than that they would add to Germany's burden. The heavier
the reparations, the more difficult it would be for Germany to
struggle to her feet again and be a threat to France. The French
are a traditionally thrifty people, but so great was their passion
for security that if they had been forced to choose between a

powerful Germany able to pay and a prostrate Germany unable to pay, they would almost certainly have chosen the latter.

At the time of the pensions decision, Wilson was opposing French demands on the Saar, the Rhineland, and other matters. This constant opposition to France on issues of seemingly vital importance may have had something to do with his willingness to yield on an issue which seemed to be of no real importance.

But it *was* important—terribly so. It bloated the bill to a point where there was grave doubt as to Germany's capacity to pay. And it gave the Germans additional moral justification for evading payment.

4

The third and final battle was waged by the Americans in behalf of a reasonable, specific lump sum to be named in the treaty and paid over a definite period of years. The Americans lost this too.

The final treaty did not stipulate the maximum Germany would have to pay, or at what time her obligations, when fixed, would end. That was left to the future—in effect a demoralizing blank check on Germany's resources. Nothing is so disheartening to a debtor as not to know how much he owes. If the figure is fixed within his reasonable capacity to pay, he has some incentive to roll up his sleeves and rid himself of the burden. But if it is beyond his capacity to pay, and if he must keep on paying indefinitely through generation after generation, there is no will to pay. There is instead every incentive to evade.

Winston Churchill has well described the Paris Conference as "a turbulent collision of embarrassed demagogues." Nowhere is this better illustrated than in the handling of the reparations problem.

The Allied leaders, Lloyd George in particular, had led their people to believe that Germany could be forced to pay the entire cost of the war which, so it seemed, had so wantonly been forced upon them. In the general election of 1918 the welkin had rung with cries of "Hang the Kaiser"; "Make Germany pay to the last pfennig"; and "Search their pockets." Sir Eric Geddes had cried: "We will get out of her all you can squeeze out of a lemon and a bit more. I will squeeze her until you can hear the pips squeak." George Creel relates that Lloyd George came to Paris grinning, as if it were all a huge joke, "Heaven only knows what I would have had to promise them if the campaign had lasted a week longer."

We may say in defense of Lloyd George—and this is admittedly a lame defense—that he started the campaign on a more moderate note; but when he sensed that this was unpopular he instinctively raised the pitch. We may also say in his defense—and this too is a lame defense—that it was Geddes, and not he, who promised to squeeze Germany until the pips squeaked. A politician cannot be held accountable for every wild outcry of his followers. The canny Welshman had said in effect: "They shall pay to the utmost farthing—*if they can do so without delaying the economic revival of the world.*" "They shall pay the maximum possible—*but what is the maximum possible must be ascertained by financial experts.*"

These were supremely important qualifications, and they provided Lloyd George with a perfect "out." But the masses either do not hear such qualifications, or rapidly forget them. They hear and remember only what they want to hear and remember. Lloyd George was an experienced enough politician to know this, and therein lay the enormity of his crime. Like a pyromaniac scattering firebrands around England, he deliberately whipped up passions at a time when peacemaking demanded a subsidence of passion; he deliberately aroused a feeling of greed when he probably knew in his heart that it could not be completely satisfied. In so doing he did perhaps more than any other one man to make impossible the insertion of a reasonable reparations figure in the treaty. And in a very real sense reparations were the heart of the entire settlement.

Lloyd George came to the Conference distinctly disheveled by his electoral gymnastics, and with the blatant and provocative posters of the recent campaign pinned to his coattails. He was displeased when the austere Woodrow Wilson declined to congratulate him on the success of his demagoguery. Wilson was too honest a Presbyterian to conceal his disgust. The essential point is that Lloyd George had whipped up unrealizable expectations. He could not collect what he had led his people to believe he could collect; but if he failed to collect they would have his head. The magnetic Welshman would have to employ his unusual talents for tightrope walking to the utmost if he was to get out of this corner.

In April, 1919, over 200 members of the Coalition in the British House of Commons, fearing that the Prime Minister was weakening on his election promises, telegraphed him a famous ultimatum, and extorted from him a renewed pledge of delivery. It is an ironical fact that in the actual making of the peace Lloyd George was more embarrassed by his victory than Wilson was by his defeat in the November elections.

5

French estimates of Germany's capacity to pay ran as high as the utterly fantastic figure of $200,000,000,000. Some calculators even included the repayment of France's indemnity to Germany, of 1871, at 5 per cent interest, plus the capital value of all French lives lost in the recent war. Additional moral justification for such colossal sums was provided by the recollection that the Germans, in their hours of triumph, had boasted of the indemnities—$500,000,000,000 was mentioned by some irresponsible persons—that they would exact from their foe. In certain German quarters satisfaction even had been expressed over America's entry into the war: rich Uncle Sam could be gouged for a pretty penny.

Two leading British experts, appropriately called the "heavenly twins," went to work on German reparations and produced the astronomical sum of $120,000,000,000. American advisers estimated that Germany could not pay more than $30,-000,000,000 at the outside. The figure as finally established by the Reparations Commission in 1921 was approximately $33,-000,000,000, but this was ultimately whittled down to about $8,000,000,000 in the Young Plan of 1929. If this sum had been settled upon in 1919, the Germans might have accepted it with good grace, and the whole story might well have been different. But the men of 1919 were looking at their problem through the colored glasses of 1919, not of 1929.

Thus it was that the estimates made so lightly in the enthusiasm of victory remained to embarrass the demagogues at the Conference. Their sober second thought recognized that Germany could not pay anywhere near these maximum figures, and that to put them into the treaty would completely remove all incentive to payment. Perhaps the Germans would refuse to sign the treaty at all, and Europe would lapse into anarchy. If they did sign and tried to pay such monstrous amounts, they might be plunged into economic chaos and not be able to pay anything. Or, worse yet, they might pull the victors down into the economic morass with them.

Yet the demagogues could not go back to their people on bended knees and say that they had made a mistake. They could not confess that Germany was unable to pay more than one-tenth of the amount expected. If they did this, they would be replaced immediately by new demagogues. And this would mean further delay in making the treaty.

There was one possible way by which the negotiators could save face, and in some measure justify a manageable sum. If the Americans would renounce all claims to the approximately $10,000,000,000 which the Allies had borrowed from them, then the Allies could reduce by that much the amount that Germany could reasonably be expected to pay.

This proposal was made repeatedly at the Conference, and repeatedly after the Conference. Wilson opposed it, his economic advisers opposed it, the United States Treasury opposed it, the United States Congress opposed it, and the American taxpayers opposed it. Our perfectly understandable attitude on the debt problem had a great deal to do with the reparations muddle.

6

The demagogues had no alternative but to postpone the fixing of the final figure. Speed was still at a premium; the Bolsheviks were on the march; pressing problems of boundaries had to be settled. There was no time to make a careful and scientific estimate of Germany's capacity to pay. A lump sum, worked out by rule-of-thumb methods, might conceivably prove too small, and leave the goose with a few unplucked feathers. Clemenceau argued that, no matter how much he got, French public opinion would demand twice as much, and call him a traitor.

The Americans, as we have seen, fought for a lump sum, based on Germany's capacity to pay, set at a reasonable figure, and paid over a thirty-year period. Norman H. Davis, one of the American experts, pleaded that "the enslavement of one generation was enough." The Allies fought for an indefinite figure, to be paid over an indefinite period, and based not upon capacity but upon Allied claims.

The Americans lost every one of these points. The crucial decisions were made when Wilson was ill with influenza, and when House was representing him on the Council of Four. On some of these matters House consulted Wilson; on others he acted on his own responsibility, thus committing Wilson to a position which he later reluctantly endorsed.

From the American point of view there was one saving feature: the all-important. Reparations Commission. This body, which grew out of the proposal of an American expert, would be clothed with enormous powers to fix and collect reparations. The United States would be represented on it; and under moderate American influence, and in a sane, peacetime atmosphere, the reparations problem would be dispassionately

studied, and the final figure set at a reasonable sum. The demagogues would save face; Germany would be fairly dealt with.
And the Americans in the end would win the battles they had
lost on pensions, on a fixed sum, and on a definite time for payment.

The supreme irony is that the United States never ratified
the treaty, and never took a seat on the Reparations Commis-

Soaked!
(Courtesy of the Columbus *Dispatch*)

sion. Control fell into other and less moderate hands, and the
purposes of the Americans were defeated by other Americans.
But this is another story.

The net result was a house-that-Jack-built debacle. Wilson
surrendered on pensions, presumably because he assumed that
the reparations figure would be fixed and reasonable. It was
neither. Colonel House and Wilson surrendered on a fixed and

reasonable figure, to be paid over a limited period, partly because they assumed that the Reparations Commission would
be moderate. It was not.

We have observed that the Americans won the first of the
three battles on reparations: that against saddling the entire
cost of the war on Germany. In the end they lost this battle too,
because the final figure was put so high as to amount in effect
to the same thing.

7

The budget of blunders does not end here. A word must be
said about Article 231 of the Treaty of Versailles—the famous
"war guilt clause," which was the preamble to the reparations
section. It reads: "The Allied and Associated governments
affirm and Germany accepts the responsibility of Germany and
her allies for causing all the loss and damage to which the
Allied and Associated governments and their nationals have
been subjected as a consequence of the war imposed upon them
by the aggression of Germany and her allies." This did not say,
as the Germans attempted to make it say, that Germany was
solely responsible for starting the war. It merely said that Germany accepted for herself *and her allies,* which included Austria-Hungary, the responsibility for causing all the losses
growing out of the war—a war brought on by the aggression of
Germany and her allies. Whatever the causes, immediate or
remote, it is clear that the fighting started when Austrian
troops invaded Serbia.

But, whether true or not, this war-guilt statement is a classic
example of how political chickens can come home to roost and
embroil international relations.

From the German point of view there were two figures:
what Germany could pay, and what she would pay. There
was a wide gap between the two sums. From the point of view
of the Allies there were two figures: what they had led their
people to think they could collect, and what they could actually

collect. There was a tremendous gap between the two sums.

By this time it was clear that nothing like the entire cost of the war could be extorted from exhausted Germany. But from a political point of view it did not seem wise to let the Hun off without some statement of liability. He should be made to confess that he was responsible for the cost of the conflict, even though he was not going to pay for it all. This, presumably, would do something to cushion the disappointment of the Allied electorates. It would also provide a moral and legal basis for collecting reasonable reparations.

The irony of this whole wretched controversy is that it was thoroughly unnecessary, because the "war guilt" clause was unnecessary, except perhaps as a weak sop to home opinion. The Armistice contract, which Germany had signed, had provided a perfect legal basis for collecting reparations for civilian damages, without dragging in the inflammatory issue of moral turpitude and punitive exactions.

The Germans did not then believe, have never believed, and will never believe that they and their allies were solely responsible for all the damage caused by the war. They even cited Wilson's pre-1917 pronouncements to the effect that no one nation had brought on this terrible catastrophe. They had the effrontery not only to deny their own guilt but to believe that the Allies were guilty instead. They cried out bitterly against having to sign such a lie as was embedded in Article 231, and when forced to sign under duress they mentally and orally repudiated what they were signing.

8

The moral indignation of the German people was kept warm by the fuel of a more practical consideration. The Allies, it was felt, were assessing reparations because Germany and her allies had been solely responsible for the war. If the Germans could prove that this was not true, why could they not reasonably demand that the burden be lightened or removed?

This seemingly innocent "war guilt" clause, which was flagrantly misrepresented by German propaganda, erupted into a veritable volcano of passion. It caused liberal sentiment throughout the world to sympathize with the Germans and encourage them. It caused German opinion to keep up a constant clatter against this clause and the entire treaty of which it was a part. And no German demagogue appealed more successfully to this anti-war-guilt prejudice than Adolf Hitler.

One finds no evidence that either Wilson or his advisers put up a fight against the "war guilt clause." Why did Wilson fail to do so? If he had statesmanlike vision at all, should he not have foreseen, even faintly, some of the evil consequences lurking in this seemingly innocent statement?

There are several possible explanations. Perhaps he was not interested in this preamble to the dull reparations section, and read it hurriedly or not at all. Perhaps he was worn down by trying to head off what were seemingly more disastrous things. It was both embarrassing and nerve-racking to have to say "No, no, no."

The true explanation probably lies elsewhere. Wilson and his advisers and practically everyone else of any consequence at the Conference believed that this simple statement of Germany's guilt was true. Whatever doubts Wilson may have had before 1917 quickly melted away when he entered the fiery furnace with the Allies. And since the ·war guilt clause was true—indeed self-evident—what was wrong with it?

Wilson breathed the same war-charged air as his contemporaries; he viewed problems through the same heavy fog of passion and prejudice. We cannot condemn him for not having seen what no one else could see. We can only regret that the peace had to be made in such an atmosphere.

CHAPTER SEVENTEEN

OPEN DISAGREEMENTS
OPENLY ARRIVED AT

"The whole world is speculating as to whether the Italians are 'bluffing' or whether they really intend going home and not signing the Peace unless they have Fiume. It is not unlike a game of poker." COLONEL HOUSE, *April 22, 1919.*

1

EVEN THE most ardent admirers of Woodrow Wilson find it difficult to explain, much less to justify, his extraordinarily inept handling of the Italian question.

Shortly after reaching Paris, and before the Conference formally convened, Wilson made his first costly blunder. He promised the Italians that their northern frontier might be drawn along the line of the Brenner Pass—which meant that more than 200,000 Austrian-Germans would be handed over to alien rule.

This was a flagrant violation of two of the Fourteen Points. Wilson had proclaimed that the frontiers of Italy should be readjusted along "clearly recognizable lines of nationality." This readjustment completely overshot the mark. He had proclaimed the sacred principle of self-determination. The Germans of the Austrian South Tyrol wanted no part of Italian overlordship.

Liberal observers were profoundly shocked and disillusioned. The area involved was not large, but the principle was. At the very outset of the Conference anxious inquirers began to ask themselves and one another: "Can Wilson be trusted?" Harold Nicolson, who was there, later wrote of the current feeling that, "if Wilson could swallow the Brenner, he would swallow anything."

No one will deny that the peace settlements contained a

number of glaring violations of self-determination. But these generally came about after long discussion and final compromise: a discussion often involving historical, geographical, economic, linguistic, religious, strategic, political, cultural, nationalistic, and racial considerations. The new boundary lines, thousands of miles in length, had to be run somewhere, and it is scarcely ever possible to draw a line without doing violence to at least one of these many factors. In some instances the negotiators decided—and properly so—that economic, strategic, and other advantages were of more importance to the inhabitants than self-determination.

But in the case of the South Tyrol, there was no long debate and no compromise. Wilson apparently asked for nothing in return. He just promised the Italians the 200,000 Germans.

Various explanations have been offered, none of them completely satisfying. Perhaps Wilson felt that this concession was necessary to enlist Italian support for the League. Perhaps he believed that he could moderate even more objectionable Italian demands in the Adriatic—much as one would moderate the appetite of a ravenous animal by throwing it a choice morsel of raw meat. Almost certainly he was impressed by the plea of the Italians that they needed the line of the Brenner as a strategic frontier against future invasion. (The Italians were careful not to point out that a defensible line excluding the great bulk of the Germans could have been drawn farther south.)

The most reasonable and least flattering explanation is that Wilson was ignorant of what he was promising. After the Conference was over he admitted to one of the experts that the decision was due to "insufficient study." The general feeling among the American delegation was that he had made the promise hastily, that he afterwards regretted it, but that he felt bound by his word.

The clarion call, "Tell me what's right and I'll fight for it," was still ringing in the ears of the American advisers. In many instances Wilson fought for what the experts recommended; in some instances he ran counter to their recommendations; in this instance he apparently did not even consult them. Wilson did not very often make similar promises out of

Proposed Italian Gains Under Treaty of London

the depths of his ignorance, but this one went far beyond the personal fortunes of the Tyrolese, who, as the result of a "deal" between Hitler and Mussolini, were brutally uprooted in 1939 and driven back onto German soil.

2

Italy, in pursuance of her policy of *sacro egoismo* ("sacred selfishness" or "consecrated selfishness"), had entered the war in response to inducements held out in the secret Treaty of London. This pact, among other things, promised Italy the Brenner frontier.

We have already noted that Wilson might have brought about a repudiation of all the secret treaties at the very outset of the Conference by a resounding declaration against them. His prompt and premature surrender on the South Tyrol indicated to the Italians that he was not only prepared to recognize but even support the unsavory Treaty of London. Italian "selfishness" became even more "consecrated," and the appetite for other forbidden fruit began to grow.

The choicest of the forbidden plums was the Austro-Hungarian port of Fiume. If Wilson would lightly yield the South Tyrol, with its 200,000 pure Germans, why would he not also yield Fiume, which contained a considerable colony of pure Italians?

The South Tyrol surrender was more than a violation of two of the Fourteen Points; it was a violation of the ABC's of diplomacy. When Wilson offhandedly promised Italy the Tyrol, he asked for nothing in return. Perhaps he expected something in return; but in diplomacy, as in other fields of human endeavor, it is usually unwise to pay in advance.

In any game—and diplomacy is no exception—a player does not discard his ace of trumps on the very first round. This is precisely what Wilson did. When the Italians later demanded Fiume, which was not promised them by the Treaty of London, Wilson had nothing to offer them in return for giving up their demands.

Technically speaking—and this Wilson conceded—the Italians were not bound by the Fourteen Points in their claims for the South Tyrol and other parts of the defunct Austro-

Hungarian Empire. The pre-Armistice contract with Germany
included the Fourteen Points, but this did not concern the
Italians because Germany had nothing they particularly
wanted. Besides, Italy had entered a mumbled reservation during the pre-Armistice negotiations in Paris regarding her
territorial aspirations. As for Austria-Hungary, which had
what the Italians wanted, there was no pre-Armistice contract
based on the Fourteen Points. The Austrians were so far gone
when they surrendered that they were in no position to claim
such a safeguard. When Clemenceau read the terms offered
them he remarked: "We have left the breeches of the Emperor,
and nothing else."

Yet there was a strong moral obligation which Wilson failed
to exploit to its full advantage. Italy, we remember, had officially accepted the Fourteen Points with regard to Germany,
though with unclear reservations. If Wilson, at the outset of
the Conference, when his prestige was still paramount, had
emphatically announced that there could be no double standard, and that Italy was also bound to observe the Fourteen
Points with regard to Austria, he might conceivably have carried the day. Having won this redoubt, he might then have
moved on to an assault against the Treaty of London.

Wilson took no strong stand at the outset, and during the
later negotiations rather weakly argued that it was immoral to
have two standards. Above all, he surrendered on the South
Tyrol, which seemed to indicate that the Fourteen Points did
not apply to Austria, and that the Treaty of London had the
full sanction of the United States.

Apologists for Wilson speak of the Tyrol decision as a "slip."
It was more than a slip: it was a blunder. And a blunder, as
the proverb has it, may be worse than a crime.

3

If the Tyrol was a "slip," what shall we say of Fiume?

The bothersome Treaty of London promised Italy certain Italian-inhabited areas along the eastern shore of the Adriatic Sea, but, contrary to the principle of self-determination, about 500,000 unwilling Slavs would have to go along with the Italians. The vital port of Fiume was not awarded to Italy: it was specifically reserved to the yet unborn Jugoslavia. Significantly, Italian opinion was not then counting on Fiume: the great battle cries were "Trento" and "Trieste."

If the Conference had moved rapidly, it is possible that Italy would have pressed no serious claims for Fiume. But as time dragged on, Italian appetite (*sacro egoismo*) increased, especially when it was noted that Italy, for all her sacrifices, was not going to get much out of the war, while France and Great Britain were making off with vast colonial empires. Verily, complained the Italian press, the scriptural dictum was being fulfilled: "For whosoever hath, to him shall be given . . ."

So the Italians entered their claim to Fiume, buttressed it by an armed occupation which angered Wilson, and pressed it with noisy insistence during the height of the crisis over the Saar, the Rhineland, reparations, and other problems. Even this early in the game it was rumored that the Italian delegation was threatening to bolt the Conference if its demands were not granted. Wilson was not unnaturally annoyed by this technique of bargain, bluff, bluster, and grab.

On the face of it, the Italians had a fairly good case. Fiume would strategically strengthen their northeastern frontier. It would enable them to dominate the Adriatic both militarily and commercially. It would stifle the military and commercial rivalry of the powerful and much-hated new Serb state. Finally, it would vindicate the principle of self-determination, for a majority of the dwellers within Fiume proper were Italians.

4

Actually, the case against Italy was very strong. She was evidently trying to play both ends against the middle: standing on the Treaty of London for the other parts of Austria-Hungary, and brushing aside the Treaty of London because it gave Fiume to Jugoslavia. She was denying self-determination to the Germans of the Tyrol, while insisting on self-determination for the Italians of Fiume.

The fine Italian hand even went so far as to produce faked photographs. Pictures were shown of a great crowd in Fiume, with uplifted hands, allegedly voting in an informal plebiscite for annexation to Italy. Upon investigation it was discovered that Italian officials had gone to this hunger-ridden city with supplies, and had asked all those who wanted bread to raise their hands.

As a matter of fact, while the heart of Fiume was Italian, the suburbs and the surrounding area were Slav. Italy had to annex thousands of Slavs in order to reclaim 30,000 countrymen: an islet of Italians in a great Slavonian sea. It was ridiculous, as Wilson pointed out, to claim little islands of nationals wherever they might be: the map of Europe would have spots all over it. The Italians might on the same basis as logically claim the hundreds of thousands of their compatriots in New York City.

The Italians disclaimed self-determination in the Tyrol; claimed it in Fiume; and then got angry when it was pointed out that Fiume was not Italian. What of it, they said? The Allied leaders had already violated self-determination in handing over Germans to the Poles in the Danzig corridor. Then why get so self-righteous, especially at Italy's expense? Baron Sonnino, who went so far as to threaten suicide, charged that Wilson, having lost his virginity in dealing with Germany, was now seeking to regain it at the expense of Italy.

The already tangled situation was further snarled by the

emergence of the new Serb-Croat state. When Italy was promised the Dalmatian coast and other parts of the Adriatic area, those places had belonged to the common enemy, Austria-Hungary. Now a new nation had arisen which not only was friendly to the Allies but had rendered them substantial help in the closing stages of the war. After all, one has to deal more generously with an ally than with an enemy.

Jugoslavia needed Fiume, because this was her only feasible outlet to the sea, and it would be inviting trouble—Balkan trouble—to bring a vigorous new nation into the world and then try to smother it economically. President Wilson had recognized this explosive situation when in Point XI he had promised the new Serb state a "free and secure access to the sea." The logical "access" was Fiume, to which Jugoslavia was also entitled by a later point, self-determination. The Treaty of London also promised Fiume to Jugoslavia, and Italy took her stand on this treaty—where it was to her advantage to do so.

Clemenceau and Lloyd George, having already disposed of the German problem, did not view the squabble with Italy as of transcendent importance. They did not like the Treaty of London; it was a disagreeable bargain. But England and France had given their word, Italy had entered the war, and there was nothing to do but honor the bond—which excluded Fiume. Italy might have Fiume or she might have the Treaty of London, but she could not have both.

The Italians had one sentimental argument that they harped on constantly: their terrible sacrifices in the war. They also insisted that they had saved the Allies five times, once in 1914 when they had declined to stab France in the back. But Clemenceau and Lloyd George were not much moved. They remembered that the Italians had hardly pulled their own weight in the boat. They had moved with painful slowness, except at Caporetto, when the roof fell in; and then they had moved very rapidly—to the rear. The situation had been saved only by the prompt diversion of French and British forces to this sagging front.

The white-bearded Serbian Premier, Nikola Pashitch, weary of listening to tales of Italian sacrifices, remarked quietly: "In battle many more men are killed in running away than in fighting."

5

Wilson's Tyrol blunder was probably the result of too little study; his Fiume blunder was perhaps the result of too much study. He worked on this problem as on no other, assimilating lengthy reports from the experts, and getting down on his hands and knees and poring over a large and specially prepared relief map of the Dalmatian coast. He finally concluded that Italy had no legal or moral right to Fiume, and there he took his stand.

At one time Wilson seriously considered making Fiume a free city, not unlike Danzig. But on this issue his best qualified experts were against him. Some of the experts, like Professor Douglas W. Johnson, were experts on this particular region, and some of them, like David Hunter Miller (the "House group") were experts on other matters. The expert experts were for denying Fiume completely to Italy; the non-expert experts were for a compromise which would save the face of the Italians by giving them actual though not nominal control.

The real experts claimed that the establishment of a free port at Fiume would be an injustice to Jugoslavia, and unworkable. Wilson was not convinced. Then they drew up an eloquent and moving appeal, reminding him of his splendid ideals, and of his pledge on the *George Washington*: "Tell me what's right and I'll fight for it." This turned the tide. They told him, and he fought to the last ditch.

This quarrel among the experts bore evil fruit. Colonel House took his stand for compromise with the non-experts, and pursued so ambiguous a course as to raise the suspicion that he was deliberately trying to deceive Wilson as to the anti-

Italian position of the real experts. The Colonel was also so indiscreet as to meet with Clemenceau and Lloyd George in his room (the "Little White House") for a secret conclave. Wilson found them there with their heads together, and in a stern voice said: "Hello, what is this about?" Colonel House's well-meaning but somewhat devious handling of this whole situation aroused Wilson's growing suspicions, and paved the way for the final break.

Ill-feeling between House and Wilson was paralleled by ill-feeling among the experts. The real experts resented the intrusion of the non-experts, and the non-experts felt that the experts were so blinded by a close study of geographical, ethnographical, and strategic maps that they could not grasp the larger and more statesmanlike view—that is, compromise. The Italians got wind of this quarrel in the American delegation, and were emboldened to stand more adamantly for their claims.

Wilson personally disliked having to oppose the Italian demands. Orlando was a delightful person, and he had supported Wilson foursquare on the League of Nations Commission. After a particularly unhappy conference with Orlando, Wilson remarked that only once before had he experienced such a distressing time. When he was President of Princeton, a woman who was about to have a serious operation came to him and pleaded for an hour and a half against the expulsion of her son, alleging that the double shock would kill her. Wilson denied her request on the ground that his responsibility to the university was greater than his responsibility for her health. The son was expelled; the mother had the operation—and recovered. Principle triumphed.

6

Wilson always had—or thought he had—one ace in the hole. He could always, as a last resort, appeal to the people—to his own people, or to the people of the world. During the war his own people had responded gratifyingly (except for the October appeal); and the people of the rest of the world had rallied magnificently to his Fourteen Points. At various times during the Conference he had toyed with the idea of making public statements to gain his point, but now was the time to cut the Gordian knot.

He would draw up a friendly appeal setting forth the unvarnished facts of the Fiume controversy, so that the people of Italy would know the exact situation, as well as the attitude of the United States. There might, he felt, be a temporary uproar; but with the passage of time his manifesto would correct the false picture presented by the poisoned Italian press.

The appeal was discussed in the Council of Four, and hence could not have been a surprise to Orlando. It was studied and approved by Wilson's advisers. It was a well written, temperate, and logical statement; and if presented through the regular channels as a diplomatic note it would have been unobjectionable. One wonders why Wilson did not address his statement first to Orlando, and then publish it in the press. In this way he could have made known his views to the world, as well as to Italy, without intolerably affronting the Italian government.

But the appeal was not sent through the ordinary diplomatic channels. It was given directly to the press, on April 23, 1919, and promptly emblazoned on the front page of every important newspaper. It was in effect an unprecedented appeal to the Italian people over the heads of their regularly constituted representatives. Lord Riddell, remembering the secrecy which had enshrouded the Conference up to this time, sneered: "Which of the Fourteen Points does that come under?"

This was open diplomacy with a vengeance, and the results were sensational. Orlando and Sonnino quit the Conference, ostensibly in high dudgeon, but not in high enough dudgeon to forget to keep their experts on the job looking after Italy's "sacred" interests. Actually Orlando left in sorrow rather than in anger, and allegedly to seek new instructions from Parliament, now that his authority had been called into question.

Upon returning to Rome, Orlando was greeted by cheering throngs like a conquering Caesar. When he shouted to an enormous crowd, "Have I properly interpreted the will of the Italian people?" he was greeted with a tremendous "Yes." From the turbulent throng came cries: "Down with Wilson! Long live America!" The Italian press and public in effect made a counterappeal to the American people over the head of Wilson to support them in their "sacred selfishness." Orlando received a tremendous vote of confidence, which was unanimous in the Senate, and 382 to 40 in the Chamber.

Wilson was a fallen idol in Italy. Lips that had blessed him now cursed him; tablets that had honored him were draped in cloth; streets that had been named after him were rechristened —Fiume or D'Annunzio. A story, probably apocryphal, drifted back to Paris of a perfervid Italian orator who was discoursing on the glory that had once been Italy's. He mentioned Tasso (loud cheers), Dante (loud cheers), Galileo (loud cheers), and finally Cristoforo Colombo (dead silence broken by a few hisses).

7

Why did Wilson make this reverberating blunder? Did he not realize that all people resent having an outsider appeal to them over the heads of their own authorities? Did he not remember enough of the five-volume American history that he had written to know that when Citizen Genêt, the French envoy in 1793, threatened to appeal over the head of Washington to the admiring masses, he too became a fallen idol?

The answer is difficult to find, the more so since Wilson's fellow commissioners knew in advance about the projected appeal, and apparently favored it. Even Clemenceau and Lloyd George impliedly approved, at least by silence.

We have already referred to Wilson's appeal habit, which no

doubt had something to do with his decision. It is also probable that his head had been turned to some degree by the
overwhelming adulation of the Italian masses in January. Only
a scant few weeks earlier, hundreds of thousands of Italians
had shouted for Wilson and a peace of justice. Did he not have
reason to feel that they would put him above Orlando; justice
above greed? If so, Wilson misread not only history but human
nature.

In one other respect Wilson revealed an almost unbelievable naïveté. It is true that the appeal was published in Italy;
but not until Orlando had prepared a misleading reply, and
had followed it up with others that utterly obscured or mis-
interpreted the facts which Wilson was trying to lay before the
Italian people. Knowing that Italy was inflamed by war passions, and that she had lost hundreds of thousands of her
sturdiest sons, and that she was greedy for territory, and that
she was getting little out of the war, and that her press was
controllable, and that her leaders were unscrupulous, how
could Wilson have hoped to present the facts to the Italians,
or to have swayed them with the facts if presented fairly?

8

In a very real sense the repercussions of this unfortunate
appeal have not to this day subsided.

The Italian withdrawal precipitated a crisis of which the
Japanese took full advantage to press their claims to Shantung.
We shall have more to say about this distressing business in
the next chapter.

The Germans, enheartened by the rift in the ranks of the
Allies, were encouraged not to sign the Treaty of Versailles,
and this added greatly to the tension of May and June.

Lloyd George took advantage of the absence of the Italians
to induce Wilson and Clemenceau to consent to a Greek landing at Smyrna, on the Turkish coast of Anatolia, an operation

which was supported by British, French, and *American* war-ships. This area had been provisionally promised to Italy, but Lloyd George was anxious to rush through other arrangements before the Italian delegates should come back to Paris. Why Wilson consented to have a hand in this secret deal is difficult to explain; Ray Stannard Baker shamefacedly dis-

"Are We Downhearted? Nein!"

(Courtesy of the Brooklyn *Eagle*)

misses it as the most "disreputable intrigue of the Conference." He thinks that Wilson was moved by the eloquence of Eleutherios Venizelos, the Greek premier, and by the fact that Smyrna was a Greek city. (Self-determination could be used to cover many sins.) In any event, the landing of the hated Greeks aroused prostrate and dispirited Turkey, and ultimately led to the undoing of the whole Near Eastern settlement.

This is not the least of the ironies at Paris. While laboring for a League to end wars, Wilson consented to unleash the Greeks against the Turks, and thus start a war which lasted for three years, and cost tens of thousands of lives.

While Orlando and Sonnino sulked, the British and French arranged to divide up Germany's African colonies, leaving the Italians completely out in the cold. Italy later accepted these arrangements with the understanding that she would receive compensations elsewhere, but these were never satisfactorily forthcoming. Here we find one basis for Italy's enduring bitterness over the final settlement, for the rape of Ethiopia in 1935, and for Mussolini's "stab in the back" of 1940.

Fiume was to the Italians but a third-rate port, and one for which they had but recently developed a synthetic appetite. History can offer few comparable instances where so small a matter set in train such momentous consequences.

American public opinion on the whole applauded Wilson's sensational excursion into the field of open covenants. This was shirt-sleeve diplomacy in the American tradition, and it was perhaps his one act at Paris that was most heartily praised. Wilson was right, or so it seemed; and those who thought that he had been wobbling badly on the Fourteen Points were delighted by this startling exhibition of backbone. Joseph P. Tumulty cabled from the White House that he had never been so proud of Wilson. A number of congratulatory telegrams poured in on the President from Serb and Croat groups in America.

But the Italian-American element did not applaud: the "old country" was not being properly treated. Henry Cabot Lodge of Massachusetts did not applaud; hundreds of thousands of indignant Italian-Americans lived in his constituency. This learned "scholar in politics" publicly informed the Italians of Massachusetts that Fiume was as essential to Italy as the mouth of the Mississippi had been to the United States in the nineteenth century. Henry White patiently wrote Lodge from Paris that this was true of Jugoslavia but not Italy. Yet the learned Senator refused to see the error of his ways. Could it be that this was because there were more Italian than Jugoslav voters in his state?

9

Yet what else could Wilson have done?

We can hardly blame him for opposing Italy's claim to an unconditional cession of Fiume, for he had the right on his side, and he was pledged to redeem his Fourteen Points. But one can hardly escape the conclusion that the appeal was a tremendous blunder, the more so since its immediate results were both avoidable and predictable.

One of the most unfortunate aspects of this whole affair is that Wilson received the blame for having robbed Italy of Fiume. The fact is that both Lloyd George and Clemenceau privately stood squarely with Wilson on this issue, and submitted their views to Orlando in a powerful *unpublished* memorandum, just as the latter was about to entrain for Rome.

Wilson was evidently led to believe, according to Ray Stannard Baker, that Lloyd George and Clemenceau would follow up the public appeal with supporting statements of their own. When they failed to do so, and when the storm broke in all its fury, Wilson, according to his wife, grew "white with anger." Mrs. Wilson says that, when an explanation was asked for, the answer was that Wilson's statement was so comprehensive that there was no point in adding anything to it.

There is no further evidence, not even in Ray Stannard Baker, that this story is correct in the sharp outlines that Mrs. Wilson gives. If it is true, then Wilson erred in not coming to a more definite understanding with Lloyd George and Clemenceau, in not arranging for the simultaneous publication of statements, and in not guarding against the unfortunate trap into which his wife claims he fell.

But one thing stands out clearly. Lloyd George and Clemenceau, though privately supporting Wilson, were quite content to let him subject his idealistic head to the delirium of indignation that burst upon it. They quite naturally had no desire to run from cover and become co-sharers of the storm. Wilson's seeming isolation enabled Orlando to give the false impression that Wilson stood alone, and this made the Italian people even more determined in their demands.

If Wilson had avoided a public scandal, the three great Allied leaders would have continued to present their views to Orlando privately, either individually or collectively, and Orlando would have been put in an intolerable position. If he had then bolted the Conference, he would not have returned to Rome as a conquering hero but as one who was publicly confessing failure. He would have been written down as a touchy, huffy person, who had bungled the game.

Things could hardly have worked out better for Orlando if he had planned them that way. Wilson played right into his hands; and Orlando became the hero, while Wilson became the "goat." The London *Morning Post* referred caustically to "Wild-west diplomacy," and added: "Mr. Wilson's name among the Allies is like that of the rich uncle, and they have accepted his manners out of respect for his means." The London *Daily Express* said that this was "open diplomacy gone mad," and urged that Wilson follow Orlando's excellent example and go home.

10

The Fiume affair has often been represented as a victory for Wilson—which it was not, except perhaps morally.

The Italians came back to the Conference just before the treaty was formally presented to the Germans. Negotiations over Fiume went tiresomely on. Lloyd George tried a new tack. He offered to buy the Italians out of Fiume with Turkish territory, to which he had no right, and when the Italians began to nibble at the bait, he sought to buy them out of

Turkish territory with Fiume, to which he had no right. The Italians were confused, as was everyone else, including Lloyd George. Wilson had to sit through these sordid discussions, and they must have been a trial to his sensitive soul. Certainly by taking part in these negotiations he sullied his raiment, and compromised the high idealism of his Fiume manifesto.

The American experts went to work on a compromise plan, under which there would be a plebiscite at Fiume. If the Jugoslavs lost, a new port would be constructed for them. Wilson finally vetoed the proposal when it became evident that only the United States had money for building seaports, and that the American people would probably balk at such extravagances. It was enough of a burden to feed Europe without going to the expense of creating fancy ports.

In 1920 a treaty between Italy and Jugoslavia recognized Fiume as a free state in perpetuity. This proving unsatisfactory, a new treaty was negotiated in 1924 giving Italy Fiume, while awarding Jugoslavia the harbor of Porta Baros and a fifty-year lease of a part of the harbor of Fiume. So Italy got Fiume, in spite of Wilson's dramatic effort.

In retrospect it seems as though Wilson's most fundamental mistake in this matter was not to press for the free-city solution. Here he was confused by the two groups of experts, each of which was right from its point of view. On the narrow grounds of race, geography, and economics Jugoslavia should have had Fiume. The non-expert experts like Colonel House did not know much about these technicalities, but they did recognize the explosiveness of the political situation and the necessity of not driving the Italians into a corner. A peace settlement of this nature cannot be made in a geological laboratory.

The basic explanation of Wilson's stubbornness on the Fiume issue is no doubt partly psychological. He had slipped badly on the Tyrol, and there was a natural impulse to retrieve his moral position, at least partially. He had been forced to yield so much to the French and the British, and had been criticized so savagely for doing so, that when the time came to stand up against Italy he did so, especially since he had an iron-clad case and also the silent backing of both Lloyd George and Clemenceau. So he stood up, and the heavens descended.

One tragedy of the Peace Conference was that men compromised when they should have stood up, and they stood up when they should have compromised. But they were mortal men, and it was not given them to see the future.

CHAPTER EIGHTEEN

THE YELLOW PERIL

*"They [the Japanese] are not bluffers, and they will go home
unless we give them what they should not have."* WOODROW
WILSON, *April, 1919.*

1

THE ATTITUDE of the Japanese delegates at Paris was something of a mystery. They were primarily concerned with the
Far East; and the Conference was essentially a European affair.
They did not claim membership on the Council of Four, but
they faithfully attended the various other councils, commissions, and committees on which they were assigned seats. They
always seemed interested and awake, which could not be said
of their Occidental associates; but what they were thinking
lay behind an impenetrable Oriental mask. They intently examined the various charts and maps which were presented, but
whether they studied them right side up or bottom side up
one could not always tell. They were the "silent partners of
the peace."

On one occasion, in a minor commission, there was a tied
vote, and the chairman turned to the Japanese delegate for the
deciding voice. "Do you vote," he asked, "with the French
and the Americans, or with the British and the Italians?" The
inscrutable little yellow man sucked in his breath and responded simply, "Yes."

If the Japanese sat like brown Buddhas when non-Asiatic
interests were involved, they left no doubt as to where they
stood when their own interests were affected. Having kept
quiet on matters that did not concern them directly, they
spoke with all the more authority when they finally broke
their silence. And they did so with directness, clarity, and
pertinacity.

The Japanese came to Paris with three demands: first, a formal recognition of the principle of race equality; second, title to the German islands of the North Pacific; third, acquisition of Germany's economic and other rights in the Chinese province of Shantung.

We have already considered the disposal of the German islands in the North Pacific, which Japan finally received under a League mandate. Let us now turn to the Japanese fight for a formal and explicit recognition of the principle of racial equality.

Some writers insist that Japan was not really sincere in pushing this proposal, but that she was merely advancing it as a bargaining lever. If, as she had reason to fear, she was rebuffed, she would be able to advance other and more tangible claims with greater force.

There can be little doubt that the racial equality issue was used as a bargaining lever, and to some extent was intended as such. But the evidence indicates strongly that the Japanese were sincere in making this proposal, and that they regarded it as of the greatest importance. One has only to follow the Japanese press during the Conference to recognize that racial equality was bracketed on a more or less equal basis with the North Pacific islands and German rights in Shantung.

2

The Japanese are a proud and sensitive people. Judged by Western standards, they are too proud and sensitive, and they ought to mend their ways. But some day we may discover that our disapproval will not cause people to change their national characteristics. The very first principle of diplomatic intercourse is that we must take people as we find them, and make due allowance for their distinctive traits.

The basic facts are that the Japanese are small in stature, and that they were then small in territory. Until 1904 they were looked down upon with a certain degree of amused tolerance by outside peoples. But this feeling quickly changed to respect when, in the Russo-Japanese War of 1904–1905, Nippon administered a sound beating to the largest and most populous of the white nations.

As a result of this bloody conflict, the Japanese began to display a certain cockiness. Not only that, but large numbers of energetic coolies began to emigrate to the sun-bathed slopes of our Pacific Coast. The white laborers, fearing for their standard of living, demanded and secured barriers against this influx, and even established restrictions against the owning of land by Nipponese.

Similar bars were erected by the Canadians and by the people of Australasia. The Australians, facing as they did the teeming hives of the Orient, and thinly peopling a vast land, lived in almost daily dread of a yellow tidal wave.

Basically, the objection to the Japanese coolie was economic. He could allegedly live on a handful of rice and beat down the living standard of the white man. The gravest part of the yellow peril was that a Japanese could apparently get rich on what a white man threw into his garbage can. But economic undesirability shades imperceptibly into social and racial undesirability, and there was undoubtedly a strong race prejudice against the Japanese in the threatened areas.

The plain truth is that Japan was suffering from an inferiority complex, for she felt that she had "arrived." She bitterly resented the interference of the European powers in 1895, when, at the close of the Sino-Japanese War, they had intervened to deprive her of some of her richest spoils. She resented the intrusion of the European powers in the Far East, and especially their blocking out of spheres of interest in China— an area which Japan looked upon as her legitimate field of exploitation. She resented knowing that her nationals were not wanted in the white man's country; that the Japanese, with their centuries-old civilization, were not good enough to associate with whites, or own land, or become citizens.

The Japanese state of mind was further colored by a consciousness that Japan had emerged from the World War as the
dominant power in the Far East. Russia had been bled white,
and was in the throes of revolution. Germany was completely
eliminated. Great Britain and France were war-weary and tax-
burdened. The United States could not even defend its own
Philippines.

Encouraged by all these factors, the Japanese were determined to make a strong bid for racial equality.

3

The big fight came in the commission which drafted the
Covenant of the League of Nations. The Japanese wanted a
specific recognition of the principle of racial equality, but they
were finally willing to compromise on a seemingly innocuous
clause in the preamble. It endorsed the "principle of the
equality of Nations and the just treatment of their nationals."
The dynamite-charged word "race" did not even appear.

Wilson was personally sympathetic with the basic principle
of this innocent-looking clause, for he favored any general
move toward international understanding. But he recognized
that it was a rock upon which his whole program might be
wrecked. Prime Minister Hughes of Australia put up an impassioned fight against racial equality, for "White Australia"
would not tolerate even the faintest suggestion of a wedge that
might be used to pry open her anti-Oriental barriers. Other
British statesmen, with their hundreds of millions of uneasy
colored subjects, preferred to sidestep the whole dangerous
issue.

The question was finally forced to a vote in the League of
Nations Commission, on April 11, 1919. Lord Robert Cecil,
the liberal-minded British statesman, acting under instructions from his government, rather shamefacedly registered an
objection. Wilson, as chairman, then called for the affirmative

vote, and the proposal received eleven votes from the seventeen members present. Wilson did not ask for the negative vote, but in line with previous decisions ruled that the motion had lost because it failed to command unanimous support. The objection of Cecil alone was sufficient to defeat the proposal.

This ruling was technically correct, and Wilson doubtless would have acted as he did even if there had not been tremendous pressure to sidetrack the explosive issue. Hughes of Australia loudly threatened, if the racial equality clause was adopted by the Commission, to tear the Conference wide apart by dragging the whole question out into the open of a plenary session. This, as Wilson well knew, would arouse colored people the world over, and inflame the Japanese-conscious Pacific Coast. Senator Hiram W. Johnson of California and others could be counted on to build up a strong backfire of opposition to the entire League.

The Japanese persisted in their demand for racial equality; but since they perceived that the fight was hopeless, and since they had apparently received assurances from the British on the Shantung deal, they declined to press it. This was the end of the troublesome issue as far as the Conference was concerned, but it was not the end as far as the Japanese were concerned.

The much-misunderstood vote on racial equality came after Wilson's return from the United States, and after he was forced to reassemble the League of Nations Commission for the purpose of considering amendments demanded by the American people. If, as we have already observed, Wilson had taken the necessary steps to anticipate some of these amendments when preparing the original draft, this embarrassment might not have arisen. The Japanese almost certainly would have pressed the racial equality issue to a bitter conclusion in the plenary session, but in this case Wilson would not have been the presiding officer, and he would not have had to make the unfortunate but necessary ruling.

One of the most distressing aspects of this entire episode is that Wilson—and indirectly the United States—was savagely condemned by the Japanese for having seemingly thwarted their desires. The Osaka *Mainichi* went so far as to charge that the President had a "female demon within him."

Premier Hughes of Australia, whom the benign Lord Robert Cecil referred to as "that shrimp Hughes," did nothing to set the record straight. He informed the Japanese delegates and the Japanese press that the Americans had strongly opposed racial equality, and had been primarily responsible for its defeat.

This was not true. It was the irascible Hughes more than any other one man who had led the fight. But whether true or false, the impression was made, and the Japanese have never forgiven Wilson—or the United States.

4

By mid-April the Japanese could point to one partial diplomatic victory, a mandate over the North Pacific islands; and one complete defeat, racial equality. They had one demand left: German economic rights in Shantung; and to Japan this was by all odds the most important, at least economically.

Tactically, the position of the Japanese delegates was strong. They had just suffered a stinging defeat on the race issue, and the natural tendency of the Allies was to appease them with something else they wanted.

The Japanese withheld their heavy fire with Oriental patience until late in April, when the desperate situation was all in their favor. Italy had just left the Conference, and might never return. Belgium, bitter over the apportionment of reparations, was seriously threatening to bolt too. If the Japanese, denied Shantung, had gone home, the Conference almost certainly would have collapsed, and with it Wilson's precious League of Nations.

The false impression has gone abroad that the Japanese demanded in fee simple the entire province of Shantung—the home of Confucius, the Holy Land of China—with its 56,000 square miles of territory and its population of some 30,000,000 Chinese. The false impression has also gone abroad that Wilson surrendered to these demands, and handed over to the

Reaching Out
(Courtesy of the San Francisco *Chronicle*)

tender mercies of the Japanese these 30,000,000 souls—a gross violation of self-determination.

The simple truth is that the Japanese did not ask for, and did not expect to get, sovereign rights over the province of Shantung. They were merely asking for the German economic rights and holdings, which were principally railroad and mining properties. They were also asking for the German leasehold at Kiaochow, but in accordance with a previous agreement with Peking, they were willing to hand it back to China if their claims to German economic holdings were recognized. This leasehold the Japanese had wrested from Germany early in the war at the cost of their own blood—not a great deal of blood to be sure, but nevertheless Japanese blood.

One of the most striking of the many ironies at the Conference is that two of the biggest disputes were stirred up over

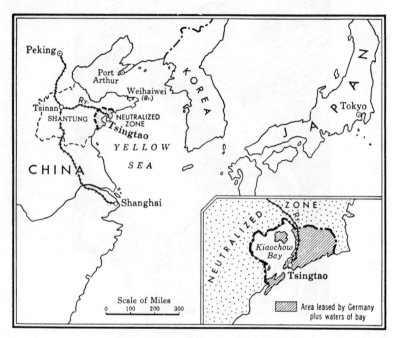

German Rights in Shantung

two of the smallest issues. Fiume, as we have seen, was from the point of view of Italy but a third-rate port. The German leasehold in Shantung, that at the bay of Kiaochow, embraced only 117 square miles. There is some little difference, as Senator Hiram Johnson and others were unwilling to recognize, between taking over 117 square miles temporarily, and 56,000 square miles in perpetuity.

It is clear that self-determination had little to do directly

with the Shantung issue, except in so far as economic privi-
leges and railroad supervision may restrict the sovereignty of
a nation. And these, it will be readily recognized, may be used
as powerful instruments of oppression.

The only Wilsonian principle that seemed directly involved
was the second of the Supplementary Points of July 4, 1918,
to the effect that "every question" "of economic arrangement"
should be based upon "the free acceptance of that settlement
by the people immediately concerned . . ."

5

The Japanese, at least as far as German rights in Shantung
were concerned, had an almost ironclad legal case. They had
been promised those rights by the secret arrangement of 1917
with Britain and France. They had also been promised those
rights by the Chinese in the treaties of 1915 and 1918, one of
which had been signed by one of the Chinese delegates at
Paris. Finally, they had captured the German holdings, and
they were apparently there to stay.

Space does not permit a discussion of the merits of the
treaties with China, which on various grounds the Chinese
now declared invalid. But the agreement of 1917 with Britain
and France was certainly binding, the more so since under it
the British were making off with Germany's South Pacific
Islands. And why apply self-determination to Japan when the
British and the French still clung to their Chinese holdings,
including the British leasehold at Weihaiwei, which was also
in Shantung province? The Japanese expressed a willingness
to yield their demands if the British and French would show
similar solicitude for China. While there was no danger that
this offer would be accepted, it was proffered, and it did bolster
Japan's moral position.

The Japanese made it unmistakably clear that if they did
not get what they were after, they would bolt the Conference

and not sign the treaty. Various compromise proposals were advanced, among them one to the effect that German rights be handed over to the Allied and Associated Powers, who in turn would deal fairly with Japanese interests. This Japan flatly rejected. She wanted to establish once and for all the principle that she was the dominant power in the Far East, and that she was privileged to settle her differences with China without the unwelcome interference of the Western Powers. She would hand Kiaochow back to China, but she would do the handing herself. In short—and this is vastly important—it was largely a matter of "face."

The Japanese delegates, with an aroused public opinion at home, dared not lose face by yielding on Shantung; the Chinese delegates, with an aroused nationalistic feeling at home, dared not lose face by failing to get the German holdings in Shantung; and Wilson, with a strong anti-Japanese element at home, dared not lose face by yielding to the Japanese demands. If he saved face by resisting those demands, he would lose even more face if and when the Japanese withdrew from the Conference and ruined his League of Nations.

6

Critics of Wilson have charged that the Japanese were merely bluffing, and that he weakly bent the knee when he did not have to. Japan, they claim, had much too vital a stake in the League to run out on the Conference. Two of Wilson's Far Eastern experts insisted that Japan was bluffing. Lansing thought so too, but we must bear in mind that he was strongly pro-Chinese, and that he subsequently served for a number of years as legal adviser to the Chinese Embassy in Washington.

Wilson did not agree with Lansing. "They are not bluffers," he said, "and they will go home unless we give them what they should not have." Colonel House agreed with Wilson.

It seems reasonable to conclude that Wilson was right; or to put it another way, he was right in not taking a chance. The Japanese are not notorious bluffers. It was generally thought that they were bluffing before they made war on China in 1894, and on Russia in 1904; when they left the League in 1933; and before they attacked Pearl Harbor in 1941. But they were not.

The Japanese had already lost completely on racial equality, and partially on the mandated islands: the Tokyo government simply could not sustain another defeat. If Japan left the Conference, what could she lose? She still had the North Pacific islands; she was entrenched in Shantung; and who was going to evict her? From the short-run point of view all that she could lose was racial equality, and she had already lost that.

If the Japanese walked out on the Conference they would have potentially formidable and dangerous company. Russia and Germany were outside the pale, and prospective partners in an alliance—an alliance which, in the case of Germany and Japan, finally took shape in 1940. If the old and discredited system of alliances and balances of power was brought into being, this would be the undoing of the League. Ray Stannard Baker believes that the possibility of Japan's joining hands with the other outcasts was one of the most decisive factors in the President's thinking.

Wilson was profoundly worried about the Shantung tangle, and at the height of the crisis he told Baker that he had not slept the previous night. If he made the wrong move, the Conference might well break up, and Europe lapse into anarchy. But if he made the right move, Japan would stay on the reservation, and the League would be saved. As for China, she would have a better chance of securing ultimate justice if Japan were in the League with her rather than outside and against her. If all else failed, the League could be used to right the Shantung wrong.

On this one issue Wilson showed a sensitiveness to home opinion that was conspicuously lacking in his dealing with certain other problems. America was as suspicious of the rising power of the Japanese as she was sympathetic with the position of the underdog Chinese. To hand German rights over to Japan instead of back to China seemed unpleasantly like awarding the loot to the policeman who recovers the stolen goods. Above all, any surrender on Shantung was bound to be attacked in the Senate, and particularly by Senators from the immigration-conscious Western states.

7

The Japanese finally won a substantial victory. They were to receive Germany's economic rights and holdings in Shantung, which was precisely what they had been contending for from the first. In a separate unsigned declaration, entirely apart from the Treaty of Versailles, they promised ultimately to withdraw their troops and restore Shantung in full sovereignty to China, retaining only the German economic holdings and the right to establish a settlement under the usual conditions at Tsingtao. They also gave certain assurances as to Chinese control of the vital railroad.

The Chinese were acutely unhappy. Coming to Paris with the hope of recovering Germany's holdings in Shantung Province, they succeeded in recovering the astronomical instruments which the German troops had baldly removed from Peking during the Boxer disorders of 1900–1901. The Chinese delegates indignantly refused to put their signatures to the Treaty of Versailles. (It was reported that their heads would be cut off if they did.) In China, schools and business houses closed their doors in protest; mass meetings were held; a boycott was begun against Japanese goods; and a few fanatical Chinese committed suicide.

In America, as Wilson feared, there was a wild outburst of condemnation. Numerous newspapers referred to "Japan, the Possessor of Stolen Goods," "The Crime of Shantung," "The Far-Eastern Alsace-Lorraine," "inexcusable injustice," "conspiracy to rob," "a damnable enterprise," "the rape of Shan-tung." Hearst's headlines blared: "SOLD—40,000,000 PEOPLE." The demagogic Senator Hiram W. Johnson, who knew bet-ter but who also knew the prejudices of his California con-stituency, branded this as "the blackest page in all our history":

> To the Japanese Empire, with only 60,000,000 of people, we turned over shamefully and cruelly 40,000,000 of Chinese. To the autocracy of the Orient we delivered 40,000,000 republicans of China. We made the Orient "safe for democracy" by dismember-ing its only democracy and handing the parts to the strongest autocracy on earth.

It would be difficult to compress more errors into fewer words; but one essential fact looms up: the Japanese kept their promise. In 1922 they made final arrangements to turn Shan-tung back to the Chinese government in full sovereignty, though they came back some fifteen years later under different circumstances. This discharge of a solemn obligation received little attention in the press, especially from those newspapers and persons who were proved false prophets.

The alleged Shantung surrender seemingly gave point to Clemenceau's biting remark that Wilson "talked like Jesus Christ but acted like Lloyd George." Writers like Harold Nicolson, forgetting that statesmen must all too often choose between the bad and the less bad, and that the greatest good is sometimes the smallest evil, condemn the Shantung settlement as "the worst surrender of all." On the contrary, it may be regarded as perhaps the most defensible of Wilson's many surrenders.

Unlike the Italians in Fiume, the Japanese had a powerful legal case, buttressed by actual possession. The final arrange-ment was one which involved the honor of Japan, and she kept her promise. The alternative was probable disruption of the entire Conference, with all that it entailed. From many points of view Wilson would have been unjustified in taking such a perilous chance.

8

Perhaps the most unfortunate thing about the so-called
Shantung surrender is that it lent itself to malicious misrepresentation. Face-saving for Japan rather than self-determination

In the Neck!
China's Nine Requests Denied

(From the Bakersfield [Calif.] *Echo;* courtesy of the
Bakersfield *Californian*)

for China was the basic issue. Yet many of the same people
who vociferously condemned Wilson for not giving the Slavs
of Fiume to Italy held up their hands in holy horror when

Shantung—or the economic holdings of Germany in Shantung —went to Japan.

Shantung, as much as any other clause except Article X of the Covenant, defeated the Treaty in the United States. But other things, which were quite avoidable, and which if avoided could have saved the pact, contributed to this end. The Shantung deal could hardly have been avoided, certainly not without running a risk which no responsible statesman should have assumed.

Wilson was acutely unhappy over the result, as he candidly confessed, but he consoled himself as best he could by saying that it was about as clean a settlement as could be made out of a "dirty past." Certainly, it was no dirtier, in fact not so dirty, as some of the things that the European powers were scheming for or actually doing at Paris. Besides, the League was specifically designed to correct such injustices.

There was one final consolation for Wilson. He had faith that when he returned home and explained the situation to the American people they would see that he had no other way out.

But other tutors, less scrupulous about facts, canceled out his efforts.

CHAPTER NINETEEN

THE DAY OF RECKONING

"The Germans don't like the peace terms, but they ought to remember that if they did nobody else would." PHILADELPHIA NORTH AMERICAN, *May, 1919.*

1

ON APRIL 14, 1919, when it seemed as though a settlement were in sight, the German delegates were summoned to Versailles to receive the Treaty. Upon arriving late in the month, they were assigned as virtual prisoners to a hotel, about which a fence was hurriedly erected to shield them from the stares of the curious and from the possible violence of the mob. This precaution was far from foolish, for several weeks later the delegates were assailed by a crowd of angry Frenchmen, and two of the Germans were injured by stones. Nothing could better illustrate the poisonous atmosphere surrounding the Conference.

The German delegates had arrived, but still there was no treaty. The explanation is that during the closing days of April the Fiume and Shantung crises came to a head, and for a while it seemed as though there would be nothing to present to the Germans. Agreement was finally reached, and the various parts of the Treaty on which the numerous committees had been working were thrown together and sent to the printer. The first printed copies were not available until the early morning of May 7, 1919—the day of the presentation of the pact to the German delegates. It is an almost incredible fact that probably no single one of the Allied statesmen had read the Treaty as a whole until the day it was handed to the Germans.

Herbert Hoover remembers that a messenger brought a copy to him on the morning of May 7, and he was so disturbed by what he found that he went for a walk in the early morning air.

He met General Smuts, who was similarly agitated, and who was also walking to cool off. The two men despondently compared notes and expressed fear for the future.

We have already noted that the various parts of the Treaty were fashioned more or less in a vacuum, and then assembled without proper editorial coordination. Lloyd George remarked in the Council of Four that he expected to find in-

Not Fourteen—Only Two—Points Left
(Courtesy of the Cincinnati *Post*)

consistencies, as one always did in a complicated bill in Parliament. He was right: there were serious inconsistencies.

As one examined the individual clauses of the Treaty by themselves the various provisions did not seem altogether unreasonable. But when they were all put together, and when it was observed that certain exactions made it difficult or impossible to carry out other exactions, the whole effect was stunning. Dr. James T. Shotwell has pointedly said that "when all the sacrifices were added together, the whole was greater than the sum of the parts."

2

The Treaty of Versailles was formally presented to the German representatives on May 7, 1919, by coincidence the fourth anniversary of the sinking of the *Lusitania*.

The scene was the Trianon Palace at Versailles. The day was one of surpassing loveliness, and brilliant spring sunlight flooded the room. Dr. Walter Simons, Commissioner-General of the German delegation, noted that "outside of the big window at my right there was a wonderful cherry tree in bloom, and it seemed to me the only reality when compared with the performance in the hall. This cherry tree and its kind will still be blooming when the states whose representatives gathered here exist no longer."

The crowd was small, for the room was small—merely the delegates of both sides, with their assistants, and a few carefully selected press representatives. The grim-visaged Clemenceau sat at the center of the main table: Wilson at his right, Lloyd George at his left.

The air was surcharged with electricity: German and Allied diplomats had not met face to face since the fateful summer of 1914. Would the Germans do something to offend the proprieties?

When all were seated, the doors swung open. At the cry, *"Messieurs les plénipotentiaires allemands!"* the whole assembly rose and stood in silence while the German delegates filed in before their conquerors and sat at a table facing Clemenceau.

The Tiger rose to his feet, and, his voice vibrant with the venom of 1871, almost spat out his speech with staccato precision: "It is neither the time nor the place for superfluous words . . . The time has come when we must settle our accounts. You have asked for peace. We are ready to give you peace."

Already a secretary had quietly walked over to the table at which the Germans sat, and laid before them the thick, two-hundred-odd-page treaty—"the book."

With Clemenceau still standing, the pale, black-clad Count Brockdorff-Rantzau, head of the German delegation, began reading his reply—*seated*.

An almost perceptible gasp swept the room, for the failure of the German to rise was taken as a studied discourtesy. Some felt that he was too nervous and shaken to stand. Others felt that he wanted to snub his "conquerors." The truth is that he planned to sit, not wishing to stand like a culprit before a judge to receive sentence.

Nothing could better reflect the spirit of the Germans. They felt that the war had been more or less a stalemate; they had laid down their arms expecting to negotiate with a chivalrous foe. As equals, why should they rise like criminals before the Allied bar?

3

If Brockdorff-Rantzau's posture was unfortunate, his words and the intonation of his words were doubly so.

The Germans had not yet read the Treaty, but they had every reason to believe that it would be severe. They had not been allowed to participate in its negotiation; they would not be allowed to discuss its provisions *orally* with their conquerors. Brockdorff-Rantzau decided to make the most of this his only opportunity to meet his adversaries face to face and comment on the unread Treaty. Both his manner and his words were sullen, arrogant, unrepentant.

Speaking with great deliberation and without the usual courteous salutation to the presiding officer, he began by saying that the Germans were under "no illusions" as to the extent of their defeat and the degree of their "powerlessness."

This was not true, for both he and his people were under great illusions.

Then he referred defiantly but inaccurately to the demand that the Germans acknowledge that "we alone are guilty of having caused the war. Such a confession in my mouth would be a lie." And the word "lie" fairly hissed from between his teeth.

Bitterly he mentioned the "hundreds of thousands" of German noncombatants who had perished since Armistice Day as a result of Allied insistence on continuing the blockade during the peace negotiations. This shaft struck home, especially to the heart of Lloyd George.

When the echo of Brockdorff-Rantzau's last tactless word had died away, Clemenceau spoke. His face had gone red during the harangue, but he had held himself in check with remarkable self-restraint. Harshly and peremptorily he steamrolled the proceedings to an end: "Has anybody any more observations to offer? Does no one wish to speak? If not, the meeting is closed."

The German delegates marched out, facing a battery of clicking moving picture cameras. Brockdorff-Rantzau lighted a cigarette with trembling fingers.

Lloyd George, who had snapped an ivory paper knife in his hands, remarked angrily: "It is hard to have won the war and to have to listen to that."

Thus, within a half-hour, was compressed one of the greatest dramas of all time.

4

Brockdorff-Rantzau's ill-timed tirade was followed with intense concentration by President Wilson. Dr. Simons noted that the German argument "obviously made its impression upon him, although not a favorable one."

This was absolutely correct. Wilson might have been deeply moved by a clear, dispassionate reference to concrete cases,

but this blanket condemnation left him indignant and stubborn. To Lloyd George he turned and said, "Isn't it just like
them!"

The German delegate undoubtedly made a grave error in
judgment. A short, tactful speech would have kept the door
open to compromise; his long, defiant diatribe forced the
victors to defend what they had done. Colonel House wrote
that if he had been in Brockdorff-Rantzau's position he should
have said: "Mr. President, and Gentlemen of the Congress:
War is a great gamble; we have lost and are willing to submit to
any reasonable terms." But Colonel House might not have
been able to say this if he had been the representative of a
starved, defeated, and embittered nation.

The Germans were allowed fifteen days—later extended—to
file written objections to the provisional terms. It will be remembered that the original plan was to allow enemy delegates
to share actively in the final negotiation, but when the preliminary conference merged with the final conference, there
was no place for German or other enemy representatives. Besides, it was feared that they might engage in intrigue of the
Talleyrand variety, and provoke further dissension at a time
when there was already enough dissension. The most serious
trouble at the Conference was caused by differences within
Allied ranks rather than by differences with the enemy. "To
the victors," remarked the Boston *Herald,* "belong the broils."

So it was that the Germans were handed the Treaty on the
point of a bayonet and told to file protests. This represented a
compromise between giving them an oral share in the discussions and giving them no part at all. The Paris Conference
was a conference only in so far as the victors conferred among
themselves.

This was most unfortunate, for there was no one during the
negotiation of the treaty to present the German point of view
to the inevitably hate-ridden victors. The very fact that the
Germans, in the short time at their disposal, and with only
written protests, were able to secure some concessions and im-

plant more doubts is proof in itself that with tactful negotiators and oral discussions the vanquished might have secured
a more moderate and workable treaty.

The reaction of German opinion to the published terms
was bitter in the extreme. President Ebert called the Treaty a
"monstrous document," and the government instituted a week
of mourning. General Ludendorff cryptically remarked: "If
these are the peace terms, then America can go to hell."

5

The days that followed were anxious and uncertain. The
Germans were studying the Treaty and preparing their replies. The Allied delegates also had to study the Treaty to find
out what was in it, for, as previously noted, few if any of them
had read it as a whole.

During this tense period of waiting for the German reply,
a strong feeling began to develop among liberal elements that
the Treaty had been made too severe, and that it ought to be
softened. This "remorse complex" was especially marked in
Great Britain and among certain members of the British delegation, and Lloyd George, the Welsh weathercock, began to
veer with it. If the Germans should refuse to sign the Treaty
on the ground that it was too drastic, the fiery Welshman
would doubtless be unhorsed. Wilson noted that he had got
into a "perfect funk"; and he insisted on ameliorating the
Treaty, notably at the expense of France rather than of Great
Britain.

Clemenceau brought Lloyd George sharply to book. Great
Britain, he said, had come off very well: German colonies,
reparations, ships, cables, the destruction of Germany's naval
power. If Lloyd George wanted to appease Germany, let him
hand back some colonies and ships, and not weaken French
security by withdrawing the Allied army of occupation, by

returning Upper Silesia to Germany, and by reducing claims for reparations.

Lloyd George's antics, if anything, confirmed Wilson in his stubbornness. During the negotiations the capricious Briton had demanded severe conditions on reparations and other matters, against the better judgment of Wilson, and now that the Germans were threatening not to sign the Treaty, he was insisting on backing down. Wilson remarked disgustedly that such people made him "tired" and "very sick." The terms of the Treaty were either just or unjust; but the time to have decided that was when the Treaty was being drafted.

There is undoubtedly much to be said for Wilson's refusal to countenance a last-moment rewriting of the pact. The race between peace and anarchy was going to be terribly close, and the peacemakers had already been at their task for more than five months. If Lloyd George was permitted to reverse himself, others would be entitled to reverse themselves. Concessions to the Germans would beget demands for further concessions, and the process would go on interminably.

On the other hand, it is possible—though we shall never know—that the importance of haste was exaggerated, and that it would have been better in the long run to take several more weeks or even months, and, if possible, thresh out a more workable treaty.

In any event, the German delegates labored frantically to prepare adequate replies in the inadequately short time allowed them. They were encouraged by learning that all was not well in the Allied camp, and they were spurred on by knowing of the terribly unsettled conditions in revolution-ridden Germany.

The waters were so troubled that a German diplomat of the caliber of Talleyrand undoubtedly could have fished to advantage. If the Germans, instead of vehemently attacking every objectionable feature of the treaty, whether minor or major, had tactfully concentrated their fire on a few essential points, they might conceivably have won substantial concessions. But they had no Talleyrand. They tactlessly and angrily filed voluminous objections to everything objectionable, and in this way forced the Allies into a blanket defense of their admittedly unsatisfactory handiwork.

The German replies, the most important of which was some 50,000 words long, protested violently against the complete loss of all colonies, against the amputation of approximately

Diplomacy!
(From the New York *Evening World;* reprinted by permission)

one-eighth of Germany's territory and one-tenth of her population, against the refusal of the victors to disarm, against Germany's ostracism from the League of Nations, and against the "financial thralldom" established by the reparations and other economic clauses, many of which were impossible of fulfillment. "Those who will sign this Treaty," wrote Brockdorff-Rantzau, "will sign the death sentence of many millions of German men, women and children."

Above all, the Germans insisted that they had laid down their arms after having been solemnly promised a peace based on the Fourteen Points, a peace of right and justice—a peace, as Wilson had said, of "no annexations, no contributions, no punitive damages." Now, they alleged, the points had been cast aside one by one, in the interest of keeping Germany economically and politically prostrate.

6

The 35,000-word Allied reply to the German counterproposals began with an unchallengeable statement: "The protest of the German Delegation shows that they utterly fail to understand the position in which Germany stands today."

Sharply rebutting the German contentions, the Allied statement asserted that the peace proposed "is fundamentally a peace of justice." The Allied conception of justice was further elaborated:

Justice is what the German Delegation ask for and say that Germany had been promised. Justice is what Germany shall have. But it must be justice for all. There must be justice for the dead and wounded and for those who have been orphaned and bereaved that Europe might be freed from Prussian despotism. There must be justice for the peoples who now stagger under war debts which exceed £30,000,000,000 that liberty might be saved. There must be justice for those millions whose homes and land, ships and property German savagery has spoliated and destroyed.

When the Germans laid down their arms on the basis of Wilson's promises of a peace of "right" and "impartial justice," they were clearly laboring under a very serious misapprehension. They were evidently thinking of "mercy" and "leniency" when they thought of "right," "fairness," and "justice." They evidently did not realize that these three words mean different things to different men and at different times. They evidently failed to observe that "justice" meant one thing to them, a different thing to the Allies, and a still different thing to the neutrals. They evidently failed to understand that what is "justice" in a war-charged atmosphere may be something different from "justice" in a peaceful atmosphere. Anyone who talked about genuine "justice" was regarded as pro-German.

Such relative and flexible terms need definition and application by impartial judges. And the Germans failed to realize that the Allies, in determining what justice should be, would be the sole determinants. Wilson, who was one of the chief judges, thought of himself as impartial and disinterested. He had in fact told his experts on the *George Washington* that they would be the "only disinterested people" at the Conference. The truth is that Wilson was not impartial or disinterested: no man could be who had passed through the recent bath of propaganda, war hatred, and atrocity stories.

"Justice" is a word that has several definitions, but a primary meaning is "merited reward or punishment."

There can be no doubt that the great body of Allied negotiators, including Wilson, felt that the severities of the Treaty were a "merited punishment"—in fact, less than a "merited punishment"—for having wantonly forced this horrible calamity upon humanity. Wilson was a stern rather than a merciful man, and his idea of justice was the Calvinist concept of an angry God meting out just deserts to depraved sinners. In his later public defense of the Treaty, he declared time and again that the pact was severe but just.

Lloyd George privately said—and the humane Herbert Hoover wrote essentially the same thing—that if "right" and "justice" were granted to the "Boches" they would be crushed out of existence. Public opinion in the Allied countries felt the same way. The press of the United States abounded in such statements as "Her offenses considered, Germany gets off lightly, indeed"; the terms were "essentially just in view of the colossal calamity which Germany brought upon the world"; "It is a harsh treaty, but it could not have been otherwise and be just."

We may not unreasonably conclude that since "justice" admits of several definitions, and since in 1919 the Allies were doing the defining, the Germans would have to seek other grounds for a legal protest.

7

On the question of the Fourteen Points the Berlin government was treading—or seemed to be treading—on firmer ground.

The Germans in their protests against the Treaty asserted that they had made a solemn pre-Armistice contract with their enemy, in which they were promised a peace based on the Fourteen Points, with one reservation and one elucidation. They now alleged that many of those Points had been broken, and as a consequence the contract had been violated.

The Allies in their reply candidly admitted that they had entered into such a contract, but they unequivocally denied that they had broken the Fourteen Points. Their defense was devastating.

It will be remembered that Berlin had sued for a peace based on the original Fourteen Points and *all the subsequent points and principles relating to peace which Wilson had set forth in his public utterances.* Unluckily for the Germans, some of these supplementary Points contradicted and wiped out all the others. The Allies made powerful use of these forgotten Points in rebutting the German claims.

At Mount Vernon, on July 4, 1918, Wilson had asserted that every "arbitrary power" which might "disturb the peace of the world" must be "destroyed," or at least reduced to "virtual impotence." The Germans solemnly signed this appalling blank check when they accepted *all* of Wilson's Points.

Assuming, as the Allies all did, that Germany was a disturber of world peace, then any measures would be justified that would reduce her to "virtual impotence," including the loss of colonies and German-inhabited areas like Danzig and Upper Silesia.

On February 11, 1918, Wilson had told Congress that each part of the coming settlement should be based not only upon "essential justice" but upon *such adjustments as are most likely to bring a peace that will be permanent.*" In short, any "adjustment" of any kind which *in Allied eyes* would make for a "permanent" peace would override any or all of the other Fourteen Points.

By using these "escape clauses," and the contradictions in the Fourteen Points, the Allies could invoke those principles that operated to Germany's disadvantage, and discard those that did not. Let it not be forgotten that in the application of the Fourteen Points the Allies were both prosecutor and judge; and from their technically defensible point of view there were no violations of the Fourteen Points at all.

8

The shyster lawyer will deliberately introduce "escape clauses" into the contract; but it is hard to believe that Wilson, with his high sense of honor, realized fully what he was doing when he made his numerous speeches. If a man in public life talks enough he will almost inevitably contradict himself.

We do not know whether the Allied leaders immediately detected these "escape clauses" and made careful note of them. The Germans probably did not, for their natural tendency was to seize upon those statements that held out promise of leniency, while overlooking the rest. It is possible, of course, that they did notice them, and rather than press for a more careful definition, preferred to take their chances with oral discussion in the negotiation of the peace—an oral discussion which never came.

But why did Wilson, the man of honor, keep quiet on this issue at Paris? Why did he not, as the author of the Fourteen

Points, issue a peremptory protest against the palpable misuse of his sacred principles? As a matter of fact, he sat through the meetings of the Council of Four while the Allied reply was being discussed, yet, according to the records now available, he merely said that the document "conveyed a slight feeling of inadequacy," and that "it would not prove satisfactory to the future historian."

The explanation is not easy to find. Perhaps Wilson resented the attacks on his Fourteen Points, and the effrontery of the Germans in quoting Wilson to refute Wilson. Perhaps his conscience hurt him so keenly over the infractions of his principles that he was willing to take refuge in technical escapes. Certainly he was angered by Brockdorff-Rantzau's defiant harangue. Certainly he saw the folly of reopening the whole issue again and further delaying the Treaty. And certainly he was counting on the League of Nations to iron out the inequities that had inevitably crept into the Treaty.

Enlightened opinion in the Allied countries knew perfectly well in a general way what the Fourteen Points meant. This was the meaning that the Germans had accepted, or thought they had accepted. But the practical application of the Fourteen Points involved, perhaps inescapably, a moral, though not a strictly legal, breach of contract.

A later generation might be tempted to call this dishonest. But the negotiators were too close to their problem and too close to their unrepentant foe not to take full advantage of these loopholes.

9

Clemenceau stood foursquare with Wilson in refusing to alter the Treaty in any fundamental way. The French press changed its tune overnight and began to praise the splendid American President. After all these voluminous interchanges with the Germans, the Allies made only a few minor concessions, and only one of any real consequence. They relented on turning over Upper Silesia, with its considerable German population and highly important industries, to the tender mercies of the Poles. Instead, provision was made for a plebiscite. (See map on p. 219.)

We need not discuss this interesting problem at length, because Lloyd George was primarily responsible for it, as he had been in making the German port of Danzig a free city rather than an outright Polish possession. In both cases Wilson, after considerable indecision, and contrary to the wishes of his pro-Pole experts, gave in. Upon mature reflection Upper Silesia seemed to him so clear-cut a case of self-determination as to require the vote of the inhabitants.

It is hardly fair to criticize Wilson because the plebiscite did not work out happily, and because the Germans were exceedingly ungrateful for the substantial part of Upper Silesia which they finally received. This was a situation of terrible explosiveness, and it seems probable that Germany would have been even more bitter if the entire area had been awarded outright to the Poles.

During the hectic weeks when these concessions were being debated, the question on every lip was: Will Germany sign? Opinion varied in every quarter, and from day to day. The Germans showed their defiance by burning certain French battle flags which they were supposed to return, and by spectacularly scuttling their battle fleet in the British harbor of Scapa Flow, rather than have it fall into Allied hands. This was a flagrant violation of the Armistice terms, and aroused the French to new bitterness. "Germany," remarked *L'Action Française* (Paris), "may one day, if we are not careful, scuttle the League of Nations as she scuttled the fleet."

At the last moment, the German government reluctantly offered to sign, subject to an abrogation of the "war guilt" clause, to a renunciation of the article providing for the surrender of German war "criminals" for trial, and to a solemn protest against shearing away all of Germany's colonial possessions.

The Allies flatly rejected these overtures. They were in no mood to dicker, and in no position to have to. Instead, they instructed Marshal Foch, on June 20th, to march into Germany if the Treaty was not approved by 7:00 P.M. on June 23rd.

There was nothing the Germans could now do but sign. Marshal Foch's armies were poised to strike, and both he and

The Fifteenth Point!

(From the New York *Herald;* courtesy of the New York *Sun*)

many of his men would have enjoyed a jaunt through Germany. The American boys of the A.E.F. were delighted with the prospect of a long-deferred march down Unter den Linden.

Germany was bankrupt, revolution-torn, starving. Thousands of Berliners were surging through the streets bearing banners that clamored for immediate signing: "We have had enough; peace, for God's sake." "We want bread not bullets."

On June 23, 1919, a few scant hours before the dead line, the terrible suspense was ended. The new German government

—the old one had resigned in protest on June 20th—announced
that it approved the Treaty, unconditionally.

10

The signing ceremony was staged in the great Hall of
Mirrors in Louis XIV's Palace of Versailles. This was the place
where the Germans had humiliated the defeated French in
1871 by proclaiming William I the Emperor of united Germany, and obviously for the purpose of a counter humiliation
it was chosen for the scene. The Hall of Mirrors was at once
the cradle and the grave of the German Empire.

The date was June 28, 1919, by coincidence the fifth anniversary of the murder of the Archduke Francis Ferdinand at
Sarajevo. The precise time was midafternoon. The occasion
lacked the dignity and suspense of the presentation ceremony
in the small room of the Trianon Palace. Everyone knew that
the Germans would sign; and the event was too elaborately
staged in too large a place. There were about a thousand people
in the audience, many of them ladies, and the air buzzed with
conversation.

The two German delegates were marched in—Brockdorff-
Rantzau had resigned with his government—and after a brief
speech by Clemenceau, they signed the Treaty. The Allied
plenipotentiaries added their signatures. Outside the hall
cannon boomed, the great fountains gushed forth for the first
time since the war began, and the assembly broke up in confusion, with autograph hunters ferreting out the delegates.

A young German was heard to say: "All passes. It will seem
so different in ten, in twenty years . . ."

Colonel House was sad. "I had," he wrote, "a feeling of
sympathy for the Germans who sat there quite stoically. It was
not unlike what was done in olden times, when the conqueror
dragged the conquered at his chariot wheels."

Two incidents marred the ceremony. General Smuts, the

South African liberal, signed under protest. "I feel," he said, "that in the Treaty we have not yet achieved the real peace to which our peoples were looking."

The Chinese refused to sign at all. They could not forget Shantung.

The Germans signed because they had to. They presented no more formal reservations; their reservations were mental. Those that they had offered so vehemently, only a few days before, they would not soon forget. They morally repudiated the Treaty while they signed it.

In Berlin, some of the newspapers announced the signing with black borders, and with captions: "Germany's Fate Sealed." The Berlin *Vorwärts*, which was regarded as a mouthpiece of the government, cried: "We must never forget it is only a scrap of paper. Treaties based on violence can keep their validity only so long as force exists. Do not lose hope. The resurrection day comes."

11

It is highly significant that much of Germany's bitterness against the Treaty turned against America, and particularly against Wilson. His name is still cursed in German.

The fall, rise, and again the fall of Wilson in German esteem was most spectacular. In 1914 he was regarded with considerable respect; from 1915 to 1917 he was branded as a sniveling hypocrite, sympathetic with the Allies and thwarting German victory; from 1917 to 1918 he was a remorseless enemy; from the Armistice to the presentation of the Treaty he was seized upon as Germany's last hope—her sole chance of being delivered from the vengeance of her enemies.

With the publication of peace terms, Wilson again became a treacherous deceiver. All Germany cried with Philipp Scheidemann, head of the German ministry, "President Wilson is a hypocrite and the Versailles Treaty is the vilest crime in history."

It would be amusing, if it were not so tragic, to note how German devotion to the pristine Fourteen Points increased in proportion as the Allies forsook them. "The further President Wilson gets away from the Fourteen Points," chortled the Washington *Post*, "the closer the Germans nudge up to them." By June, 1919, the Germans were far more enthusiastic about the original Wilsonian program than anyone else.

American public opinion was not impressed by German "bleating" about the Fourteen Points. Journals like the New York *World* insisted that Wilson's principles had been generally carried out, which was not difficult to establish, depending on one's premises. Other newspapers bluntly reminded the Germans that they would have fared much less well if it had not been for Wilson and his Points, which was undoubtedly true. Others insisted that Germany had not been disarmed by the Fourteen Points at all but by several million Allied bayonet points, including those of American doughboys.

Other explanations or justifications were more cynical. The Philadelphia *Public Ledger* reminded its readers that the purpose of the Fourteen Points was to "impale German militarism," and this they were doing, and doing well. A good many Republican newspapers shrugged aside the Points by saying that they were Wilson's Points, and they did not represent the wishes of the American people—which was probably more true than Wilson wanted to believe. The *Wall Street Journal* went a step further in perverting history. It declared that the American people had "repudiated the Fourteen Points at the Congressional election in November," when a Republican majority was elected "on the straightforward slogan of 'unconditional surrender.'"

While there was some doubt in America as to the status of the Fourteen Points, there was none as to Germany's general attitude. She had clearly signed under great protest, and she regarded this treaty as another "scrap of paper." She was, in the judgment of the St. Louis *Star*, "a disarmed trickster rather than a reformed conspirator." The Kansas City *Journal* agreed: "It took force to make Germany sign. And it will take force to make her honor the signature." This situation was regarded in certain quarters as all the more reason why the United States should protect itself by joining the League of Nations.

12

The American people wasted little sympathy on the Hun. The press abounded with references to his "yellow streak" in surrendering before taking his beating, to his cowardly and treacherous sinking of his fleet, and to his constant "yawping" for food. There was little appreciation of the terrible straits to which the German population had been reduced by the Allied hunger blockade, which was kept on in some fashion for eight full months after the Armistice. When Congress, in February, 1919, finally appropriated $100,000,000 to provide food for devastated Europe, Germany and her allies were specifically denied a single crumb of bread or a single drop of soup. The Philadelphia *Evening Ledger* caught the spirit of the hour when it declared: "If Germany can be made safe only by hunger and torment and relative poverty, then it is better for the rest of the world that she be made to endure hunger and torment and poverty."

It is a fact of the greatest significance, particularly in view of the later unpopularity of the Treaty in the United States, that there was no serious objection to its severity, except among a numerically small group of liberals. Everywhere there was satisfaction that this was a "hard" peace, and not a "soft" one, such as the Republicans had feared that the dreamy Wilson would make. "The wild beast that sprang at the throat of civilization has been muzzled," rejoiced the New York *Tribune*. Most of our newspapers regarded the terms as just, even merciful, when judged in relation to Germany's offense against civilization. The Atlanta *Constitution* felt that the Germans, "instead of bewailing the fact that they must consign themselves to the mercies of God, should be thanking God that they got off so lightly." "It's a hard bed, Heinie, but who made it?" gibed the Cleveland *Press;* while the Chicago *Daily News* sneered: "What did Germania think—that the nations were going to make her Queen of the May?"

An occasional jarring note was introduced by the liberals, the pro-Germans, the Socialists, and others.

The liberal *New Republic* published a telling indictment of the Allied breach of faith, and concluded that the Treaty "gives the Germans too many reasons for feeling themselves thoroughly abused." The Springfield *Republican,* a liberal newspaper, declared: "The Treaty was dictated in a paroxysm of hate."

The German-language New York *Staats-Zeitung* discreetly refrained from comment on its editorial page and merely published the Fourteen Points.

The Socialist New York *Call,* branding this a "peace that passeth all understanding," cried with savage irony: "Accept it, children, with faith and resignation—and prepare for the next Armageddon."

CHAPTER TWENTY

BLESSED ARE THE
PEACEMAKERS

*"How splendid it would have been had we blazed a new and
better trail!"* COLONEL HOUSE, *June 29, 1919.*

1

SHORTLY AFTER the signing ceremony, Wilson left Paris
for Brest, where he was to board the *George Washington* for
home. A large and enthusiastic crowd, many of them notables,
saw him off at the Paris railway station. For the last time the
red carpet was rolled out, and he and Mrs. Wilson walked
between potted palms to their train.

Just before leaving, Wilson gave a mass interview to some
two hundred newspaper correspondents. To the query of
Lincoln Steffens he replied: "I think that we have made a
better peace than I should have expected when I came here to
Paris." His opinion was probably colored, as he privately
wrote, by "the consciousness that the results are so much better
than at one time I feared . . ."

Nevertheless Wilson was so deeply disturbed by France's
blocking of his plans that he had seriously considered declining an invitation to a farewell dinner given by President
Poincaré. Fortunately for international amity, Wilson was dis-
suaded by Henry White and others from administering such
a resounding rebuke. But it is evident that he was in a fighting
mood.

House had a final word with the departing President. He
pointed out that if Wilson were as conciliatory in dealing with
the Senate as he had been with his foreign colleagues in Paris,
all would be well. Ominously, Wilson rejected this counsel of
compromise and concession, and said: "House, I have found

one can never get anything in his life that is worth while without fighting for it."

House replied that "Anglo-Saxon civilization was built up on compromise . . ." Into these few words were compressed the divergent viewpoints of the two men.

They never saw each other again.

2

What manner of treaty was Wilson carrying home for the hostile scrutiny of the United States Senate?

It has been fashionable in recent years to condemn the Treaty of Versailles as thoroughly bad. The truth is that it contained much that was good and much that was bad. We need not try to determine whether the good outweighed the bad; but, all things considered, it is remarkable that the defects were not more numerous, more pervasive, and more glaring. One could even go so far as to say that the most surprising thing about the Treaty is not that it was unsatisfactory but that any kind of treaty came out of the madhouse at Paris. Certainly no other conference was ever confronted with such a complex of problems, and certainly none has ever dealt with a comparable task more scientifically and expeditiously. As compared with other great conferences of the past, this one moved at a dizzy pace.

We have considered the blunders—at least some of the blunders—that the statesmen made. But in all fairness it must be pointed out that there were certain conditions over which the negotiators had no control whatsoever, and these conditions would have left their imprint on any peace at that time.

The vision of the delegates and of their people was clouded by the passions of a war that was still too close. The Peace of Versailles was almost literally negotiated on the ruins of a smoking battlefield. As Lloyd George told the House of Commons: "I am doubtful whether any body of men with a difficult task have worked under greater difficulties—stones crackling on the roof and crashing through the windows, and sometimes wild men screaming through the keyholes." The tragedy is that in order to win the war the Allies had been forced to whip up such passions at home as to make difficult if not impossible the winning of the peace. "Once lead this people into war," Wilson had said in 1917, "and they'll forget there ever was such a thing as tolerance."

The Bolshevik menace, rising like an ominous flood, cried aloud for haste. Its red rivulet licked into Hungary, into Bavaria. There was every temptation to build hastily and quickly, rather than permanently and well. "Better a bad treaty today," was the saying, "than a good treaty four months hence."

The situation in Central Europe was nothing short of chaotic. Succession states were rising like phoenixes from the ruins of the ramshackle Austro-Hungarian empire. They could not wait for the quiet dictates of the Conference; they moved in and took what they wanted, thus presenting the negotiators with accomplished facts. In many cases the oppressed became the oppressors, and all the more savage because of their soul-searing experience.

Men cried, "Peace! Peace!" but there was no peace. While the peacemakers were busy in Paris, the warmakers were busy in Russia and Central Europe. It would in fact be difficult to name a single year following the Armistice when a serious armed disturbance was not agitating some part of the world. Bonar Law told the House of Commons, a few days before the Germans signed the treaty, that twenty-three different wars were raging in various parts of the world. It was as if some giant monster, threshing about in death agony, had broken into twenty-three convulsive parts. No wonder men spoke cynically of "the terrors of peace."

Peace is not in itself a condition: it reflects a condition. We should never forget that one of the insuperable obstacles at Paris was that the frock-coated negotiators were expected to produce a settlement in lands where there was no settlement, in lands where their authority did not extend.

3

There were several other conditions over which the negotiators could have no control.

Behind everything and permeating everything were politics. Clemenceau, Lloyd George, and Orlando—yes, even Wilson—were but the servants and mouthpieces of their people. If they yielded too much, if they did not bring back the spoils of victory, they would be thrown out and replaced by men of sterner stuff. Clemenceau and Lloyd George generally tried to give the public what it wanted. They survived. Orlando failed to give the people what they wanted. He was unhorsed. Wilson tried to give the people what *he* wanted. He was broken.

Where there were so many clashing interests, there had to be compromise or there would be no settlement. The representatives of great nations will not voluntarily consent to sit down at a table and be outvoted by an unfriendly majority. Compromise between two groups is often difficult and always unsatisfactory; but at Paris there had to be compromise among four or five of the great powers, and this increased the difficulty and dissatisfaction vastly more than four- or five-fold. It was simply impossible for Wilson to have his own way all—or perhaps most—of the time, even though he had powerful economic weapons in his arsenal. The marvel is that he got as much of his program written into the Treaty as he did. The explanation probably is that the European nations, despite the muttering in the American press and the sniping in the Senate, did not realize the extent to which he was losing his hold on public opinion.

Not a single one of the great powers was satisfied with the Treaty. This was because it had to be a compromise, and no compromise, as we have observed, is ever completely satisfactory to all the parties concerned. Each power felt that it had yielded too much and received too little. In France, Clemenceau was condemned as the dupe of Wilson and Lloyd George; in England, Lloyd George as the dupe of Wilson and Clemenceau; in America, Wilson as the dupe of Clemenceau and Lloyd George.

Another unavoidable difficulty at Paris was that the peace was a coalition peace, just as the war had been a coalition war; and a coalition can seldom move with complete singleness of purpose.

Napoleon once remarked that his brilliant victories had been easy because he was fighting a coalition of enemies. The Allies of 1914–1918 had prosecuted the war in a disorganized fashion, until the spring of 1918, and they framed the peace in a disorganized fashion, under the additional handicap of having disposed of the enemy who had forced them to unite. When we consider that it is on the whole a more delicate and complicated task to make an enduring peace than to prosecute a successful war, it is all the more surprising that the results were not less satisfactory.

4

Finally—and ominously—Russia, the blind Cyclops of the East, had no part in the Conference.

It is not altogether clear that this was an avoidable blunder. Russia was in the throes of one of the bloodiest civil wars in history, and it was impossible to tell which group of officials represented the nation. Wilson and others backed an attempt to bring the discordant elements together on the isle of Prinkipo in the Sea of Marmora; but this failed, partly because of Russian recalcitrance, and partly because of French opposition. It is probably true that the problem was an insoluble one, but the fact is that France ruined whatever scant prospects there were for success. She would have no traffic, in the colorful phrase of Winston Churchill, with the "foul baboonery of Bolshevism."

Repeated reference has been made in these pages to the Big Four. It was really the Big Five. Lenin was the fifth member—an invisible member occupying an invisible chair. He was more important than Orlando. He held the Conference to its labors, and applied the whip and spur. Russia was more important at Paris than Prussia; Prussia had no voice, Russia had a loud though ghostlike voice.

Thus the peace settlements of 1919 embraced only Western and Central Europe and Turkey, with due attention to Germany's overseas empire. The powers could delineate Poland's western borders; but they could not delineate her eastern borders. These could be settled only between her and Russia.

It seems self-evident that there can be no European settlement without Russia, for Russia is about one-half of Europe. It seems self-evident that there can be no world settlement without Russia, for Russia is about one-seventh of the world.

So it came about that peace—an uneasy peace—was made with only one side of Europe. The other side was still in chaos. The wonder is that the settlements lasted as long as they did.

5

Wilson at Paris conceived of the problem before him as a dual one. He tried to make peace with Germany, which was the immediate task, and at the same time reorder international relations, which was the long-run task. The two became hopelessly entangled, and neither was satisfactorily handled.

One of the results—and a fatal result—was that the Treaty of Versailles fell between two stools. It was neither a thoroughgoing victor's peace nor a peace of accommodation.

There are two ways of dealing with a fallen foe. The one is to make a peace so generous that he may forgive and forget. Whether Germany would have responded favorably to such treatment is still a matter of speculation, but there was a possibility that it might have worked. The second method is to impose a victor's peace, with the purpose of keeping the con-

"Chust See If I Don'd Get Oudt of It Yet!"
(Courtesy of the Baltimore *American*)

queror's heel on the enemy's neck as long as physically possible. This method is certain to breed another war.

The Treaty of Versailles contained some of the most severe terms that one civilized nation has ever imposed on another, while elsewhere it soared heavenward in the lofty idealism of the Covenant of the League of Nations. It was harsh enough to humiliate and anger the Germans but not drastic enough permanently to enchain them—assuming that this could ever be done. It was idealistic enough to create the illusion of workable peace machinery, but selfish enough to make that machinery unworkable in a real crisis.

The seeds of war were planted by the statesmen at Paris in many of the articles of the Treaty, but in that impassioned atmosphere they knew not what they were doing. Before 1914, France was the aggrieved power, nursing memories of Alsace-Lorraine and vanished *gloire*, while preparing for a war of revenge; after 1919, Germany was the aggrieved power, nursing memories of Danzig and lost colonies and frustrated plans of European domination, while preparing for a war of revenge. The "guilt clause" was a verbal Alsace-Lorraine.

Wilson recognized that there were inequities in the Treaty, but he confidently counted on the League to iron them out at a later date and in a saner atmosphere. This was a splendid ideal, but utterly unworkable, because Article V of the Covenant called for a unanimous vote in the Assembly and Council on all questions of substance. France, Poland, and others could always be counted on to veto any proposition that would show leniency toward Germany or her vanquished satellites. This was one of the prices that Wilson had to pay for France's adherence to the League of Nations.

Wilson also had to yield to French insistence that Germany be kept out of the League, which she was until 1926. The opposition of France was natural, but it had the most unfortunate result of causing the League to appear like a new Anglo-French alliance—a kind of exclusive international club from which Germany was excluded because of her moral blemish. This weakened the League in the eyes of both Germany and the other non-member nations, and subjected it to an incessant barrage of criticism and denunciation.

In the final analysis the League of Nations turned out to be an organization designed to freeze the status quo and keep the victorious Allies permanently in the saddle. The League was in essence an alliance of the victors, without the binding force of a true alliance. It evolved into an organization designed not to create a new balance of power but to preserve the existing imbalance of power.

This, of course, was not what Wilson wanted. "You cannot go forward," he said, "with one foot in the Old Order and the other in the New." But this was the best he could bring back from Paris, and he hoped that it would work out better than it did. Ironically, the very concessions that he was forced to make in order to give life to the League were the very concessions that ultimately gave it death.

The New Order, far from being established, merely "fouled the Old"—to use the phrase of Harold Nicolson. In the view of many Europeans the idealistic bungler from America should have stayed at home and allowed the Europeans to make a good old-fashioned victor's peace. War probably would have followed, but perhaps it would have been delayed for two generations instead of one. Possibly that is the best humanity can hope for. But Wilson was unable to resign himself to such defeatism.

6

A strong point should be made of the fact that a large part of Wilson's achievement at Paris was purely negative. It can even be argued that his most important contribution was not what he did but what he prevented others from doing, notably in connection with the Saar, saddling Germany with the entire cost of the war, and dividing Germany's colonies on a purely imperialistic basis, illusory though all of these solutions may have been.

It is true that many things went through which he did not approve. But there were so many iniquitous heads popping up at Paris that he could not tilt a lance at every one he saw. He concentrated his efforts on what he regarded—in some cases mistakenly—as the most iniquitous. It is worth repeating that the punitive parts of the Treaty undoubtedly would have been more harsh had he not been at Paris.

The critics of Wilson almost unanimously charge that his most conspicuous failure at Paris had to do with self-determination. Instead of Poles being forced to live under German domination, Germans were forced to live under Polish domination; instead of Italians being forced to live under Slavs, Slavs were forced to live under Italians. New if smaller minorities were seemingly exchanged for old.

Most conspicuous of all, the nearly seven million Germans of Austria were forbidden to join hands with their compatriots in Germany. The French, with their decimated man power and declining birth rate, found it unthinkable that Germany should emerge from this bloody war with a larger population of Germans than in 1914. Austria was to be made so independent that she could not exercise the right voluntarily to yield her independence. She was left an economic shell: a tremendous capital without a hinterland; a heart without a body. In all this Wilson reluctantly acquiesced.

The most glaring violations of the principle of nationality were in some instances avoidable, in others unavoidable. But on the whole the Paris settlement was a victory for self-determination. This principle was far more often honored in the observance than in the breach. Many more millions of minority groups were released from alien domination than were consigned to alien domination. The result was the closest approximation that modern Europe has ever had to an ethnographic map coinciding with a political map.

This raises the question whether an ethnographic map was what Europe needed: whether it would not have been better to have fewer states rather than more, whether it would not have been better to have more economic self-sufficiency and less self-determination, less abstract justice and more economic viability. Man does not live by bread alone, but he cannot live without bread.

7

The critics of Wilson say that at Paris he sacrificed his Fourteen Points one by one in order to save the League, just as a mother would throw her younger children to the pursuing wolves in order to save her first-born. Harold Nicolson, at least by indirection, accuses Wilson of having abandoned nineteen of his twenty-three points and principles.

This statement is pure nonsense, but it should be examined to determine how intelligent men can arrive at so erroneous a conclusion.

Critics like Nicolson assume that because a point, like self-determination, was not fully achieved, it was completely betrayed: 90 per cent success is total failure. This, in all honesty, is unfair. Winston Churchill estimated that fewer than 3 per cent of the people of Europe were condemned to live under governments whose nationality they repudiated. On the whole, the territorial readjustments in Europe were the most reasonable part of the settlement, and they generally benefited the small states rather than the great powers.

Nicolson takes it for granted that because a point was not achieved at Paris, it was completely betrayed. This also is unfair. Wilson assumed, for example, that the League of Nations would take care of freedom of the seas, and he had confidence that the machinery specially set up by the League would deal satisfactorily with disarmament. It did not do so, but that was not because he betrayed his principles, but because others betrayed the League.

Certain other points could not be carried out at Paris, notably those having to do with Russia and Turkey, because the confusion in those places had not sufficiently subsided.

When we rule out Russia and Turkey, and consider what the League was supposed to do, and include those points that were in large part carried out either in letter or in spirit, we have a far different picture. This is why men like Secretary

Lansing could honestly testify, after the Treaty of Versailles was signed, that in so far as circumstances then permitted, the Fourteen Points were "substantially" carried out. This could not have been said a few years later, but by that time a situation had developed over which Wilson could have no control.

Even so, the fact cannot be blinked that when the Germans laid down their arms they were tendered a solemn contract promising, with specified exceptions, the Fourteen Points. The contract did not say that the points would be "substantially" carried out, or carried out in so far as circumstances would permit. The contract was terribly binding; and from the German point of view no excuses were valid.

In any case, the word "betrayal" is far too strong when applied to Wilson and his Fourteen Points. There are errors of commission and errors of omission. Most of the criticism of Wilson is directed not at what he did but at what he failed to do. Most of his critics assume that he should have forced his Points fully and completely upon colleagues who did not want them, and who under no circumstances would accept them. Not even Wilson could do the impossible. The original error was to permit his name to be used in giving currency to the belief that he could.

Wilson was never willing to confess—and probably never believed—that he had betrayed his Points. He told the newspaper men before leaving Paris that he had secured more than he had expected when the Conference began, and he insisted that the general spirit of the Fourteen Points had permeated the discussions. As for betraying Germany, he declared to the very end that the Treaty was severe but just.

Allied apologists not only agreed with him on this last point; they also made much of the fact that the Treaty of Versailles was not so bad as that of Brest-Litovsk, which the Germans had imposed upon a vanquished Russia early in 1918.

This is all beside the point. It is true that Brest-Litovsk was a bad peace, so bad in fact as to provide unanswerable justification for the charge that the Germans would have dictated a

Carthaginian treaty had they been the victors. But two wrongs still do not make a right. The task before the negotiators at Paris was not to pay off old scores, or to make a treaty as bad as Brest-Litovsk, or as bad as the Germans might have made had they won, but to construct a workable and lasting peace which both the victors and the rest of the world so desperately needed.

8

The Treaty of Versailles in general and Wilson in particular have been savagely blamed for many sins that they did not commit.

Much of the Treaty was concerned with righting century-old wrongs. A wrong that old sometimes ceases to look like a wrong. The aggressions of Prussia, for example, had netted her territory, notably in Poland, which on the basis of self-determination had to be taken away. Yet the eggs had long been scrambled, and the unscrambling process created newer but perhaps lesser wrongs. It was no easy problem to thrust back into Central Europe a populous nation which had passed out of existence during the Presidency of George Washington in America. The ghosts of those who had partitioned Poland in the eighteenth century stalked through the halls of Versailles.

The men of Paris were blamed for creating the quarrelsome "succession states" of Czechoslovakia, Jugoslavia, and Poland, all of which were destined to sow dragon's teeth of trouble in Central Europe. But the Conference did not create these states. They sprang into being before the negotiators could meet. The task at Paris was to delineate their boundaries and erect safeguards to insure that they would live in peace with their minorities and their neighbors.

The Treaty of Versailles has been blamed for all the ills that befell Europe from 1919 to 1939. The truth is that there had been a grueling, demoralizing conflict of more than four years' duration before the Conference met. It has been competently estimated that the war alone cost Germany $100,000,000,000. If the negotiators at Paris had been angels from heaven they could not have drawn up a treaty which would have prevented many of the calamities of exhaustion and reconstruction. Europe was sick, desperately sick; and Harold Nicolson is correct when he says that those who write about Versailles are not describing a conference but a serious illness.

Lloyd George insists that most of the sins of the Treaty must be laid at the doors of the men who carried it out—or who failed to carry it out. With all due allowance for exaggeration, we must concede that the former prime minister has put his finger on a fundamental truth. Commissions were to be set up, plebiscites were to be held, reparations were to be determined and collected. The treaty in itself was no magic formula; no man-made document can be. Everything depended on the energy, intelligence, loyalty, broad-mindedness, and singleness of purpose of those who were charged with administering it. In many respects the executors of the Treaty are unquestionably far more censurable than its makers.

There is one final observation. The Treaty of Versailles— the treaty with Germany—was but one part of the European settlement. The treaties with Austria, Hungary, Bulgaria, and Turkey were intimately connected with it, just as Wilson had planned and later boasted. The very first section of every one of these treaties was the Covenant of the League of Nations. Not only was the Covenant the first section of the Treaty of Versailles, but other provisions of the same treaty were interlocked with it, and all the treaties were interlocked with one another. The Reparations Commission established by Versailles, for example, was charged with supervising the collection of reparations under the treaty with Austria.

The essential point is that the interlocking postwar settlements were a complicated and topheavy structure which could only endure if its most important foundation stone was put into place. The whole edifice was erected on the assumption, and with Wilson's assurances, that the United States would bear its share of the responsibility for guaranteeing the new world order. The Europeans did not like the architecture of the new building, but they accepted it as a cheap price for the cooperation of a powerful America.

Milestones

(From the St. Louis *Republic;* courtesy of the
St. Louis *Globe-Democrat*)

The most important foundation stone, as we all know, was never put into place. The precarious structure teetered along for more than a decade, and then crashed in ruins.

If the Europeans had been told at the outset that they could not count on our support, they would have built a different structure. Whether it would have been better, one cannot say;

but it would have been different, and perhaps it would have lasted longer.

9

We have already considered the blunders of the Paris negotiation at such length that their applicability to a future conference should be self-evident. But for purposes of re-emphasis and summary, it seems desirable to stress certain basic principles which the American people should keep in mind in connection with a general peace at the end of a great world conflict.

War aims should be unambiguous, practicable, acceptable to American public opinion, and closely correlated with the pronouncements of our allies.

The people should be so led during the conflict that their emotionalism will be held in leash. The greater the passions aroused by the fighting, the greater the difficulties in making a lasting settlement. One may win the war but lose the peace, as we did last time. The objective should be to pace one's self so as to win both.

American public opinion should be educated *in advance* to its responsibilities in world affairs, and more particularly to its responsibilities in executing the peace treaty. This campaign should be undertaken as early in the war as possible, for when the fighting ends the time is always too short for adequate instruction. Wilson made an heroic attempt to educate the country *after* the treaty was completed, but by that time the Senate had gained too big a head start.

Unconditional surrender on the part of the enemy is imperative, unless the conditions are defined with unmistakable clarity, unless they are capable of fulfillment, and unless the victors intend in good faith to fulfill them. Even so, unconditional surrender is no sure guarantee of an enduring peace.

The American peace commission should be bipartisan, with

adequate representation accorded the two great political parties, as well as the Senate of the United States.

The President should enter into the closest and most cordial possible relations with the leaders of both parties in the Senate —*before*, *during* and *after* the negotiations.

A preliminary peace should precede the final treaty, and it should speedily outline the military and other terms most pressingly in need of solution. This will enable the world to adjust itself to a peacetime footing, while giving passions time to cool off. At a later date the negotiators can approach the general settlement with greater deliberation and clearer vision.

The defeated powers should be privileged to discuss, both orally and in writing, the terms of the definitive treaty *while they are being drawn up*. This is the only practicable way in which the reasons for the unworkability of certain provisions may be adequately set forth.

The detailed covenant for a new world organization, if any, should not be written into the treaty of peace. General provision may be made in the pact for creating some such system at a subsequent time and under different auspices. Making peace with the enemy should not be confused with making a constitution for a new order.

No treaty can last unless it provides *workable* machinery for peaceful change in the light of changing conditions.

The victor can have vengeance, or he may have peace, but he cannot have both. In 1919 the Allies got neither, for vengeance was incomplete and short-lived. No great nation can be kept in bondage forever. The vengeance of 1919 enlisted neutral sympathy, created a "remorse complex" in the minds of liberals in the victor nations, and revived German nationalism. Germany needed to be persuaded that war was bad; instead she was convinced that the peace was bad. All these factors contributed to the final undoing of the Treaty of Versailles.

The Constitution should be amended so as to reduce the great obstructive power of the one-third minority in the Senate. Opponents of any treaty are armed with two votes; the proponents with only one. This is illogical, undemocratic, and in 1919 it was probably disastrous. The same thing could easily happen again. The sooner the Constitution is changed the better, because amendment takes time, and procrastination is easy. When treaty-making is not in prospect, the two-thirds rule seems unimportant; when it is in prospect, time is too short for amendment. If we wait for Congress to take steps to reduce its own power, we shall doubtless have to wait a long time. But the Constitution provides adequate machinery for the states to initiate and ratify amendments without the voluntary action of Congress.

The President of the United States should never again make promises which the Senate cannot reasonably be counted on to honor or public opinion to support. It will be a long time before the world recovers from the disillusionment of 1919.

The temple of peace must be built on the foundations of what people are likely to accept and what they will accept, not on what they should ideally accept.

Wilson had a noble vision but he made the tragic mistake of thinking that mankind, without the proper preparation and education, could attain a kind of international millennium at a single bound. As he told his associates on the *George Washington,* "If it won't work, it must be made to work." He assumed that human nature—with its suspicion, fear, selfishness, and greed—could be substantially changed overnight, especially American human nature. He took it for granted that our people would respond gladly to his gospel of unselfishness, speedily assume responsibilities commensurate with their new power, and willingly shoulder burdens from which they could expect no direct gains. Unto America much had been given; she should repay her debt to the rest of the world. It was to be a new era of joy through service.

Instead, we got Harding and "normalcy."

Statesmen must ever remember that mankind is shortsighted and perverse, and that he who would make haste too fast will almost inevitably fail. We shall not see the millennium in our day, or in our children's day; the best we can hope for is a substantial step forward on the tortuous path of international understanding and cooperation. If we can but learn the lessons from our last experience which are there for all to see, the price paid for them, though far too high, will not have been spent altogether in vain.

BIBLIOGRAPHICAL NOTES

INTRODUCTION

THIS BOOK is primarily a synthesis, not a research project on a monographic scale. It is largely, though by no means solely, a reinterpretation of facts that have for some little while been generally available, and for this reason, among others, it has not seemed desirable to present elaborate footnote documentation. Bibliographical comments are confined to moot questions, or to problems which need further amplification.

The bibliographies here listed are not exhaustive, but in a general way they indicate the most important sources of information, as well as the materials from which the basic facts have been drawn. This is primarily a study of the peace from the American point of view, and more particularly from that of Wilson, and consequently no effort has been made to present extensive references bearing upon purely European problems, though there exists a vast body of literature on this phase of the subject. Where translations exist, the English version is cited. Interest in the Treaty of Versailles has been so great that fortunately for the general reader most of the important French and German secondary accounts have been translated.

This study is particularly concerned with the reactions of American public opinion, and extensive use has been made of the newspaper press, notably the New York *Times,* and of the periodical press, notably the *Literary Digest.* Use has also been made of the important documentary collections in print, as well as other published materials, official or otherwise. It has been necessary to borrow heavily from the researches of others, and it can only be hoped that they have been given adequate recognition. In most cases it would have been a profitless expenditure of time to go behind their findings.

The archives of the Department of State are not currently available to investigators, though the publication by the Department of the first four volumes of its monumental peace collection has done much to fill this gap. The Woodrow Wilson papers in the Library of Congress were returned from their evacuation center in time to be consulted during two hurried vacation trips; and while the limitations of time did not permit so careful an examination as this great collection deserves, it was possible to consult, among other things, all of Wilson's "out" letters and cablegrams during the Conference period, and in addition a file of the secret minutes of the Council of Four. Fortunately, the task was simplified by Ray Stannard Baker's earlier researches with these papers. The manuscript minutes of the Council of Ten were originally examined in the Hoover Library, Stanford University, though they were subsequently published in the Department of State series referred to above.

The writer was also privileged to examine the House Papers, at Yale University; and certain other manuscript collections in the Library of Congress, notably those of Robert Lansing, Henry White, Ray Stannard Baker, and Senator Gilbert M. Hitchcock. Most of these collections have to some extent been worked over, and, with certain exceptions, they contributed shading to the picture rather than striking new lines. The most significant new revelations bear upon the fight for the ratification of the treaty, which will be dealt with in a sequel volume.

In the bibliographies and notes that follow, the full citation is given the first time only; thereafter the shortened form.

THE ROAD TO WAR

FOR EXTENDED bibliographies relating to this chapter, consult Samuel Flagg Bemis and Grace Gardner Griffin, *Guide to the Diplomatic History of the United States, 1775–1921* (Washington, 1935), pp. 655–672, and the bibliographies and footnotes of my *A Diplomatic History of the American People* (2nd ed., New York, 1942), chaps. XXXVII–XXXVIII. Among the better secondary accounts, one must single out for special mention C. C. Tansill, *America Goes to War* (Boston, 1938); Charles Seymour, *American Diplomacy During the World War* (Baltimore, 1934); Harley Notter, *The Origins of the Foreign Policy of Woodrow Wilson* (Baltimore, 1937); Edwin M. Borchard and W. P. Lage, *Neutrality for the United States* (New Haven, 1937); and Charles Seymour, *American Neutrality, 1914–1917* (New Haven, 1935). These are all substantial works by recognized scholars.

THE QUESTION OF PUBLIC OPINION. The role of American public opinion in connection with our entrance into the war in 1917 has been largely neglected by scholars, probably because the subject is not only enormous but nebulous. Yet it is of the greatest importance, because one indisputable fact is that Wilson would never have asked Congress to declare war unless certain that public opinion was ripe for it. Two unpublished studies have been of value: Emlyn David Jones, "Pacific Coast Press Opinion and the Break with Germany, 1917" (MS. master's thesis, Stanford University, 1942), and Albert Russell Buchanan, "European Propaganda and American Public Opinion, 1914–1917" (MS. doctoral dissertation, Stanford University, 1935). Dr. Buchanan has revised this study in the light of an extensive examination of newspaper and manuscript materials in the Library of Congress, and the present writer has been privileged to consult it in unpublished form. Dr. Buchanan has also published a valuable analysis of the editorial opinion of sixty-eight newspapers, from forty-eight states, for the month immediately following our entrance into the war, "American Editors Examine American War Aims and Plans in April, 1917," *Pacific Historical Review*, IX (1940), 253–265. Granted that newspaper opinion is not a thoroughly satisfactory index to public opinion, the fact is that this is the only study of its kind that has yet been published, and scholars would do well to examine it. Significantly, the newspaper editors overwhelmingly agreed on one thing: the United States had been forced into the war (p. 254).

WAR CAUSES AND WAR AIMS. The present chapter is concerned largely with pre-1917 attitudes and war aims, because any real understanding of the defeat of the Treaty of Versailles in the United States must go back to them. As George Creel well says: "The peace tangle will not unravel unless related to war aims, and war aims stand unsupported and somewhat overstrained unless related to the various emotional stages that marked the period of our neutrality" (*The War, the World and Wilson* [New York, 1920], p. 39).

WERE THE ALLIES LOSING EARLY IN 1917? During February and March, there was relatively little military news on the front page of the New York *Times*, and it was uniformly favorable to the Allies. Many reports were printed regarding starvation in Germany, and these stories were confirmed by the returning Ambassador Gerard (*ibid.*, March 12, 23, 1917). Shipping losses made the first page, but they were not spectacularly more serious than those of the months before the unrestricted submarine campaign was begun. By mid-March, it was recorded that the sinkings were slackening off (*ibid.*, March 15), though the toll became terrific late in April, *after* we entered the war. See J. A. Salter, *Allied Shipping Control* (Oxford, 1921), pp. 357–358. It is true that the Russian Revolution occurred in mid-March, but this was not generally regarded as an ominous portent: it was in fact widely believed that the Russians would fight harder now that they were becoming democratized. Further evidence of Allied strength and German weakness is to be seen in the Austrian peace overtures, begun in February, 1917; the confident paper partition of Germany by France and Russia in February, 1917; the Allied offensive under Nivelle in April and May, 1917; and the Reichstag resolution of July, 1917, favoring a liberal peace.

FEAR OF GERMANY IN THE UNITED STATES. It is undoubtedly true that there was much unreasoning fear of a German victory in the United States, but that this has been overemphasized is indicated by the delay with which the American people accepted the German submarine challenge. More than two months elapsed between the submarine announcement and the actual declaration of war, and during this time there were a number of incidents that could be regarded as "overt acts." At the Cabinet meeting of Feb. 2, 1917, two days *after* the German announcement, Wilson said, in response to a question as to which side he "wished to see win," that "he didn't wish to see either side win . . ." (A. W. Lane and L. H. Wall, eds., *The Letters of Franklin K. Lane* [Boston, 1922], p. 234). About one o'clock of the very same morning on which he presented his war message to Congress, Wilson exclaimed to Frank Cobb, "If there is any alternative, for God's sake, let's take it" (John L. Heaton, comp., *Cobb of "The World"* [New York, 1924], p. 270). The story of this interview was told by Cobb to one of his associates, who later recorded it. For this reason the exact words may be doubted, but the statement is in character. Both what Wilson said in Cabinet meeting and what he told Cobb indicate that he was not impressed with the German menace. On Jan. 4, 1919, Colonel House, Wilson's closest adviser, scoffed at the fear-of-Germany argument (Charles Seymour, *The Intimate Papers of Colonel House* [Boston, 1926], IV, 268). There is some reason to believe that the chief concern of Wilson and others was what would happen to American institutions if they had to be revamped so as to stand guard against aggressions on the part of German militarism. If the American people had felt themselves to be in immediate danger from Germany, it is difficult to understand why they were so leisurely in their war preparations, and why they delayed so many months before undertaking to send a large A.E.F.

WILSON'S CONFUSION OF CAUSES AND OBJECTIVES. This analysis is based on a reading of all of Wilson's published writings and addresses relevant to the problem. See Woodrow Wilson, *War and Peace: Presidential Messages, Addresses, and Other Papers (1917–1924)*, eds. Ray Stannard Baker and William E. Dodd (2 vols., New York, 1927), I, 22, 50, 158, 169, 170, 179, 198, 206, 259, 380, 397, 527, 538, 549, 637; II, 117, 118, 162, 211, 258, 366. Wilson's letter to Heflin (May 22, 1917) shows that at this time he still had the distinction between causes and objectives clearly in mind. On Aug. 19, 1919, testifying before the Senate Foreign Relations Committee, Wilson made the often quoted statement that we would have gone to war with Germany anyhow without the submarine attacks. (*Sen. Docs.,* 66 Cong., 1 sess., no. 76, p. 40). Whether this was another instance of Wilson's memory being warped by current war hatreds, or a projection of a "wish-phantasy" into the past, one cannot say. It should be noted that in this same testimony he said that he knew nothing of certain of the secret treaties before reaching Paris, which was not true. On Nov. 8, 1918, George Creel wrote Wilson that, while Wilson's leadership had made it a war to "make the world safe for democracy," it "was not that sort of war when we entered it" (*The War, the World and Wilson,* p. 145). Yet Wilson told the Council of Four, on April 20, 1919, that when he wrote his war aims he was writing the point of view of the American people, and on these principles the United States had entered the war (Woodrow Wilson Papers, IX–C).

LIMITED-LIABILITY WAR. This is a highly significant point which has never been adequately stressed. Two revealing symposia on the subject appear in the *Literary Digest* (March 3, 1917, pp. 538–539; April 7, 1917, pp. 965–967—the leading article).

THE BALANCE OF POWER IDEA. It is difficult to understand why latter-day writers, like Nicholas John Spykman, in *America's Strategy in World Politics* (New York, 1942), and Walter Lippmann, in *U.S. Foreign Policy* (Boston, 1943), assert that we entered the war primarily to insure our own safety and preserve the balance of power, except that this theory so closely fits the situation in 1941. Lesser minds than these have fallen into the error of reading the present back into the past. Such a theory presupposes that the Allies were visibly collapsing, and that we were in mortal fear of Germany, neither of which was the case. It would doubtless have been better, from the standpoint of America's acceptance of her share of world responsibility, if this had been true; and the fact that we ran out so lightly on our obligations in 1919–1920 is further evidence that it was not. For Wilson's abhorrence of the balance of power, see Woodrow Wilson, *War and Peace,* I, 257, 353, 410, 411.

CHAPTER TWO

THE PEN IS MIGHTIER

THE BEST source for Wilson's war-aims addresses is Woodrow Wilson, *War and Peace*, vol. I. Valuable background material appears in Ray Stannard Baker, *Woodrow Wilson: Life and Letters* (New York, 1939), vols. VII and VIII; and more generally in F. L. Paxson, *America at War, 1917–1918* (Boston, 1939). The publicity given to the Fourteen Points is described by its director, George Creel, in *How We Advertised America* (New York, 1920), and more briefly in the same author's *The War, the World and Wilson*. A revealing account of more recent date is James R. Mock and Cedric Larson, *Words That Won the War* (Princeton, 1939). For the effect of Allied propaganda on the German collapse, see George G. Bruntz, *Allied Propaganda and the Collapse of the German Empire in 1918* (Stanford University, 1938). David Lloyd George's *Memoirs of the Peace Conference* (2 vols., New Haven, 1939), vol. I, has a useful introductory chapter on Allied war aims. Lloyd George takes credit to the Allies for having anticipated Wilson in the formulation of war aims, and he believes that they were substantially carried out in the Treaty of Versailles. A useful study of this important subject is Ebba Dahlin, *French and German Public Opinion on Declared War Aims, 1914–1918* (Stanford University, 1933). An indispensable compilation is James B. Scott, ed., *Official Statements of War Aims and Peace Proposals, December 1916 to November 1918* (Washington, 1921).

WILSON AND SELF-DETERMINATION. While the idea of self-determination was not original with Wilson, he was doubtless attracted to it because it was so closely in harmony with American tradition as embodied in the Virginia Bill of Rights and the Declaration of Independence. It is also worth noting that Wilson was a Southerner, reared in war-ravaged Georgia; and the war fought by the South was one of the most perfect examples of self-determination in modern history. Wilson's expression of faith in self-determination preceded America's entry into the war. A clear statement appeared in his address of May 27, 1916 (Woodrow Wilson, *The New Democracy: Presidential Messages, Addresses, and Other Papers* [1913–1917], eds. R. S. Baker and W. E. Dodd [2 vols., New York, 1926], II, 187). For Wilson's assertion that the Fourteen Points were not his but an expression of the will of the American people, see Woodrow Wilson, *War and Peace*, II, 410.

Wilson's Fourteen and Supplementary Points

ADDRESS TO CONGRESS, JANUARY 8, 1918

1. Open covenants of peace, openly arrived at, after which there shall be no private international understandings of any kind but diplomacy shall proceed always frankly and in the public view.

2. Absolute freedom of navigation upon the seas, outside territorial waters, alike in peace and in war, except as the seas may be closed in whole or in part by international action for the enforcement of international covenants.

3. The removal, so far as possible, of all economic barriers and the establishment of an equality of trade conditions among all the nations consenting to the peace and associating themselves for its maintenance.

4. Adequate guarantees given and taken that national armaments will be reduced to the lowest point consistent with domestic safety.

5. A free, open-minded, and absolutely impartial adjustment of all colonial claims, based upon a strict observance of the principle that in determining all such questions of sovereignty the interests of the populations concerned must have equal weight with the equitable claims of the government whose title is to be determined.

6. The evacuation of all Russian territory and such a settlement of all questions affecting Russia as will secure the best and freest cooperation of the other nations of the world in obtaining for her an unhampered and unembarrassed opportunity for the independent determination of her own political development and national policy and assure her of a sincere welcome into the society of free nations under institutions of her own choosing; and, more than a

welcome, assistance also of every kind that she may need and may herself desire. The treatment accorded Russia by her sister nations in the months to come will be the acid test of their good will, of their comprehension of her needs as distinguished from their own interests, and of their intelligent and unselfish sympathy.

7. Belgium, the whole world will agree, must be evacuated and restored, without any attempt to limit the sovereignty which she enjoys in common with all other free nations. No other single act will serve as this will serve to restore confidence among the nations in the laws which they have themselves set and determined for the government of their relations with one another. Without this healing act the whole structure and validity of international law is forever impaired.

8. All French territory should be freed and the invaded portions restored, and the wrong done to France by Prussia in 1871 in the matter of Alsace-Lorraine, which has unsettled the peace of the world for nearly fifty years, should be righted, in order that peace may once more be made secure in the interest of all.

9. A readjustment of the frontiers of Italy should be effected along clearly recognizable lines of nationality.

10. The peoples of Austria-Hungary, whose place among the nations we wish to see safeguarded and assured, should be accorded the freest opportunity of autonomous development.

11. Rumania, Serbia, and Montenegro should be evacuated; occupied territories restored; Serbia accorded free and secure access to the sea; and the relations of the several Balkan states to one another determined by friendly counsel along historically established lines of allegiance and nationality; and international guarantees of the political and economic independence and territorial integrity of the several Balkan states should be entered into.

12. The Turkish portions of the present Ottoman Empire should be assured a secure sovereignty, but the other nationalities which are now under Turkish rule should be assured an undoubted security of life and an absolutely unmolested opportunity of autonomous development, and the Dardanelles should be permanently opened as a free passage to the ships and commerce of all nations under international guarantees.

13. An independent Polish state should be erected which should include the territories inhabited by indisputably Polish populations, which should be assured a free and secure access to the sea, and whose political and economic independence and territorial integrity should be guaranteed by international covenant.

14. A general association of nations must be formed under specific covenants for the purpose of affording mutual guarantees of political independence and territorial integrity to great and small states alike.

ADDRESS TO CONGRESS, FEBRUARY 11, 1918

15. That each part of the final settlement must be based upon the essential justice of that particular case and upon such adjustments as are most likely to bring a peace that will be permanent;

16. That peoples and provinces are not to be bartered about from sovereignty to sovereignty as if they were mere chattels and pawns in a game, even the great game, now forever discredited, of the balance of power; but that

17. Every territorial settlement involved in this war must be made in the interest and for the benefit of the populations concerned, and not as a part of any mere adjustment or compromise of claims amongst rival states; and

18. That all well-defined national aspirations shall be accorded the utmost satisfaction that can be accorded them without introducing new or perpetuating old elements of discord and antagonism that would be likely in time to break the peace of Europe and consequently of the world.

ADDRESS AT MOUNT VERNON, JULY 4, 1918

19. The destruction of every arbitrary power anywhere that can separately, secretly, and of its single choice disturb the peace of the world; or, if it cannot be presently destroyed, at the least its reduction to virtual impotence.

(17) (Compare with No. 17 above.) The settlement of every question, whether of territory, of sovereignty, of economic arrangement, or of political relationship, upon the basis of the free acceptance of that settlement by the people immediately concerned, and not upon the basis of the material interest or advantage of any other nation or people which may desire a different settlement for the sake of its own exterior influence or mastery.

20. The consent of all nations to be governed in their conduct towards each other by the same principles of honor and of respect for the common law of civilized society that govern the individual citizens of all modern states in their relations with one another; to the end that all promises and covenants may be sacredly observed, no private plots or conspiracies hatched, no selfish injuries wrought with impunity, and a mutual trust established upon the handsome foundation of a mutual respect for right.

(14) (Compare with No. 14 above.) The establishment of an organization of peace which shall make it certain that the combined power of free nations will check every invasion of right and serve

to make peace and justice the more secure by affording a definite tribunal of opinion to which all must submit and by which every international readjustment that cannot be amicably agreed upon by the peoples directly concerned shall be sanctioned.

ADDRESS IN NEW YORK CITY, SEPTEMBER 27, 1918

(15) (Compare with No. 15 above.) The impartial justice meted out must involve no discrimination between those to whom we wish to be just and those to whom we do not wish to be just. It must be a justice that plays no favorites and knows no standard but the equal rights of the several peoples concerned;

21. No special or separate interest of any single nation or any group of nations can be made the basis of any part of the settlement which is not consistent with the common interest of all;

22. There can be no leagues or alliances or special covenants and understandings within the general and common family of the League of Nations.

23. And more specifically, there can be no special, selfish economic combinations within the League and no employment of any form of economic boycott or exclusion except as the power of economic penalty by exclusion from the markets of the world may be vested in the League of Nations itself as a means of discipline and control.

24. All international agreements and treaties of every kind must be made known in their entirety to the rest of the world.

CHAPTER THREE

AN ARMISTICE
THAT WAS NOT AN ARMISTICE

THE BEST account in some detail is Charles Seymour, *American Diplomacy During the World War*. The same author has made available many of the invaluable papers of Colonel House in *The Intimate Papers of Colonel House*, vol. IV. House was Wilson's representative in the Paris negotiations. David F. Houston, *Eight*

Years with Wilson's Cabinet, 1913 to 1920 (2 vols., Garden City, N.Y., 1926), vol. I, contains records of Cabinet discussions of the German peace overtures. Valuable background material appears in R. S. Baker, *Wilson,* vol. VIII, and Joseph P. Tumulty, *Woodrow Wilson As I Know Him* (Garden City, N.Y., 1921). Tumulty was Wilson's private secretary. The standard life of General Bliss, based on his private papers, is Frederick Palmer, *Bliss, Peacemaker* (New York, 1934); see also Tasker H. Bliss, "The Armistices," in *American Journal of International Law,* XVI (1922), 509–522. Bliss, an American, was on the Supreme War Council, and his observations are of great value. C. E. Callwell, *Field-Marshal Sir Henry Wilson* (2 vols., New York, 1927), vol. II, reflects British bitterness at Wilson's lone-hand conduct of the pre-Armistice negotiations. An able defense of the Armistice is J. J. H. Mordacq, *La guerre mondiale, pages vécues: la vérité sur l'armistice* (Paris, 1929) ; and a penetrating discussion of the series of armistices has recently been published by the distinguished military writer, Sir Frederick Maurice, *The Armistices of 1918* (London, 1943). See also George B. Noble, *Policies and Opinions at Paris, 1919* (New York, 1935), chap. II; and Harold Nicolson, *Peacemaking, 1919* (New York, 1939), chap. I. Important documents bearing upon the negotiation of the Armistice may be found in *Foreign Relations of the United States, 1918,* Supp. 1 (Washington, 1933), vol. I; and James B. Scott, ed., *Preliminary History of the Armistice: Official Documents Published by the German National Chancellery by Order of the Ministry of State,* transl. by the Carnegie Endowment for International Peace, Division of International Law (New York, 1924). See also Gabriel Terrail, *Les négociations secrètes et les quatre armistices* (Paris, 1921).

WILSON AND THE ARMISTICE NEGOTIATIONS. Wilson's willingness to enter into negotiations may be explained in part by his statement to Colonel House that he did not want the stain of invading and ravaging Germany to tarnish Allied arms. Charles Seymour, *House Papers,* IV, 83. Wilson's pressure on the German people to get rid of the Kaiser seems to have been a latter-day development. It may have been in part a throwback to his earlier policy of trying to force undesirable rulers out of the Latin American countries, notably Huerta in Mexico.

CHAPTER FOUR

THE MAN WITHOUT A COUNTRY

AN EXHAUSTIVE study of the campaign of 1918 needs to be done, with attention to trends in preceding and succeeding elections. The most careful investigations to date are Selig Adler, "The Congressional Election of 1918," *South Atlantic Quarterly*, XXXVI (1937), 447–465; and Denna Frank Fleming, *The United States and the League of Nations, 1918–1920* (New York, 1932), chap. II. These should be supplemented by Charles P. Howland, ed., *Survey of American Foreign Relations, 1928* (New Haven, 1928), which pays some attention to an analysis of the contests in the various states. Valuable background material appears in R. S. Baker, *Wilson*, vol. VIII; George Creel, *The War, the World and Wilson;* D. F. Houston, *Eight Years with Wilson's Cabinet,* vol. I; J. P. Tumulty, *Woodrow Wilson As I Know Him;* H. C. Lodge, ed., *Selections from the Correspondence of Theodore Roosevelt and Henry Cabot Lodge, 1884–1918* (2 vols., New York, 1925), vol. II. See also A. D. H. Smith, *Mr. House of Texas* (New York, 1940), pp. 272–276. The text of the October appeal may be conveniently found in Woodrow Wilson, *War and Peace,* I, 286–288.

REPUBLICAN INCONSISTENCY. It is an ironical fact that there was ample Republican precedent for the Democratic appeal, notably in 1898, when President McKinley asked for support on the eve of the negotiations with Spain. Young Theodore Roosevelt and Henry Cabot Lodge, who were later to criticize Wilson for doing essentially the same thing, vigorously applauded their President. It should be noted, however, that earlier appeals were less spectacular or less bald than that of Wilson. This subject is well treated in Fleming, *op. cit.,* pp. 47–51.

WILSON AND THE PURGE IDEA. During the summer of 1918 Wilson had interfered with some success in the Democratic primaries to secure the election of loyal Democrats. This, of course, was not the same as urging the defeat of Republicans; but it may have given Wilson false notions. See *Literary Digest,* Aug. 24, 1918, pp. 10–11.

DEMOCRATIC DISORGANIZATION. The Democratic national organization had suffered because the able national chairman, Vance C. McCormick, had been devoting his energies to the War Trade Board, while the Republican Committee, under Will Hays, was very active. Wilson's influence with the party was not so strong as it might have been, in part because he was certain to go out of office in 1921. The current influenza epidemic prevented public meetings, which the Democrats would have found useful in combating the last-minute Republican misrepresentations inspired by Wilson's appeal. Ray Stannard Baker interviewed Mr. McCormick, July 15, 1928, on the subject of the October appeal, and an interesting memorandum of this interview appears in the Baker papers, Library of Congress.

THE FORD-NEWBERRY ELECTION. Spencer Ervin, in *Henry Ford vs. Truman H. Newberry: The Famous Senate Election Contest* (New York, 1935), presents a strong brief in support of the proposition that Newberry was more sinned against than sinning. Whatever the technicalities of the case, the election was very close, and may have been decided by too liberal a use of money by the Republicans.

F. D. ROOSEVELT AND THE 1942 CONGRESSIONAL ELECTION. Wilson lost 5 seats in the Senate and 25 in the House. In 1942, also in the midst of war, Roosevelt lost 9 in the Senate and 46 in the House. (See *The American Year Book,* 1942, p. 66.) Roosevelt's defeat, though numerically more severe than Wilson's, did not result in a loss of control of either body. The Republicans in 1942 actually polled more than 50 per cent of the popular vote. Roosevelt issued no appeal, and was criticized by many Democrats for not having provided the necessary leadership. Perhaps he was deterred by Wilson's unfortunate experience, and his own rather unhappy attempts at "purging." In any event, this shows that in time of war Congressional reverses may be suffered, with or without a Presidential appeal. In 1942 few informed persons seriously claimed that Roosevelt was a repudiated President.

CHAPTER FIVE

JOVE STEPS DOWN FROM OLYMPUS

THE MOST important new material appears in *Papers Relating to the Foreign Relations of the United States, 1919: The Paris Peace Conference* (Washington, 1942), vol. I. (Hereafter cited as *U.S. Peace Documents.*) This is the monumental series of documents currently being published by the Department of State. Considerable light is thrown on the problem of Wilson's going by R. S. Baker, *Wilson,* vol. VIII, and Charles Seymour, *House Papers,* vol. IV. Observations by those close to Wilson appear in D. F. Houston, *Eight Years with Wilson's Cabinet,* vol. I; J. P. Tumulty, *Woodrow Wilson As I Know Him;* Robert Lansing, *The Peace Negotiations: A Personal Narrative* (Boston, 1921); and George Creel, *The War, the World and Wilson.* See also Allan Nevins, *Henry White: Thirty Years of American Diplomacy* (New York, 1930).

WAS WILSON PERSUADED TO STAY IN PARIS? Robert Lansing, in his *The Big Four and Others of the Peace Conference* (Boston, 1921), pp. 13–14, says that, for two or three weeks after Wilson reached Paris, Clemenceau and his colleagues exerted all of their powers òf persuasion to induce Wilson to stay as a delegate. David Lloyd George, in his *Memoirs of the Peace Conference,* I, 89, publishes what purports to be evidence along the same lines. While it is doubtless true that Clemenceau relaxed his opposition to Wilson's presence after the latter reached Paris, it is clear that from the very beginning Wilson had every intention of acting as a guiding force, and he needed no persuasion to do so. As early as Nov. 13, 1918, he cabled House that he expected to preside. (*U.S. Peace Documents,* I, 129. See also Charles Seymour, *House Papers,* IV, 209.)

CHAPTER SIX

WILSON AND HIS "ERRAND BOYS"

THE MOST important new light appears in *U.S. Peace Documents,* I. See also R. S. Baker, *Wilson,* vol. VIII; Charles Seymour, *House Papers,* vol. IV; J. P. Tumulty, *Woodrow Wilson As I Know Him.* A good brief discussion is in D. F. Fleming, *The United States and the League of Nations.* For Lansing, see Robert Lansing, *The Peace Negotiations.* For House, consult Charles Seymour, *House Papers,* vol. IV, and A. D. H. Smith, *Mr. House of Texas,* the only full-length biography of House, and undocumented. Also the unreliable but suggestive George Sylvester Viereck, *The Strangest Friendship in History* (New York, 1932). For White, see Allan Nevins, *Henry White,* one of the most revealing biographies of the period. For Bliss, consult Frederick Palmer, *Bliss,* which is based on Bliss's private papers. On Root and Taft, see Philip C. Jessup, *Elihu Root* (2 vols., New York, 1938), vol. II, and Henry F. Pringle, *The Life and Times of William Howard Taft* (2 vols., New York, 1939), vol. II, both of which are outstanding biographies.

COMMISSION POSSIBILITIES. There was considerable pressure from labor groups to put Samuel Gompers on the Commission, and there was also some talk about having a woman and a representative from the West. Wilson sternly resisted all efforts to secure group representation (see *U.S. Peace Documents,* I, 173). Secretary of the Treasury McAdoo and ex-President Charles W. Eliot of Harvard were prominently mentioned, but apparently were not seriously considered by Wilson. There was also some support for Bryan, but Wilson dismissed him for obvious reasons. Wilson planned to take his Secretary of War, Newton D. Baker, as a representative on military matters; but when it was learned that Secretary McAdoo was going to resign, it seemed unwise to weaken the Cabinet further and thus disquiet the country. General Bliss was then chosen. Most of the above facts are taken from *U.S. Peace Documents,* I, 155–192.

REPUBLICAN ALTERNATIVES. So far as the records reveal, Wilson never planned to take more than one Republican out of five. He seriously considered asking the pro-Wilson Governor McCall of Massachusetts, who would have been most distasteful to his fellow Republicans. He actually did invite Republican Justice Day of the Supreme Court, a veteran of the 1898 negotiations with Spain; but the aged jurist declined (*ibid.*, p. 159), presumably for reasons of health, but possibly also because it seemed unwise to involve the Court in peacemaking. Wilson then turned to Henry White.

THE ROLE OF ROOT. Root had served as head of an American mission to Russia in 1917, and apparently some friction developed between him and Wilson as a result of it. Root was doubtful whether he would have accepted a place on the Commission after Wilson announced he was going as a delegate (P. C. Jessup, *Root,* II, 380). Shortly before Wilson left for Paris, House enthusiastically seconded a suggestion that Root be invited to come as general adviser with the title of Counsel to the American Plenipotentiaries. Wilson declined on the ground that to appoint Root at that time would suggest a lack of confidence in the delegation as formally constituted (*ibid.*). Whether this was the real reason or a good one, the fact is that Wilson did not want Root along. In connection with Taft, Hughes, and Root, it is to be noted that Lloyd George was also criticized for not appointing his political rival, Herbert Henry Asquith. Clemenceau likewise ignored commanding political figures. See Geoffrey Bruun, *Clemenceau* (Cambridge, Mass., 1943), p. 187.

CHAPTER SEVEN

THE COMING OF THE MESSIAH

FOR THE work of the Inquiry, see James T. Shotwell, *At the Paris Peace Conference* (New York, 1937), an important work by one of the members. Consult also the account by Dr. Sidney E. Mezes (the Director) in Edward M. House and Charles Seymour, eds., *What Really Happened at Paris* (New York, 1921), chap. I; also Ingram Bander, "Sidney Edward Mezes and 'The Inquiry,'" in *Journal of Modern History,* XI (1939), 199–202. Wilson's remarks to the experts on the *George Washington* are conveniently found in Charles Seymour, *House Papers*, IV, 280–283; Wilson's speeches on his European tour, in Woodrow Wilson, *War and Peace*, vol. I. Revealing comments on Wilson's ovations appear in David Lloyd George, *Memoirs of the Peace Conference*, vol. I; Norval Richardson, *My Diplomatic Education* (New York, 1923), an account by an American diplomat in Italy; Irwin Hood Hoover, *Forty-two Years in the White House* (Boston, 1934), which is a rather superficial description by the White House usher; George Creel, *The War, the World and Wilson*, by the Chairman of the Committee on Public Information; and especially Edith Bolling Wilson (Mrs. Woodrow Wilson), *My Memoir* (Indianapolis, 1939), which is intimate and stresses the feminine viewpoint. The biographies of Wilson by David Lawrence and William Allen White contain some color and anecdote. The reactions of the French press are well presented in George B. Noble, *Policies and Opinions at Paris*, chap. III, and in R. C. Binkley, "Reactions of European Public Opinion to Woodrow Wilson's Statesmanship from the Armistice to the Peace at Versailles" (MS. doctoral dissertation, Stanford University, 1927). See also H. H. Merriman, "The French and Woodrow Wilson, 1912–1918: A Study in Public Opinion" (MS. doctoral dissertation, Harvard University, 1937).

ATTEMPTS TO KEEP WILSON FROM THE MASSES. The incident in Italy is taken from Creel, *op. cit.*, pp. 168–171, and is corroborated by Mrs. Wilson's *My Memoir*, p. 217. Mrs. Wilson also tells how a group of French soldiers were deliberately kept in quarters while Wilson was visiting the devastated regions, but were set at liberty as soon as the Presidential party had passed (p. 235).

CHAPTER EIGHT

BLUNDERING BEGINNINGS

FOR GENERAL bibliographies on the Peace Conference, consult S. F. Bemis and G. G. Griffin, *Guide to the Diplomatic History of the United States*, pp. 673–684; Nina Almond and Ralph H. Lutz,

An Introduction to a Bibliography of the Paris Peace Conference (Stanford University, 1935); and two outstanding bibliographical articles, R. C. Binkley, "Ten Years of Peace Conference History," *Journal of Modern History,* I (1929), 607–629; and Paul Birdsall, "The Second Decade of Peace Conference History," *ibid.,* XI (1939), 362–378. The same author has the most scholarly single-volume analysis of the whole problem in *Versailles Twenty Years After* (New York, 1941).

On the whole, the most valuable work on the Conference from the point of view of Wilson and the United States is still Ray Stannard Baker's *Woodrow Wilson and World Settlement* (3 vols., Garden City, N.Y., 1923). It supersedes Mr. Baker's sketchy *What Wilson Did at Paris* (Garden City, N.Y., 1919). Though the larger work is marred by too sympathetic an attitude toward Wilson, it reproduces many documents from the Wilson collection, notably from the secret minutes of the Council of Four, which to this day have not been published. No less useful in many ways is Charles Seymour's *House Papers,* vol. IV, which corrects Baker's *World Settlement* on a number of points. An extremely valuable narrative and diary by one of the American experts is J. T. Shotwell, *At the Paris Peace Conference.* A series of lectures by experts who were at the Conference was published in E. M. House and Charles Seymour, eds., *What Really Happened at Paris.* Charles Seymour has a brief but sound general account, *Woodrow Wilson and the World War* (New Haven, 1921). Two leading experts, Charles H. Haskins and Robert H. Lord, collaborated in writing *Some Problems of the Peace Conference* (Cambridge, Mass., 1920). H. J. Coolidge and R. H. Lord, in *Archibald Cary Coolidge: Life and Letters* (Boston, 1932), present some interesting data on an American expert who was primarily concerned with the Central European settlement. Herbert Hoover has some brief observations from the isolationist point of view, chiefly on the economic questions, in his *America's First Crusade* (New York, 1942).

H. W. V. Temperley, ed., *A History of the Peace Conference of Paris* (6 vols., London, 1920–1924), is a cooperative work in the nature of a semiofficial British history. The British point of view is further set forth in David Lloyd George's *Memoirs of the Peace Conference;* in Winston S. Churchill, *The World Crisis, 1918–1928, The Aftermath* (New York, 1929); and in Harold Nicolson, *Peace-*

making 1919, which, though out of focus in its characterization of Wilson and other persons, is a brilliantly penetrating account of the Conference. The present writer is indebted to this work for a considerable number of his ideas. Valuable glimpses also appear in *Lord Riddell's Intimate Diary of the Peace Conference and After, 1918–1923* (New York, 1934); in C. E. Callwell, *Field-Marshal Sir Henry Wilson,* vol. II; and in Henry Borden, ed., *Robert Laird Borden: His Memoirs* (2 vols., New York, 1938). See also R. H. Beadon, *Some Memories of the Peace Conference* (London, 1933). The French point of view is most ably set forth by André Tardieu, one of the French Commissioners, in *The Truth About the Treaty* (Indianapolis, 1921). Consult also Geneviève Tabouis, *The Life of Jules Cambon* (London, 1938, trans. by C. F. Atkinson). G. B. Noble, *Policies and Opinions at Paris, 1919,* discusses French policy and opinion against the general background of the Conference.

Among the numerous books by British journalists, one must single out H. Wilson Harris, *The Peace in the Making* (New York, 1920), which is remarkably fair and accurate for the time; Sisley Huddleston, *Peace-Making at Paris* (London, 1919), which is less satisfactory; the same author's *In My Time* (New York, 1938); Henry Wickham Steed, *Through Thirty Years, 1892–1922* (2 vols., Garden City, N.Y., 1924), whose author was close to some of the leading statesmen; and E. J. Dillon, *The Inside Story of the Peace Conference* (New York, 1920), which is not trustworthy.

Material of some value by American journalists may be found in O. G. Villard, *Fighting Years;* C. T. Thompson, *The Peace Conference Day by Day* (New York, 1920), which is in the nature of a newspaper diary; Harry Hansen, *The Adventures of the Fourteen Points* (New York, 1919); Lincoln Steffens, *The Autobiography of Lincoln Steffens* (2 vols., New York, 1931); and Ella Winter and Granville Hicks, eds., *The Letters of Lincoln Steffens* (2 vols., New York, 1938). See also M. P. Briggs, *George D. Herron and the European Settlement* (Stanford University, 1932).

The most important single documentary collection that has appeared in full to date is David Hunter Miller's monumental *My Diary at the Conference of Paris* (21 vols., New York, 1924–1926), though it is being superseded in part by *U.S. Peace Documents.*

Other titles have already been cited, or will be cited in successive Bibliographical Notes.

On the general subject matter of Chapter VIII, R. S. Baker, *World Settlement,* vol. I, and Charles Seymour, *House Papers,* vol. IV, are especially valuable. Baker's chapter on publicity is revealing; he was in a position to know as much about the problem as anyone else. On the question of the locale of the Conference, *U.S. Peace Documents,* I, 119–127, provides important new information. See also David Lloyd George, *Memoirs of the Peace Conference,* vol. I. On the problem of publicity see J. P. Tumulty, *Woodrow Wilson As I Know Him,* and J. T. Shotwell, *At the Paris Peace Conference.* Shotwell was in Paris with the American delegation, while Tumulty watched the home front. The viewpoint of the journalists is effectively set forth by the well-known American liberal, O. G. Villard, *Fighting Years,* and by the British liberal, H. W. Harris, *The Peace in the Making,* and by the internationally known correspondent, Sisley Huddleston, *Peace-Making at Paris.* The French point of view on these problems is well described in G. B. Noble, *Policies and Opinions at Paris.*

WILSON AND OPEN COVENANTS. While Wilson did not publicly explain his precise views on the subject of open covenants, he did make several feeble gestures in the interest of clarification. On March 12, 1918, he wrote a letter to Secretary Lansing, setting forth exactly what he had in mind. This was transmitted to Congress, and finally embalmed in the *Congressional Record* on June 12, 1918 (*Cong. Record,* 65 Cong., 2 sess., p. 7653). Wilson also approved the explanation of open covenants prepared by Messrs. Lippmann and Cobb in their glossary on the Fourteen Points. But this was not made public until long after the Conference. At Paris, Wilson set forth his views at a secret session of the Council of Ten (Jan. 13, 1919), but this statement was not published until much later. See *U.S. Peace Documents,* III, 536. Speaking at Tacoma, Washington, on September 13, 1919, while touring the country on behalf of the Treaty, Wilson still failed to make it clear that there must be secret discussions preliminary to open covenants. See Woodrow Wilson, *War and Peace,* II, 178.

CHAPTER NINE

THE PERILS OF IMPRECISION

ON THE organization of the Conference see R. S. Baker, *World Settlement*, vols. I, II; Charles Seymour, *House Papers*, vol. IV; Robert C. Binkley, "New Light on the Paris Peace Conference," in *Political Science Quarterly*, XLVI (1931), 335–361; 509–547; C. H. Haskins and R. H. Lord, *Some Problems of the Peace Conference;* Robert Lansing, *The Peace Negotiations* and *The Big Four;* and Harold Nicolson, *Peacemaking 1919*, chaps. IV–VI. The text of the French proposal of Nov. 29, 1918, may be found in R. S. Baker, *World Settlement*, III, 55–63. On the secret treaties, see R. S. Baker, *Wilson*, vols. VII, VIII; Charles Seymour, *House Papers*, III, chap. II; *Senate Docs.*, 66 Cong., 1 sess., no. 76 (Wilson before Senate Foreign Relations Committee); and *ibid.*, no. 106 (Hearings on the Treaty of Versailles); also *Papers Relating to the Foreign Relations of the United States: The Lansing Papers, 1914–1920* (Washington, 1939–1940), II, 23–25.

PUBLICATION OF THE SECRET TREATIES. The material in the text on the republication by American newspapers is taken largely from R. S. Baker, *World Settlement*, I, 32 n. The figures given by Oswald G. Villard, editor of the New York *Evening Post*, which first published the treaties in the United States, are somewhat different. He says that the treaties were syndicated in nine other daily newspapers, and then reprinted in pamphlet form and sold on the news stands of New York, Boston, Philadelphia, Chicago, Washington, and other cities. Two copies were also mailed to the White House. Colonel House apparently received two of them. See Villard, *Fighting Years*, pp. 470–472.

WILSON'S UNTRUTHFULNESS. Only the naïve will be shocked at Wilson's misstatements before the Senate Committee. Few men have gone far in politics without having occasionally "to chip the cube of truth to make it roll." A careful analysis of the writings and addresses of politicians, especially if they make many speeches, will almost invariably reveal inconsistencies and contradictions. There are a number in Wilson's speeches. Two days before he sailed to Europe, for example, he told Congress that the Allied governments "desire my personal counsel," which does not square with his anger over their opposition to his coming. See Woodrow Wilson, *War and Peace*, I, 322. Although, as pointed out in the text, Wilson was clear on many details of the Conference while before the Senate Committee, he did not remember that he had invited China to sever relations with the Central Powers in 1917, which he had and which was an important step (*Senate* Docs., 66 Cong., 1 sess., no. 76, p. 30).

CHAPTER TEN

THE OLYMPIANS

THE BEST general characterization of the Big Four as a group is Robert Lansing's *The Big Four*, which is penetrating. There are few books bearing upon the Conference which do not contain some reference to the Big Four, but one must single out for special mention R. S. Baker's *World Settlement;* Charles Seymour's *House Papers*, vol. IV; Harold Nicolson's *Peacemaking 1919;* and Gabriel Terrail, *Le combat des trois* (Paris, 1922), which contains excerpts from the yet unpublished and confidential minutes of the Council of Four. Nicolson, though brilliant, must be used with caution, for in his unfriendly characterization of Wilson he is as far from the mark as J. M. Keynes in his *The Economic Consequences of the Peace* (New York, 1920). Lloyd George stands self-revealed (and partially self-concealed) in his *Memoirs of the Peace Conference*. Glimpses of Lloyd George appear in Winston S. Churchill's brilliant if somewhat lurid *The World Crisis;* in Lord Riddell's *Intimate Diary of the Peace Conference and After;* in C. E. Callwell's *Field-Marshal Sir Henry Wilson*, vol. II (Wilson is bitterly outspoken); and in H. W. Steed's *Through Thirty Years*, vol. II, which is by a high-grade journalist who had intimate contacts with the leading statesmen. Georges Clemenceau's *Grandeur and Misery of Victory* (trans. by F. M. Atkinson, New York, 1930), is an embittered defense of his making of the peace; while the most recent and most useful biography of the Tiger is Geoffrey Bruun, *Clemenceau*. Colonel Stephen Bonsal, an American interpreter, saw a good deal of Clemenceau during the latter's convalescence, and sets forth some amusing anecdotes in *Unfinished Business* (Garden City, N.Y., 1944), Pt. III. An excellent bibliography on Wilson is published by Charles Seymour in the *Dictionary of American Biography*, XX, 367–368. Intimate glimpses appear in Edith Bolling Wilson, *My Memoir*, and I. H. Hoover, *Forty-two Years in the White House*. Of the various biographies of Wilson, that by William E. Dodd suffers from an excess of sympathy; that by William A. White from a lack of sympathy. David Lawrence, *The True Story of Woodrow Wilson* (New York, 1924), is worth consulting. Two outstanding character sketches of Wilson are in Gamaliel Bradford's *The Quick and the Dead* (Boston, 1929), chap. II; and D. F. Houston, *Eight Years with Wilson's Cabinet*, II, 155–254.

CHAPTER ELEVEN

THE WHITE MAN'S BURDEN

AMONG THE numerous works touching upon the adoption of the mandate system, one must particularly mention David Lloyd George's *Memoirs of the Peace Conference*, I, chap. X; R. S. Baker's *World Settlement*, I, chap. XV; Charles Seymour's *House Papers*, vol. IV; David Hunter Miller, *The Drafting of the Covenant* (2 vols., New York, 1928), chap. IX; and G. L. Beer, *African Questions at the Paris Peace Conference* (New York, 1923). Beer was one of the American experts on colonies. The views expressed by the Germans at Paris are conveniently compiled in Alma Luckau, *The German Delegation at the Paris Peace Conference* (New York, 1941). For an excellent brief discussion see Paul Birdsall, *Versailles Twenty Years After*, chap. III.

ORIGINS OF THE MANDATE IDEA. Wilson apparently conceived of the idea independently of General Jan C. Smuts, of South Africa, who is sometimes given credit for it. Smuts would have applied the scheme only to territories formerly belonging to Russia, Austria-Hungary, and Turkey, and not to the former German colonies (Charles Seymour, *House Papers*, IV, 284–285).

THE IDEA OF AN AMERICAN MANDATE. Late in Oct., 1918, Colonel House reported to Wilson that Lloyd George had suggested that the United States take over the trusteeship of German East Africa. House was under the impression that the British wanted the United States to secure something so that the British could with better grace take what they desired (*U.S. Peace Documents*, I, 407). This was undoubtedly one of the motives behind the later request that the United States assume a mandate for Armenia and Constantinople.

THE ARMENIAN MANDATE. Professor William L. Westermann, one of the American experts at Paris, is strongly critical of America's failure to assume its responsibilities toward Armenia. See his chapter in E. M. House and Charles Seymour, *What Really Happened at Paris*, chap. VIII. Herbert Hoover recalls that he was approached by Colonel House on the subject of being named governor of the Armenian mandate (Herbert Hoover, *America's First Crusade*, p. 48). On May 21, 1919, Wilson told his colleagues on the Council of Four that while in his judgment the American people would oppose taking a mandate over any part of Asia Minor where they had no material interests, he was nevertheless hopeful that he could secure acceptance of a mandate over Armenia and Constantinople, where the United States had missionary and other interests (Woodrow Wilson Papers, IX–C).

JAPANESE MANDATED ISLANDS. The conclusions here expressed regarding the 1898–1899 negotiations between Germany and Spain for the Pacific islands are based primarily on the manuscript records of the Department of State for that period, now in the National Archives. There is also considerable material in *Die Grosse Politik der Europäischen Kabinette*, Band XV, Kapitel XCVIII. It is possible that Wilson attached little importance to the islands, partly because he expected that America would leave the Philippines, in line with Democratic policy, and in that event we should not need bases for strategic support of our possessions in the Far East. A number of years later, Admiral A. T. Mahan, the world-famous naval authority, recalled: "When the Caroline and Ladrone Islands were about to be ceded to Germany by Spain in 1898, I received more than one letter urging me to use any influence I could exert to induce our government to resist the step. My reply was that, besides having no influence, I saw no sufficient reason for our opposition." (*Armaments and Arbitration* [New York, 1912], p. 80.) It is hardly fair to blame McKinley for not seeing what Admiral Mahan could not see.

Under date of Dec. 14, 1918, Third Assistant Secretary of State Breckinridge Long prepared for the United States peace delegation a memorandum of extraordinary interest. His plan was that at the Conference the United States should work for the return of the islands to Germany, and then, when the Conference had adjourned, take them over on an indemnity or some other basis. There is no evidence that this proposal was looked upon favorably; certainly not by such a stern advocate of morality in international dealings as Wilson. It is interesting that Long did not make any mention of the islands as potential air bases. (*U.S. Peace Documents*, II, 512–515.)

On Feb. 13, 1919, the Intelligence Section of the American experts at Paris submitted a lengthy report ("Black Book") on the German North Pacific islands. It recommended that they be turned over to Japan as a mandate, with proper safeguards regarding fortification. The American experts concluded that the islands had "slight importance," except "possibly" from the standpoint of military strategy. The possible strategic value of the islands seemed even more negligible to the experts in view of the prospective establishment of the League of Nations and the possible abolition of the submarine. The report concluded that the United States had no legitimate claim to the islands, and that to demand them would not only offend Japan but undermine America's strong moral position at the Conference. (Woodrow Wilson Papers, IX–A.)

CHAPTER TWELVE

A LIVING THING IS BORN

THE MOST important single work is D. H. Miller, *The Drafting of the Covenant*. The author was an American expert and one of the chief architects of the finished Covenant. Consult also his monumental *My Diary*, and his brief account in E. M. House and Charles Seymour, *What Really Happened at Paris*, chap. XVII. Colonel Stephen Bonsal, who was the interpreter for Wilson and House on the League of Nations Commission, has just published his contemporary notes under the title *Unfinished Business*. While they add little to Miller and Seymour on the formation of the Covenant, they reproduce a good deal of useful color and corroborative data. The difficulties of transacting business through the medium of an interpreter are effectively portrayed. See also Charles Seymour, *House Papers*, vol. IV, and Robert Lansing, *The Peace Negotiations*. Lord Robert Cecil tells his part in the story in *A Great Experiment* (London, 1941). There is also some important light on the place of the Covenant on the agenda in André Tardieu, *The Truth About the Treaty*. R. S. Baker's *World Settlement*, vol. II, contains an important account, which tends to overstress European opposition to the League idea. Lloyd George, in his *Memoirs of the Peace Conference*, vol. I, chap. XIV, swings the pendulum violently the other way. On the question of origins, consult Theodore Marburg, *Development of the League of Nations Idea* (2 vols., New York, 1932); Florence Wilson, *The Origins of the League Covenant* (London, 1928); and Charles Howard-Ellis, *The Origin, Structure, and Working of the League of Nations* (Boston, 1928). Useful secondary accounts are G. B. Noble, *Policies and Opinions at Paris*, chap. IV; and Paul Birdsall, *Versailles Twenty Years After*, chap. V.

THE INTEGRAL PRINCIPLE. David Hunter Miller is of the opinion that the incorporation of the Covenant in the treaty was "itself of the substance of the pre-armistice agreement," and something which was owing to Germany under it. See E. M. House and Charles

Seymour, *What Really Happened at Paris,* p. 399. Wilson believed that the Covenant should be in the treaty, for in this way Germany could be made to approve the League and would not later be in a legal position to challenge the arrangements under it. If she signed the treaty and not the Covenant, there would be no way of compelling her to do so at a later date. At least, this was Wilson's argument before the Senate Foreign Relations Committee (*Sen. Docs.,* 66 Cong., 1 sess., no. 76, p. 16). Yet in the Treaty of Versailles, Germany was compelled to approve, sight unseen, the yet unmade treaties of the Allied and Associated Powers with her former allies. If this could be done, it seems evident that she could have been forced to approve the yet unborn League Covenant.

The incorporation of the Covenant in the Treaty was a source of great embarrassment to the neutrals who wanted to join the League, but who did not want to be associated with the Treaty. As late as 1937 the Assembly of the League of Nations was still debating the question of separating the Covenant from the Treaty. See J. T. Shotwell, *At the Paris Peace Conference,* p. v.

The workability of the plan for putting the general outlines of the League into the Treaty is borne out by the Covenant itself. Article XIV embodies the idea of the Permanent Court of International Justice, which was later worked out by a Committee of Jurists. Article XXIII of the Covenant and Part XIII of the Treaty made rather detailed provision for the International Labor Organization, which was later brought into being. In both of these creations the neutrals played an important role.

CHAPTER THIRTEEN

A PROPHET IS NOT WITHOUT HONOR

THE BEST brief secondary account is D. F. Fleming, *The United States and the League of Nations.* Henry Cabot Lodge's own embittered account of the Round Robin is given in his *The Senate and the League of Nations* (New York, 1925). See also J. P. Tumulty, *Woodrow Wilson As I Know Him;* George Creel, *The War, the World and Wilson;* Allan Nevins, *Henry White.*

THE LITERARY DIGEST POLL. A breakdown of the figures by party is most revealing (*ibid.,* April 5, 1919, p. 14):

DEMOCRATIC NEWSPAPERS

Yes	4,327,052
No	121,912
Conditional	508,384
Total	4,957,348

REPUBLICAN NEWSPAPERS

Yes	1,911,256
No	1,249,264
Conditional	3,836,417
Total	6,996,937

INDEPENDENT NEWSPAPERS

Yes	3,648,141
No	2,955,706*
Conditional	2,447,660
Total	9,051,507

WILSON'S INDISCREET SPEECH. On Feb. 28, 1919, Wilson spoke to the Democratic National Committee at the White House, and while some of his remarks were reported in the press the text was not published until 1921, when it appeared in J. P. Tumulty's *Woodrow Wilson As I Know Him,* pp. 367–379. Wilson referred to the opponents of the League (clearly meaning among them the Senators) as "of all the blind and little, provincial people, they are the littlest and most contemptible. It is not their character so much that I have a contempt for, though that contempt is thoroughgoing, but their minds. They have not got even good working imitations of minds." There was much more in the same vein. Here Wilson betrayed his characteristic contempt for people with "bungalow minds"; and though his speech was presumably not meant for public consumption, he should have known that his remarks would leak out and do nothing to smooth the already ruffled feathers of the Republicans in the Senate.

* Including the 2,488,976 circulation of the Hearst papers.

WILSON AND LEAGUE AMENDMENTS. While it is true that Wilson expected to amend the Covenant to some extent upon his return to Paris, it seems clear that he was hoping for nothing more serious than minor verbal changes in the interests of clarification. See Wilson to Senator Thomas J. Walsh, Feb. 26, 1919, Woodrow Wilson Papers, IX–A. It is interesting also that when Colonel House cabled from Paris advising that the League be put into operation at once, Wilson declined to do so, except possibly on a very provisional basis. He feared that the Senate would resent an attempt to railroad the Covenant through. This indicates that Wilson, then in America, was becoming increasingly aware of the temper of the Senate, while Colonel House experienced an extraordinary lapse from his usual political acuteness. (Wilson to House [cablegram], March 3, 1919, Woodrow Wilson Papers, IX–A.)

CHAPTER FOURTEEN

THE BATTLE BEGINS

ON THE dropping of the preliminary conference see Charles Seymour, *House Papers*, vol. IV; R. S. Baker, *World Settlement*, vols. I, II; and Harold Nicolson, *Peacemaking 1919*, chap. IV. On the amending of the League Covenant, consult David Hunter Miller, *The Drafting of the Covenant;* Stephen Bonsal, *Unfinished Business;* Seymour, *op. cit.;* Baker, *op. cit.;* and D. F. Fleming, *The United States and the League of Nations.* Harold and Margaret Sprout, *Toward a New Order of Sea Power* (Princeton, 1940), have an excellent analysis of the naval problem at Paris. On the Saar, there is an exceptionally able discussion by Professor Haskins in C. H. Haskins and R. H. Lord, *Some Problems of the Peace Conference.* Haskins was one of the American experts and was generally regarded as the prospective head of the Saar Commission. See also Paul. Birdsall, *Versailles Twenty Years After,* chap. IX. The French point of view is ably set forth in André Tardieu, *The Truth About the Treaty;* also in G. B. Noble, *Policies and Opinions at Paris,* chaps. VI, IX. See also Seymour, *op. cit.;* Baker, *op. cit.;* and

David Lloyd George, *Memoirs of the Peace Conference*, vol. I, chap. VIII. The standard work on the subject is Sarah Wambaugh, *The Saar Plebiscite* (Cambridge, 1940).

THE "SIDETRACK PLOT." The alleged plot in its most dramatic form is set forth in R. S. Baker, *World Settlement*, vol. I, chap. XVII. Many of the details are sharply challenged by Charles Seymour, *House Papers*, IV, 363–376. Winston S. Churchill enters the lists against Baker most vigorously in *The World Crisis*, pp. 187–191. Robert C. Binkley ably analyzes the whole controversy in "Ten Years of Peace Conference History," *Journal of Modern History*, I (1929), 612–621, and acquits Baker of dishonesty in handling the evidence. The truth seems to be that while there was no real plot, Wilson evidently thought that Colonel House had compromised too far, and that there was real danger to the League.

SUMMONING THE GEORGE WASHINGTON. There is also a controversy over the effectiveness of the summoning of the *George Washington*. R. S. Baker, in his *World Settlement*, II, 57–62, stresses its influence. Charles Seymour, in his *House Papers*, IV, 403–404, belittles it. It is certainly true, as Seymour says, that this incident marks no sharp turning point in the Conference, for in the subsequent days the President himself yielded ground, as well as the French, in effecting compromises over vital issues. On the other hand, Henry White wrote repeatedly in his letters that the possibility of an American withdrawal filled the French and others with consternation. (Allan Nevins, *Henry White*, p. 438 n.) Dr. Grayson, Wilson's personal physician, who presumably knew more about medicine than politics, cabled Tumulty that the *George Washington* incident had had a "castor oil effect" on the slow-moving French (April 10, 1919, Woodrow Wilson Papers, IX–A). Certainly the incident was headlined luridly in the press. Perhaps the fairest conclusion is that the affair has been overplayed, but that it was probably not without some effect. It is to be noted that the original cablegram of April 7, 1919, from Admiral Benson to the Navy Department, did not order the *George Washington* to sail, but asked how soon she could sail. (The text is in Charles Seymour, *House Papers*, IV, 403.) For alleged irregularities attending the sending of this cablegram from London, and for the sailing of the ship on the afternoon of April 11 from New York, see *New York Times*, April 11, 12, 1919.

CHAPTER FIFTEEN

THE PHANTOM OF FRENCH SECURITY

A SPIRITED and able defense of the French position on the Security Treaty appears in André Tardieu, *The Truth About the Treaty,* chap. VI. Tardieu was one of the French commissioners, and the right-hand man of Clemenceau. The Tiger defends himself with less fact and more emotion in *Grandeur and Misery of Victory.* Robert Lansing has an informative statement of the problem in his *The Peace Negotiations,* chap. XV. There is also useful material in David Lloyd George's *Memoirs of the Peace Conference;* in R. S. Baker's *World Settlement,* vols. II, III; and Charles Seymour, *House Papers,* vol. IV. An excellent analysis of French policy, chiefly as reflected in the press, is G. B. Noble, *Policies and Opinions at Paris,* chap. VII. See also C. H. Haskins and R. H. Lord, *Some Problems of the Peace Conference,* chap. IV. There are a number of books on French backgrounds of Rhine policy, but they add little or nothing to the above references with regard to Wilson and the policy of the United States. A summary account appears in Paul Birdsall, *Versailles Twenty Years After,* chap. VIII.

THE RHINELAND DEAL. It is commonly but erroneously supposed that France gave up her demands for the annexation of the Rhineland in return for the Security Treaty. There was never any official demand at the Conference for outright annexation. It is also sometimes thought that the French gave up occupation of the Rhine in return for the treaty. The facts are as stated in the text: France got limited occupation *in addition* to the treaty. It is also a common error to say that France foolishly gave up real security for the fancied security of the treaty. As pointed out in the text, she had ample technical safeguards in addition to the treaty.

THE SECURITY TREATY. Some critics are disposed to blame Britain for exercising her indisputable right to withdraw from the agreement when the United States declined to ratify. They feel that the history of postwar Europe would have been different if Britain had been willing to accept a dual alliance. It is interesting to note that there was considerable support for the Security Treaty in the press of the United States, and it seems probable that public opinion was considerably ahead of the Senate on this issue. See *Literary Digest*, May 3, 1919, p. 20; July 19, 1919, p. 12; and Dec. 31, 1921, pp. 5–9. This last article was based on a newspaper poll on the idea of aiding France. On the other hand, there was strong opposition in the American isolationist press to the proposed Security Treaty, even while it was only in the rumor stage. See Tumulty to Wilson (cablegram), April 22, 1919, Woodrow Wilson Papers, IX–A.

CHAPTER SIXTEEN

MAKING THE PIPS SQUEAK

T H E M O S T exhaustive study of the subject from the American point of view, and a model of its kind, is Philip Mason Burnett, *Reparation at the Paris Peace Conference from the Standpoint of the American Delegation* (2 vols., New York, 1940). The present study has drawn heavily on this work for some of its conclusions. The most important volume to come down to us from one of the American experts is Bernard M. Baruch, *The Making of the Reparation and Economic Sections of the Treaty* (New York, 1920). A brief chapter by another expert, Thomas W. Lamont, is published in E. M. House and Charles Seymour, *What Really Happened at Paris,* chap. XI. The French viewpoint is set forth in André Tardieu, *The Truth About the Treaty;* the British, in David Lloyd George, *Memoirs of the Peace Conference,* vol. I, chap. IX. John Maynard Keynes, a British economic expert who resigned from the British delegation in protest, wrote a daring and on the whole farsighted analysis in his *The Economic Consequences of the Peace,* which he supplemented with *A Revision of the Treaty* (New York, 1922). Additional material appears in Charles Seymour, *House Papers,* vol. IV; and R. S. Baker, *World Settlement,* vol. II. Brief secondary accounts appear in Paul Birdsall, *Versailles Twenty*

Years After, chap. X; and G. B. Noble, *Policies and Opinions at Paris,* chap. VI.

THE FRENCH RESERVATION ON REPARATIONS. The French, during the Armistice negotiations, succeeded in inserting into paragraph 19 of the final agreement a clause "that any future claims and demands of the Allies and the United States of America remain unaffected . . ." (*For. Rels., 1918, Supp. 1,* I, p. 466). The French later used this seemingly innocent safeguard to support their demands for war costs and pensions. The circumstantial evidence is overwhelming that no such construction was then accepted or could properly be made. John Maynard Keynes concludes that the clause was "merely the usual phrase of the draftsman, who, about to rehearse a list of certain claims, wishes to guard himself from the implication that such list is exhaustive." *Economic Consequences of the Peace,* p. 114. The whole controversy is ably discussed in Burnett, *op. cit.,* I, 7–8.

THE PENSIONS DECISION. The American experts reconciled themselves to this decision on the ground that even if the swollen figure was finally accepted, it would be too big for Germany to pay anyhow, and hence the burden on her would be substantially the same in the long run (Burnett, *op. cit.,* I, 64–65).

THE REPARATIONS COMMISSION. The British apparently did not want American representation; the French, for various reasons, did. Wilson finally threw his weight in favor of American participation. He later told the Senate Committee on Foreign Relations that the United States did not want membership, but that he yielded to the importunities of those nations who "wanted our advice and counsel" (*Senate Docs.,* 66 Cong., 1 sess., no. 76, p. 55). He contemporaneously (April 15, 1919) wrote to Herbert Hoover, who had protested against American participation, that "that commission will undoubtedly need an umpire, and I am afraid we must take the necessary risks in that matter" (Herbert Hoover, *America's First Crusade,* p. 48).

WAR GUILT CLAUSE. A great controversy has raged over the question whether the "war guilt clause" implied moral turpitude on the part of the Germans. It is clear that this clause was originally designed primarily as a political safeguard and not as a moral indictment. A careful reading of the text of the Treaty gives strong support to those who claim that no sense of wrongdoing was implied. But if the instrument is taken in connection with the German replies and the Allied rejoinders, as it must be to determine the intent of the framers, the opposite is true. The Germans took the ground that the clause did involve moral guilt, and that they were blameless. The Allies, whether they wanted to or not, were placed in a position where they had to deny German claims of innocence. The whole controversy is academic, however, because the Germans *thought* that theirs was the correct interpretation, and what they thought in this case was supremely important. Burnett, *op. cit.,* vol. I, chap. XVII, has a penetrating and well balanced discussion of this mooted question.

CHAPTER SEVENTEEN

OPEN DISAGREEMENTS OPENLY ARRIVED AT

THE FULLEST account, based largely on yet unpublished documents, is R. S. Baker, *World Settlement,* vol. II. David Lloyd George's *Memoirs of the Peace Conference,* vol. II, also reproduces significant documents, but is less reliable. There are important materials in Charles Seymour, *House Papers,* vol. IV, and also in J. T. Shotwell, *At the Paris Peace Conference.* Dr. Shotwell was intimately concerned with the quarrel among the American experts over Fiume. Allan Nevins, *Henry White,* pp. 430–433, is revealing on Senator Lodge's attitude regarding Fiume. Professor Douglas W. Johnson, a geographical expert on the Dalmatian area who was on the whole sympathetic toward Jugoslavia, has a compact chapter, which avoids controversial political issues, in E. M. House and Charles Seymour, *What Really Happened at Paris,* chap. VI. Johnson is the authority (p. 117) for the statement herein made regarding a defensible frontier south of the Brenner. Edith Bolling Wilson, *My Memoir,* gives intimate feminine glimpses of Wilson during this dispute. See also George Creel, *The War, the World and Wilson,* chap. XIX. Of the purely secondary accounts, that by René Albrecht-Carrié, *Italy at the Paris Peace Conference* (New York, 1938), is outstanding, and embodies the fruits of the most recent scholarship. The same author also has published "New Light on Italian Problems in 1919," *Journal of Modern History*, XIII (1941), 493–516; "Italy and Her Allies, June 1919," *American Historical Review*, XLVI (1941), 837–843; and "Italian Colonial Problems in 1919," *Political Science Quarterly*, LVIII (1943), 562–580. For brief analyses see Harold Nicolson, *Peacemaking 1919*, chap. VII; and Paul Birdsall, *Versailles Twenty Years After*, chap. XI.

WILSON'S APPEAL HABIT. It will be remembered that Wilson twice toyed with the idea of a public appeal at the time of the Armistice negotiations (Charles Seymour, *House Papers*, IV, 168, 183), in connection with the mandates question *ibid.*, (298 n.), and in connection with the Allied demand for war costs (*ibid.*, 343 n.). His summoning of the *George Washington* was in the nature of a public appeal, and in the case of Fiume he actually went through with it. Wilson should have been a keen enough student of human nature to know that it is one thing to appeal to one's own people; another to appeal to strangers over the heads of their own government. The time was not especially well chosen, because only a few months before, in the October appeal, he had apparently not been able to induce his own people to respond favorably. This experience with the Italians apparently did not change Wilson's views as to the efficacy of direct methods. On May 11, 1919, he told the Council of Four (Orlando absent) that he was so deeply angered by Italian machinations in Asia Minor that he could not much longer refrain from exposing Italy's course to the entire world, and thus visiting upon her the reprobation of mankind (Woodrow Wilson Papers, IX–C).

THE WILSON–HOUSE "BREAK." It is a curious fact that Colonel House often said he never knew precisely when the break actually occurred or what caused it. (See G. S. Viereck, *The Strangest Friendship in History*, chap. XXXV.) A. D. H. Smith, in his *Mr. House of Texas*, pp. 270–272, quotes the Colonel as later seeing the beginnings of coolness when, in the spring of 1918, Smith published a series of laudatory articles under the title, "The Real Colonel House." Mrs. Wilson seems to date the rift from Wilson's first return to Paris, at the time of the alleged "sidetrack plot"

(*My Memoir,* pp. 245–246). J. T. Shotwell, in his *At the Paris Peace Conference,* p. 200, stresses the Fiume affair. The incident regarding Wilson's having been annoyed by House's conclave with Lloyd George and Clemenceau appears in Lloyd George's *Memoirs of the Peace Conference,* I, 159. Shortly after House's death, a statement which the Colonel is said to have given to newspapermen was published by the press. In it he recounts two instances when Wilson was annoyed because Clemenceau and Lloyd George were seeking him out rather than Wilson. From the second of these incidents House is reported to have said that he dated the end of his friendship with the President. See North Adams (Mass.) *Transcript,* May 3, 1938, as quoted in Paul Birdsall, *Journal of Modern History,* XI, 372. This account is subject to some suspicion because House apparently on no other occasion was prepared to date the break so definitely. See also Viereck, *op. cit.,* pp. 247, 262. There can be no doubt that busybodies were at work during the Conference turning Wilson against House, and that the events of the Fiume controversy did nothing to restore the President's peace of mind. It is also clear that there was a "drifting apart" rather than an outright "break." See Seymour, *op. cit.,* IV, 506–517.

ORLANDO AND THE COUNCIL OF FOUR. Contrary to a common misconception, Orlando did not immediately bolt the Conference after Wilson's appeal, and he did not leave in anger. He and Sonnino met with the Council of Four the next day (April 24, 1919), and Orlando said that his esteem for Wilson was unshaken; that he believed Wilson's attitude to be that of a friend; that he had no intention of bolting the Conference (his authority had been called into question, and he must return home to seek new instructions); and that he owed his thanks to Wilson for the latter's "noble declaration." This was in response to the President's explanation that he had never thought of his appeal as going over the head of Orlando to the Italian people; that if this were the effect he personally regretted it; and that he had felt it necessary to issue the appeal because the French and Italian press was not setting forth the true facts. Near the end of the discussion, Orlando said that he had to leave to catch his train, whereupon Sir Maurice Hankey, on behalf of Lloyd George and Clemenceau, handed him the joint letter of April 23, 1919, signed by the British and French premiers. (Minutes of the Council of Four, Woodrow Wilson

Papers, IX–C.) The untrustworthy Lloyd George (*Memoirs of the Peace Conference,* p. 546) leaves the false impression that this letter was handed to Orlando *the day it was dated,* which was the day of Wilson's appeal. Actually it was presented the next day.

ORLANDO AND THE MANDATES. It is not true, as alleged by several writers, that the mandates were finally parceled out while Orlando was absent. The semifinal steps for their allocation were taken while the Italian premier was in Italy, but he was present at the afternoon meeting of May 7, 1919, when the final division was made. He rather mildly protested against Italy's being excluded from African mandates, but did not press the point, presumably because he expected compensations elsewhere. (Minutes of the Council of Four, May 7, 1919, Woodrow Wilson Papers, IX–C.) Some of the confusion probably arises from the fact that there were three meetings of the Council of Four on May 7. Orlando, who had just arrived, came late to the one which met at 11:00 A.M.; was not present at the one which met at noon (here the Smyrna decision was taken); and was present at the one which met at 4:15 P.M. House relates that Sonnino told him on May 8 that both he and Orlando greatly regretted the intemperate things that had been printed and said in Italy, and had tried to curb them. (House to Wilson, May 8, 1919, Yale House Collection.)

CHAPTER EIGHTEEN

THE YELLOW PERIL

ON THE Japanese problem at Paris, see David Hunter Miller, *The Drafting of the Covenant.* The account in R. S. Baker, *World Settlement,* vol. II, is useful, as is that in Charles Seymour, *House Papers,* vol. IV. Robert Lansing, *The Peace Negotiations,* chap. XVIII, is highly critical of Wilson. See also Frederick Palmer's *Bliss,* chap. XXXVI, for an account of Bliss' vigorous protest against the Shantung deal. Wilson's own thinking on this matter is best revealed in his testimony before the Senate Foreign Relations Committee, Aug. 19, 1919 (*Sen. Docs.,* 66 Cong., 1 sess., no. 76), and in his speeches in behalf of the Treaty which are published in Woodrow Wilson, *War and Peace,* vol. II. See also Lansing's testimony before the Senate Committee in *Sen. Docs.,* 66 Cong., 1 sess., no. 106. An excellent monographic account of the problem, with emphasis on Shantung, is T. E. La Fargue, *China and the World War* (Stanford University, 1937). George Creel has a spirited and on the whole able defense of Wilson in *The War, the World and Wilson,* chap. XVIII.

WAS RACIAL EQUALITY A BLUFF? An examination of the *Japan Times and Mail* (Weekly Edition), which reproduced translations of leading editorials in the Japanese press and which also maintained an excellent news service, reveals that Japanese opinion was much concerned over this issue (*ibid.,* XL, 153, 254, 333, 380, 391, 417, 457, 515, 524–525, 568, 571). See particularly the statement of Viscount Uchida, Minister of Foreign Affairs, before the Diet, in which he said that the issue was one of great importance (*ibid.,* p. 420). It is interesting to note that while opinion in the United States felt that Japan got too much at Paris, opinion in Japan was critical of the Japanese negotiators. There was a widespread feeling that Japan, as in 1895 and 1905, had been outmaneuvered by the great powers. But this feeling was not uncommon in the press of all the participating nations.

THE RACE EQUALITY VOTE. Various secondary accounts state that the vote was 11 to 6. This perfectly natural error probably stems in part from the statement in Charles Seymour, *House Papers,* IV, 428 n., which was written without benefit of David Hunter Miller's revelations. While it is true that eleven members did vote in the affirmative, six did not vote in the negative because no negative vote was called for. Thus the votes of the United States (Wilson and House) and Great Britain (Cecil, with Smuts absent) and Portugal, Poland, and Rumania were not recorded. It is not safe to assume that they all would have been negative if asked for; possibly some would have refrained from voting. Wilson, previous to the vote, spoke against the amendment, not because he opposed it in principle, but because he thought that it should not go into the Covenant. (He doubtless was thinking of the opposition which such a clause might arouse among the anti-Japanese elements in the United States.) For this episode see D. H. Miller, *The Drafting of the Covenant,* I, 461–466; also Miller, *My Diary,* VIII, 259.

Wilson's ruling that the motion had lost because it failed to secure unanimous support was objected to by one of the French delegates. Wilson stood his ground, declaring that the practice had been to insist upon unanimity unless those in the opposition were willing to let the motion pass with a reservation. The one apparent exception involved the selection of Geneva rather than Brussels as the seat of the League; but in this case the Belgians did not insist on their point, and any other procedure would have made a decision impossible. See Miller, *op. cit.,* I, 442; II, 392.

CHAPTER NINETEEN

THE DAY OF RECKONING

T H E P R O T E S T S presented by the Germans at Versailles, together with the Allied replies, are all conveniently printed in Alma Luckau, *The German Delegation at the Paris Peace Conference.* The relevant pages in R. S. Baker, *World Settlement,* vol. II, and Charles Seymour, *House Papers,* vol. IV, are revealing, as are those in C. E. Callwell, *Field-Marshal Sir Henry Wilson,* vol. II, and Herbert Hoover, *America's First Crusade.* There are materials on the "funk period" in David Lloyd George's *Memoirs of the Peace Conference,* vol. I, chap. XVI. See also G. B. Noble, *Policies and Opinions at Paris,* chap. X. The German point of view is ably presented in Karl F. Nowak, *Versailles* (trans. by Norman Thomas and E. W. Dickes, London, 1928); Victor Schiff, *The Germans at Versailles, 1919* (trans. by Geoffrey Dunlop, London, 1930), an expert on the German delegation; and Alfred von Wegerer, *A Refutation of the Versailles War Guilt Thesis* (trans. by Edwin H. Zeydel, New York, 1930) . For purposes of comparing Versailles with the Treaty of Brest-Litovsk, consult John W. Wheeler-Bennett, *The Forgotten Peace: Brest-Litovsk* (New York, 1939).

BROCKDORFF-RANTZAU'S FAILURE TO RISE. The stock explanation is that the German delegate was so nervous that he found it difficult or physically impossible to stand. There can be no doubt that he betrayed signs of extreme nervousness, but the evidence as presented in Dr. Simon's diary is conclusive on the point that he had decided in advance not to rise like a criminal before the bar of justice. See Luckau, *The German Delegation at the Paris Peace Conference*, p. 119.

WILSON'S CONCEPT OF JUSTICE. Wilson seems not to have doubted for one moment that the treaty was just, for he believed with his associates that Germany's sins were far greater than she could atone for. She must be punished severely lest she sin again. On his "swing around the circle" in behalf of the Treaty, Wilson told an audience at Columbus, Ohio, on Sept. 4, 1919: "She [Germany] attempted an intolerable thing, and she must be made to pay for the attempt. The terms of the treaty are severe, but they are not unjust." (Woodrow Wilson, *War and Peace*, I, 590–591. For similar expressions on the same tour see *ibid.*, pp. 591, 592, 644; II, 34, 104, 266, 400.)

CHAPTER TWENTY

BLESSED ARE THE PEACEMAKERS

M A N Y O F the works already cited are relevant to this concluding chapter. General commentaries appear in Paul Birdsall, *Versailles Twenty Years After*, chap. XII; Harold Nicolson, *Peacemaking 1919*, chap. VIII; René Albrecht-Carrié, "Versailles Twenty Years After," *Political Science Quarterly*, LV (1940), 1–24; W. C. Langsam, "Maladjustments of the Peace Settlement," *Annals of the American Academy of Political and Social Science*, CLXXV (1934), 1–10. Sketchy generalizations, some by British experts, are published in Lord Riddell, *et al.*, *The Treaty of Versailles and After* (London, 1935). See also T. E. Jessop, *The Treaty of Versailles: Was It Just?* (London, 1942), an able but biased brief for the treaty. For a French indictment see Alcide Ebray, *A Frenchman Looks at the Peace* (trans. by E. W. Dickes, New York, 1927); for a British, with emphasis on reparations, J. M. Keynes, *A Revision of the Treaty;* for a German, Wilhelm Ziegler, *Versailles: die Geschichte eines missglückten Friedens* (Hamburg, 1933); for an American, Frank H. Simonds, *How Europe Made Peace Without America* (Garden City, N.Y., 1927). See also Hermann Stegemann, *The Mirage of Versailles* (New York, 1928, trans. by R. T. Clark), another unfavorable discussion from the German point of view; and W. H. Dawson, *Germany Under the Treaty* (London, 1933), which is critical of the treaty. The minorities problem is discussed in William O. Molony, *Nationality and the Peace Treaties* (London, 1934); and L. P. Mair, *The Protection of Minorities* (London, 1928), which is an account of the minorities treaties under the League of Nations. W. E. Stephens, *Revisions of the Treaty of Versailles* (New York, 1939), though useful, contains little that is directly relevant to the United States. J. T. Shotwell, *What Germany Forgot* (New York, 1940), shows that the war and not the Treaty was responsible for many of Germany's ills. Critics of Versailles in America and elsewhere also forgot this.

VIOLATIONS OF THE FOURTEEN POINTS. In this connection, see the discussion of the contradictions and the "escape clauses" in Chapter XIX, above. If there was bad faith, it was not on the part of Wilson, who on the whole sincerely tried to honor his bond.

For the text of the Fourteen Points and their supplements see pp. 333–336 above. Point I (open covenants) was fulfilled in the sense that Wilson intended, though certainly neither he nor anyone else could have put an end to secret understandings. Henceforth treaties were to be registered with the League (Article XVIII of the Covenant). Point II (freedom of the seas) was not discussed at Paris. The British were hostile to it, and Wilson assumed that under the League there would be no neutrals, and consequently no issue involving maritime rights. (See R. S. Baker, *World Settlement*, I, 383.) It has often been remarked that the Treaty of Ghent, which ended our conflict with England in 1814, made no mention of freedom of the seas, one of the primary causes for our declaring war. Exactly the same thing may be said of Versailles.

Point III (removal of economic barriers *"so far as possible"*) was carried out literally "so far as possible," which meant that the principal immediate reductions were at the expense of Germany. The rest was left to Article XXIII of the Covenant. Point IV (arms reduction) was left to Article VIII of the Covenant. Point V (impartial adjustment of colonial claims) was presumably though only partially fulfilled in the mandate system. Point VI (Russia) could not be carried out at Paris, owing to current disorders; but Germany was forced to renounce the Treaty of Brest-Litovsk, and Wilson refused to support with American troops any schemes for crushing the Bolsheviks.

Point VII (restoration of Belgium) was completely discharged, as was Point VIII (restoration of France). Point IX (Italian frontier on lines of nationality) was more than carried out, though a number of aliens were thrown in for good measure, contrary to self-determination. Point X (autonomous development for the peoples of Austria-Hungary) was eventually worked out in the "succession states." Point XI (Balkan restoration) was generally fulfilled. Point XII regarding Turkey could not then be carried out because a settlement had not been effected. Point XIII (an independent Poland) was substantially discharged, as was Point XIV (a League of Nations).

The supplementary points were more nebulous in character, and on them some of the most serious of the German charges were based. Point 15 (essential justice of each case) was carried out only in part. Point 16 (non-bartering of peoples) was certainly more honored than not. The same thing may be said of Point 17 (territorial and other settlements in the interests of the people), at least in regard to Europe. In some cases it was discovered that where economic or other ties would be severed, or general interests would not be served, the people were better off without self-determination. A number of these decisions were made on the urgent recommendation of the American experts, and if blame must be apportioned it would be fairer to attack them than Wilson. Point 18 (recognition of national aspirations) was generally observed. Point 19 (destruction of arbitrary power) was certainly carried out, temporarily, in the case of Germany and her allies. Point 20 was the expression of a noble ideal which could hardly be realized as long as national states are what they are. Point 21 (no special interests) was only partially carried out. Point 22 (no alliances within the League) was apparently violated by Wilson in the Security Treaty with France; but this was an interim arrangement. Besides, the League, when founded, did not regard defensive alliances as reprehensible provided they contained no secret clauses. Point 23 (no economic combinations within the League) was carried out at least in part. Point 24 (registration of treaties) was achieved by the League.

It is impossible to tell an accurate story in these few brief words; the whole subject with all its ramifications would fill a book. For unfavorable judgments on the carrying out of the Fourteen Points, consult Harold Nicolson, *Peacemaking 1919*, pp. 43–44, 202–205; and Herbert Hoover, *America's First Crusade*, pp. 66–72. Both writers stress the nonobservances, rather than the important observances. Nicolson blames Wilson for his sins of omission; Hoover blames the wicked Europeans. He says (p. 71) : "America has been accused of running out on Europe after the treaty. As a matter of fact, Europe ran out on America in twenty of the Twenty-five Points." Hoover further confuses the picture by turning up with another set of supplementary points than Nicolson has, or than is conventionally accepted. For evidence that every one of the original Fourteen Points was faithfully observed in Paris, in so far as conditions would permit, see Lansing's testimony before the Senate Committee (*Sen. Docs.*, 66 Cong., 1 sess., no. 106, p. 169); also George Creel, *The War, the World and Wilson*, chap. XX. David Lloyd George is unable to "discover a single particular" in which the Allies departed from their war aims (*Memoirs of the Peace Conference*, I, 88) .

THE OTHER TREATIES. The Treaty of Versailles was the first to be signed (June 28, 1919), but the main lines of the others were blocked out before the Big Four went home. The final details were left to the members of the delegations who remained behind. The Treaty of St. Germain, with Austria, was signed on Sept. 10, 1919. Undersecretary of State Frank L. Polk, Henry White, and General Tasker H. Bliss acted for the United States. The Treaty of Neuilly, with Bulgaria, was signed on Nov. 27, 1919, with the same three men affixing their signatures. The Treaty of Trianon, with Hungary, was signed on June 4, 1920, with Hugh Campbell Wallace representing the United States. The Treaty of Sèvres, with Turkey, signed on Aug. 10, 1920, was not subscribed to by the United States, for we had not declared war on Turkey. All these treaties were modeled to a considerable extent on the Treaty of Versailles, and the Covenant of the League of Nations was Part I of each of them. A convenient compilation is *The Treaties of Peace, 1919–1923* (2 vols., New York, 1924), published by the Carnegie Endowment for International Peace. A highly useful abstract is Arthur P. Scott, *An Introduction to the Peace Treaties* (Chicago, 1920).

INDEX